Reagan's Rescue:

A Grandfather's Journal,
A Grandfather's Journey

Greg Williams

Greg Williams

Printed in the United States of America

ISBN-13: 978-0692678626

Cover design by Julia Megan Sullivan

Star Dust

And now the purple dusk of twilight time
Steals across the meadows of my heart
High up in the sky the little stars climb
Always reminding me that we're apart
You wander down the lane and far away
Leaving me a song that will not die
Love is now the stardust of yesterday
The music of the years gone by
Sometimes I wonder why I spend
The lonely night dreaming of a song
The melody haunts my reverie
And I am once again with you
When our love was new
And each kiss an inspiration
But that was long ago
Now my consolation
Is in the stardust of a song
Beside a garden wall
When stars are bright
You are in my arms
The nightingale tells his fairy tale
A paradise where roses bloom
Though I dream in vain
In my heart it will remain
My stardust melody
The memory of love's refrain

--Hoagy Carmichael

Table of Contents

Preface

The name of this book is <u>Reagan's Rescue: A Grandfather's Journal, A Grandfather's Journey</u>. It is about a journal that I started in 2004 for my first grandchild. It is about an unexpected journey that I began in 2006, a journey that I continue to this day. It is, ultimately, about the power of a little girl, Reagan, to rescue her grandfather from oblivion.

This is not my story alone. I represent family, friends, and acquaintances who have all been touched by Reagan's brief but important life.

Reagan was a victim of Shaken Baby Syndrome, a form of child abuse. Four grieving grandparents came together to create a public charity and child advocacy organization called Reagan's Rescue. We could not save Reagan from domestic violence, but it was our hope that, in her memory, we could save others from a similar fate. What we did not anticipate was how Reagan could also save us.

On the evening of the day that Reagan died, I asked my wife, Marsha, if it would be okay to continue writing to Reagan in her journal.

"Of course it would be okay to write to her," was her understanding and compassionate response.

At first, I looked at the journal entries as a way to keep communicating with my granddaughter. I envisioned her spirit—an invisible Reagan, really—standing next to me as I wrote. I assumed that she would have acquired the ability to read what I was writing or, at least, to understand what was in my head and my heart. Later, the purpose of the journal began to change; I realized that I was writing as much for me as for her as I tried to maneuver through the various stages of grief. Eventually, I began to wonder if my experience and insight could somehow help others who were on their own journeys of loss and confusion.

Preparing this book meant transcribing Reagan's journal and that, of course, meant reliving much of what I had stored away. The painful memories were agonizing. The happy memories were life-affirming. Both types brought tears. The tears were good and necessary.

Often, I could only transcribe one painful entry before crying began, but the crying was a link to those days in early July of 2006. The crying was my connection. Tears meant I had not forgotten. I somehow enjoyed the pain. If you've ever had a toothache and purposely pressed down on the sore tooth with your tongue to make it throb just a little, you might understand how crying, let out in small doses, helped.

Other times, I transcribed numerous happier entries with abandon, grateful that I had taken the time to write down memories that would have otherwise been forgotten. These memories were little bits of Reagan discovered and rediscovered, like coming across a photo yet unseen and gaining another second or two with her.

To all fellow parents and grandparents: photos and videos are not enough; they only tell a part of the story. You must take the time to write down the little things which are done or said. Trust me, the little things will be important enough. If you don't preserve memories through writing, you will lose those moments forever. Anne Morrow Lindbergh, the wife of pilot and hero Charles Lindbergh, said that she had to write it all down: "Writing is thinking. It is more than living, for it is being conscious of living."

Themes—motifs, maybe—emerged as I reread these entries. I turned to literature of all kinds for guidance— books, poetry, song lyrics, scripture, posters, the wisdom printed on the side of a paper cup. I wrestled with questions of doubt and faith. I regularly fluctuated between hope, numbness, and despair. I looked for signs. I apologized to Reagan over and over. I took comfort in ritual. Certain words were often repeated from entry to entry—pain, tears, grief, love, miss, sorry.

The journal also became a repository of items associated with Reagan's life and memory—pictures, notes, copies of letters or e-mails, a hat from a Christmas cracker, manuscripts from speaking engagements, and so on—the many volumes an archive bulging with treasures.

Everything in this book is based on what I knew at the time of its writing. My intention is not to hurt anyone. It is an honest account of what happened by someone who was there to experience it. Do I have all the answers? No. The sad fact is that we will never know all the details, and, frankly, I am not really sure I could handle knowing everything that happened although I have certainly played out various forms of events in my head, especially when it comes to Reagan's last months and weeks in the house where her life was taken. I am not pointing fingers at anyone, yet I am accusing all of us of contributing to her death. As you read on, you will discover why.

So why publish this book? It is meant primarily for those of you who are just beginning your journey of grief, especially if your loss was the result of violence or tragedy. I am farther down the road. I can help you make your way. Your grief—your road—will be different from mine. The ups and downs will not be the same. The directions you travel and the speed with which you make your journey will be different as well. But I can offer some general roadside assistance. I can provide some warnings, a few maps, and, I hope, some encouragement, too. This is a journey with a destination you will never reach for you never really get over a loss this traumatic. You *can* get through it.

GW

Introduction

My granddaughter's favorite book was called <u>Where is Maisy?</u> Reagan, two and a half, would bring the book to me, climb on my lap, and have me read to her. Maisy is hiding, and each turn of the page reveals a new location, a question, and a lift-the-flap answer: "Is Maisy in the house?...Oops! Not here!"; "Is Maisy in the barn?...Oops! Not here!" We would look for Maisy in the boat, the closet, and the tree as well. Each lift of the flap, manipulated by her tiny, persistent fingers, would reveal the answer: "Oops! Not here!" Finally, the last page would say "Knock, knock. Who's there?" And Reagan would uncover, behind the door, the Nickelodeon mouse and the words "It's Maisy!" I cherished those moments.

Reagan was the product of an unmarried couple—my son, Ian, and his girlfriend, Tracy Green. Though my wife, Marsha, and I had reacted to the pregnancy with a mixture of surprise, disappointment, and concern, we welcomed Reagan into the family on Twelfth Night, January 5, 2004. She was our Little Christmas gift, and she soon captivated my heart—"The light of my life," I would tell people. We recognized very early on that she was an intelligent child, somehow wise beyond her years. She had penetrating deep brown eyes that could look right through a person. She was neat and particular. She had a dramatic flair, an impishness. She loved music and dancing and making an array of faces. We were fortunate to see her regularly the first year since Marsha took care of her during the day while Tracy worked.

Although she would go to anyone, she was Papa's girl. As soon as she entered our house, she would call out for me—"Papa? Papa?" —then open her arms widely and run in my direction. When we hugged, she fit just right. Our routine normally included the reading of her favorite board books—including Where is Maisy?—and the singing of songs, Reagan lying relaxed in my lap as I rocked gently back and forth. Each time she left, I could not help but recall a line from a Truman Capote short story: "As for me, I could leave the world with today in my eyes." I loved her more than life itself.

A frantic phone call changed our lives on Sunday, July 2, 2006. When I returned home from church with my seventeen year old, Mallory, my fifteen year old daughter, Flyn, met us on the front porch in hysterics. About fifteen minutes earlier, Tracy had called, shrieking something indecipherable about Reagan. Marsha was able to conclude that our granddaughter had lost consciousness at home, and paramedics had attempted to revive her. Marsha had already rushed to the hospital; Mallory and I took off immediately. When we arrived at the emergency room, I found Marsha in the hallway, her right hand tightly clutching a tissue, her eyes red and tear-streaked. She collapsed in my arms and told me that our little Reagan was gone. Numb and shaking in disbelief, we were ushered in to a private waiting room by Sister Joanne, a grief counselor on staff. I saw through tears a blur of faces— some of Tracy's family, police, the coroner, and our pastor, Don Vanzant, who had been contacted already. I heard distant moans of "No...no" and "It's not true." Marsha sobbed, "Our baby." Sister Joanne commented on "what a beautiful child she was...so peaceful." I needed my father, a United Methodist minister, so I fumbled for the phone, couldn't get a line out, and dictated the number to someone who dialed.

Soon more family arrived—my dad, Jim, and stepmother, Roberta; Reagan's father, my son, Ian; Flyn; daughter Blythe and her husband, Shane—and each time we shared the horrible news, an eruption of wailing and tears would commence. My dad called my sisters, Elaine and Heather, who both live in Colorado, and their voices were choked with an anguish I had never heard from them before. My stepmother volunteered to tell our youngest daughter, Bailey, who was staying at a neighbor's house.

The explanation we were given by Tracy's live-in boyfriend was that Reagan had been fine one minute, playing with toys, and then sat on the couch and lost consciousness. Something didn't seem right. I found the coroner and pleaded, "I hope you investigate his story." With the arrival of an investigator from the Vermilion County Sheriff's Department, a search for answers did, in fact, start up. For the next two hours, we sat around the hospital as several of us were taken into a small room for questioning—Tracy, her boyfriend, Ian, and I all took our turns. When I told the coroner and investigator of a journal I was keeping for Reagan (to be given to her on her eighteenth birthday), in which I had written, in part, of fears of child abuse that had been going on for months, they asked if I could bring the book in and share it with them. Somehow I managed to drive home, retrieve the journal, and bring it back, haltingly reading through relevant pages.

Late Sunday afternoon, we returned home with the promise from the coroner that an autopsy would be performed and preliminary results would be available the next day. We sat in stunned silence, hoping that this death was from some unknown natural cause but fearing that Reagan had been injured…killed. The next twenty-four hours were agony. Marsha's parents and my mom and stepfather all arrived, reopening the fresh wounds with embraces and tears and attempts at comforting words. Sleep came in fits if it came at all. At a quarter to four the next morning, I woke up, unable to fall back asleep. I wandered through the dark house, whimpering, "Papa? Papa?" just like Reagan had done so often. I needed to hear her voice.

I managed to think clearly enough to go out in the backyard and check on our pool. Since rain was coming down, I had to lower the sides and let water out in order to avoid the pool caving in on itself and collapsing, causing a flood. There in the pouring rain, I heard the sound of a music and a female voice coming from the dark. I soon realized that it was a Barbie Boom Box, one of Reagan's favorite toys, left in the yard and running on its own. I hoped it was a sign, some validation that she was really there.

The next afternoon, while being visited by church friends, the coroner called to confirm our worst fears, that Reagan had received "closed head trauma." I made it a point to write it down.

"Does that mean that she was shaken?" I asked.

"It looks like it," the coroner responded, "although we will not have all the test results back for six weeks or so. You will have to be patient and let this investigation run its course."

I called Marsha and Ian into the den, closed the door, and gave them the news. Again, the tears came, along with resentment and frustration. We had sought help from the local Department of Children and Family Services, but our efforts were thwarted on several occasions.

"She was the best baby ever. How could anyone harm such an innocent, loving child?" Marsha cried. Ian breathed in and out deeply and fiercely. All I could manage, through sobbing, was "I know...I know" as I held them close.

"Don't share this information with anyone," the coroner had warned. "We don't want the investigation compromised in any way," and so we had to keep this horrible revelation a secret. Our visiting friends had, no doubt, surmised the gist of the phone call and immediately contacted Pastor Don to be there with us as we struggled with this new and disturbing revelation. Now, we not only had Reagan's death to deal with but the violent replaying of it in our minds. And the guilt. Both Marsha and I suddenly were consumed by overwhelming guilt that we could have and should have done more to save her. This would prove to be the hardest emotion to control, especially at night when we would try to fall asleep.

The days that followed brought painful duties—making arrangements with the funeral home, buying flowers, choosing an outfit for Reagan to wear, writing an obituary—each disrupted, without warning, by often uncontrollable tears of regret. The emotions were debilitating. We were grieving Reagan's loss, angry toward the person responsible, guilty that we might have done something to prevent this violent act. Numb and withdrawn, we needed some relief or escape.

The theatre director in me came out as I threw myself into planning the service. I gave Don a poem by the Puritan writer Anne Bradstreet entitled, appropriately, "In Memory of My Dear Grandchild." The last four lines summed up what I wanted to feel, what we all needed to believe:

> Farewell, dear child: thou ne'er shalt come to me,
> But yet a while and I shall go to thee.
> Meantime my throbbing heart's cheered up with
>   this—
> Thou with thy Savior art in endless bliss.

The sentiments in Bradstreet's tribute reflected the words of King David in 2 Samuel 12: 23 when his son by Bathsheba dies: "...now that he is dead, why should I fast? Can I bring him back again? I will go to him, but he will not return to me." That scripture passage gave me hope that Reagan had merely gone on ahead and that, if I lived my life accordingly, I would one day meet her at Heaven's door. In addition to the literary passages, I also let Don borrow the Maisy book, confident he would know how to use it.

I felt somehow led in both my choice of music and the recordings on which I settled. Two of the songs I sang to Reagan as part of our ritual were "You Are My Sunshine" and "Tell Me Why." Flyn and I found perfect tracks on the Internet, featuring pure voices, guitars, simple harmonies, as if they had been recorded just for this occasion. Listening to them, however, caused my first major meltdown. As the line "Please don't take my sunshine away," was repeated over and over again, I broke down in convulsions of sobbing. "They took my sunshine away," I lamented, Marsha cradling me in her arms. I felt the agony woeful King Lear must have experienced when he carried out his dead daughter, Cordelia, in his arms.

Two other songs seemed to present themselves as well. We felt drawn to the hymn "It is Well with My Soul" but wanted to avoid an "old person" rendition. For some reason, I went to my CD collection and pulled out an unopened disc by the Christian singer/composer Danny Byram, who lives in Evergreen, Colorado; there, on the song list, was his soulful version with simple, unobtrusive piano accompaniment. It was perfect and would, hopefully, provide a transition in the service from the devastation of mourning to the peace of God's promise. Finally, at a local bookstore, while purchasing a Mizpah necklace for Reagan and myself with Genesis 31: 49 printed on it, I turned to a Christian music display and spotted a CD of songs inspired by the film The Chronicles of Narnia: The Lion, the Witch, and the Wardrobe. One title caught my eye—"Remembering You" by Steven Curtis Chapman, an upbeat Celtic-sounding tune which, for me, captured all that was Reagan's spirit—her warmth, her sense of humor, and her love of dancing. The words spoke to the grief of "The brave death, the last breath/The silence whispering all hope was lost" but then celebrated the promise of resurrection in "The thunder, the wonder/A power that brings the dead back to life." I wanted family

[21]

and friends assembled in that chapel to emerge with some kind of hope as we made our way to the cemetery.

The visitation and service on that cloudless, sunny Friday were attended by so many friends and family. Each new arrival elicited from us a gasp of surprise and, then, gratitude. The staff at the mortuary, visibly touched by the circumstances, bent over backwards to help us in any way they could. Don stood nearby to lend support. He had admitted to me that this was going to be the most difficult funeral he had ever performed as there were simply no words of comfort that could make up for the loss, save one: "Jesus." During his meditation, he reminded us that we now had a personal connection to Heaven. He encouraged us to seek solace in a God who is still good. After reading Where is Maisy? aloud, lifting each worn flap, he explained that we would look for Reagan behind each corner, in each unexplained sound, in the activity of other children on a playground, just as we were searching for Christ's comfort and assurance. Later, at the grave site, the cousins, aunts, parents, and two generations of grandparents let pink and white balloons go. They sailed straight up and into the sun until we were nearly blinded for one last look.

When the official mourning rituals were over, the flowers began to fade, family members left to go back to their own homes, and the house got quieter. Left with our thoughts and a silence unbroken by Reagan's voice, Marsha and I continued to long for our beautiful granddaughter. I verbally challenged God to show Himself like He once did to Abraham, Moses, and all the others in the Bible. I would have accepted a burning bush. Faith was not enough in this; we wanted to feel Reagan's presence, to know, beyond faith, that she was resting in the Lord's arms. I wanted to be able to see through that thin veil which separated us, if only for a brief moment. Despite the lingering grief, however, I heard myself say something else in those early days—something surprising. In the midst of this unthinkable tragedy, we felt, strangely, blessed. In grieving, we were not alone. In losing, we had gained.

Beginning on the afternoon of Reagan's passing, there came frequent knocks at the front door as neighbors, friends, and, especially, our church family stopped to visit. They came with hugs; they offered to help "any time." And they brought food—smoked turkey, an entire spiral ham, pulled pork, Italian beef, fried chicken, meat and cheese trays, breads, buns, casseroles, salads of all sorts, fresh fruit, chips, soft drinks, bottled water, cookies, pies, cakes, brownies. They also brought surprising but useful gifts—plastic cups, paper plates, plasticware, coupons for food when our supply ran out, movie tickets so that we might forget, even if momentarily. After the first week, when we were alone, members of our praise band (to which daughter Mallory and I belong) divided up the week and brought a new meal each night. On Monday it was homemade chicken and noodles, followed on Tuesday by a casserole, on Wednesday by spaghetti and meatballs, on Thursday by a beef roast, and on Friday by pizza. Eating was not a priority in those early weeks; food was not sustaining us but, rather, the offering, the act of giving that went on. People also sent checks or cash to be used at our discretion; we promptly opened a memorial fund in Reagan's honor, the gifts we received to be used for local children's causes, specifically those dealing with child care and domestic abuse. We received e-mails and cards from around the country. We were on prayer chains from coast to coast. The cast and parents involved with a local children's theatre production of Honk! raised $100 to be given in Reagan's name to Your Family Resource Connection, a shelter that we had designated as a place to which contributions could be made; other friends and acquaintances had already sent hundreds in donations. Marsha and I were truly unprepared for this outpouring of support; we were not grieving alone but as "the community of Reagan." One elderly member of our church took my head in her gnarled hands and whispered, "You are strong. You have faith. You will move on. We are praying for you." Another church friend made it clear: "We love you. Your family is ours." It was hard not feeling a little bit like George Bailey at the end of It's a Wonderful Life as residents of Bedford Falls stream through his front door.

One day, an envelope arrived filled with a note of condolence and some pamphlets sent by Sister Joanne at the hospital, including a short piece entitled "Comfort for Those Who Mourn." The last paragraph resonated deeply: "The tears that dampen our eyes in times of mourning…are tears of longing for our loved ones. But it is we who are away from home, not they! Death has been for them a doorway to an eternal home. They are still with us, lovingly and tenderly waiting for the day when we, too, will enter the doorway of our eternal home." There was the door again, the threshold that King David and Anne Bradstreet planned to cross one day; it was the door we, too, would enter for a reunion of indescribable joy.

I do not believe that God makes bad things happen. I struggle with the idea that Reagan's death was God's will. I refuse to believe, as well-meaning people have suggested, that God needed Reagan in Heaven. A human being with free will did this to her, the violence a result of losing Eden. What we do in the wake of this terrible event will ultimately determine whether we grow in our faith and commitment or implode in self-pity and anger. In the meantime, Reagan would want us to dance in anticipation of that reunion day. We are committed to make something good out of our loss. That is how we survive. Still, the rest of our lives will be diminished because she will not be here.

Two weeks after Reagan's passing, I transferred all the video we had of her to a DVD. I watched my son Ian hold her after she was born. I watched her hug her Tickle Me Elmo. I watched Marsha care for her so expertly—gently, lovingly, and proudly. I smiled as Reagan opened Christmas presents. I laughed at her smearing blue icing from her first birthday cake all over her face and hair. And I cried at the last footage we had of her as she played peekaboo—behind a bathroom door.

"Where's Reagan?" I ask from behind the camera. In her usual playful way, she stares at me with a coy grin then shuts the door with a click of the latch. That is the final image—Reagan hiding just behind the door.

Then I think of Maisy, knocking on the door, and little fingers pulling back the flap to reveal the long lost mouse. I know that we will look for Reagan in the coming days and years. When our front door opens, we will expect to hear delicate footfalls and "Papa? Papa?" Myriad little things will remind us of her short but significant life. And we will certainly look forward to that glorious day when we will enter the gates of Heaven and be reunited with her. Until then, we will rely on Jesus, who stands at the door of our broken hearts and knocks, ready for us to let Him in.

2006

Reagan's Journal

Volume One

8/28/05

Yesterday, while holding you so that you'd take a nap, you raised your head from my shoulder, took my face in your tiny hands, looked me in the eyes, and said "Papa"— your name for me—before putting your head back on my shoulder to fall asleep. It was one of those moments one can't capture on video and one we frequently share, you and I. That's why I'm starting this journal for you.

A year ago, a few days before your cousin Aubrey was born, I began a journal for her. I had read an article earlier that week about how keeping a journal for a grandchild is one of the greatest gifts a grandparent can give. By the time I read that you were already about 8 months old. I didn't think starting a record of your life 2/3 through your first year would be complete enough; the journal needed to have an immediacy about it, and I had lost too much time.

Well, recently I decided, late or not, I'd begin a journal for you and hope you'll forgive my shortsightedness. The first year and a half of your life will be through my recollections, probably mixed with day to day events, the whole thing to be given to you on your 18th birthday.

I was afraid that, when Aubrey was born, she'd always think of herself as second in importance. I made a big deal out of how she was the first daughter of my first daughter. That's another reason why I started a journal for her. To be honest, however, I began to feel like I was cheating you, more so because you and I have always had this very special relationship. I could always get you to sleep or to stop crying when others couldn't. I danced with you and sang to you and took naps with you and played with you and began teaching you what I could very early on. And I love you more than words can say. And remarkable as it is, you seem to love me back.

So I begin this journal, over a year and a half late but with as much care and dedication as I've used for your cousin, Aubrey. My memories of your life so far are still clear. I hope that this book will one day explain to you just what a miracle you are. And how much you've blessed my life.

So I start this journal today to be opened on your 18th birthday.

8/29/05

I remember clearly the day we heard you were on the way. Your dad sat us down in the den, saying he had something to tell us. From the sheepish look on his face, we figured it out before he told us. Our concern was that he be there for your mom, and he assured us that he would. They stayed together, too, for about a year and a half until you were about eight months old when your dad decided to move out. We didn't understand why he reached that decision; in fact, to this day, we've never gotten a complete answer. Since he wasn't around you as much, and because your grandma and I felt responsible for the choices he made, we thought it was important to be there for your mom and for you. Your grandma was an LPN, working part-time at a nursing home, studying for her RN licensure tests, and watching you during the day while your mom worked two jobs to help support you. I was proud of both of them, making sacrifices for you. It was tough on your grandma, but it was also rewarding. Many days I would come home from school to see you and your grandma sitting on the front porch waiting for me. I looked forward to those afternoons. That was the beginning of a beautiful relationship—Reagan and her grandpa.

I'm getting ahead of myself. There was, of course, the night you arrived. January 5, 2004. We have many Christmas traditions in our family—when we get the tree, what Christmas movies we watch, what foods and goodies we make for the holidays, when we open presents, how long we leave the tree up. That's where you come in.

We like to observe the 12 days of Christmas, a tradition found in England. Your grandpa fancies himself an Anglophile. He also gets extremely blue after the holidays are over, and this custom extends Christmas to the 12th day, really the 12th night—January 5. Little Christmas it is sometimes called. It is the night before Epiphany, the time set aside in the Church to remember the visit of the Wise Men to the Christ Child. On 12th night, we take down the decorations, remove the tree, vacuum up the pine needles, and, when everything is done, exchange one last smaller gift. Okay, sometimes it ends up being a few smaller gifts.

But the greatest Little Christmas gift we ever got was our Reagan Emery. And now that custom, that day, is made more sacred because of you.

January also became more important because you joined other family members with January birthdays— Uncle Shawn, me, Great Grandpa Dave, Great Grandma Cookie, and Aunt Mallory. And you usher them all in.

I think your dad chose Reagan as your first name. I don't know whether your mom liked it or not, but she went along with it. As for your middle name, I made that suggestion. My grandma, Thelma Baker Williams, who just turned 96 this week, had 3 brothers—Owen, Frank (also in his 90s and one of my favorite relatives), and Emory. Emory died when he was a boy. I guess that means you were named for your great-great-great uncle.

I'll tell you more about your family tree later.

It was the best of all possible gifts, the Christmas you arrived at Provena United Samaritans Medical Center with family and friends looking on. Amazing how such a tiny thing could have such an influence over the lives of others. You changed us forever.

9/24/05

Today, you attended the Viking Invitational, the marching band competition at Danville High School. Thirty years ago I was in the marching band. Many years later, your Aunt Blythe played flute as a freshman and sophomore before becoming drum major as a junior and senior. Your dad played tenor sax all four years.

As you watched each band perform, you were wrapped up in the sights and sounds. You stared for long stretches of time, smiled, and applauded enthusiastically.

You saw the 2005-2006 Band of Vikings perform their show. Aunt Mallory was in Color Guard, and Aunt Flyn played trumpet. We couldn't help but wonder if you, too, will one day take the field for competition, carrying on the family tradition.

As we carried you through the crowds, you waved at complete strangers. You are such a friendly, relaxed, and intelligent little girl. You are precise in your movements, careful with things. You love books. And I was really taken today as you stood in the sunlight just how red your hair is. That makes me especially happy.

We hadn't seen you for a couple of weeks, and, frankly, we missed you. I'm glad you could spend the day with us.

10/26/05

My precious little one, I am so frightened for you. We found out that you got hurt over the weekend while your mom's boyfriend, Ryan, was watching you. We first heard that you fell off the couch and then that you ran into a glass coffee table while Ryan was in another room getting a drink. When your mom and dad took you in to see Dr. Legett, he suspected that the extent of your injuries did not match the story and that abuse might have happened. Someone from the Dept. of Children and Family Services is supposed to come out and investigate.

I'm writing about this now because my heart is breaking. My little Reagan is injured, and I want so much to hold you and sing to you and read to you and play together—anything to keep you from harm. You have been the light of my life. I've been your Papa. And I want you to be healed and happy. I never realized how tough being a grandpa was.

On Monday you have to go in for an extra procedure—a kind of X-ray to make sure you have no skull fractures. I want so much to be there.

I'm worried about more than your injuries. Since your mom and dad are not together, it places you at greater risk for so many challenges and difficulties as you grow up and go through school. Your Grandma Marsha and I both agree that we'll do everything we can to help you.

Because you are our first grandchild, you'll always have a special place in our hearts.

10/28/05

Your dad brought you by the house yesterday and today. If I'm in the den, I can hear "Papa? Papa?" as you walk through the kitchen and approach the basement stairs.

It was such a wonderful feeling to be able to hold you and give you kisses. You looked like a little raccoon with your two black eyes. I really dreaded seeing what you looked like, but your injuries were beginning to heal, so you didn't look as bad as I expected.

Today, the black under your eyes was starting to turn yellow and green. I hope this is the last injury we have to worry about.

You've started putting puzzles together. Each time you'd put a piece in the wrong place, you'd say "Noooo." Eventually, you would find the right slot. You are such a smart little girl. You really always have been.

I have to admit that now, because your dad is spending more time around you, I'm getting really jealous. You should be close to him—that's only natural, but there was something so great about my being your favorite. It used to be "Papa," and now it's more "Dada." And that's how it should be. Still, I don't like sharing you.

I wonder, in sixteen years, will you still be "Papa's girl"?

10/31/05

A rainy Halloween night. Your mom brought you over for a little while dressed in a pumpkin costume. You posed for pictures, ate puppy chow, and played with Aubrey's cheerleader pompoms. Aubrey played with Bailey's Padme Amidala light saber.

At one point I managed to get a big hug from both my granddaughters at the same time. My cup runneth over! I could die with the memory of that hug.

11/24/05

Thanksgiving Day! We ate around 1:30. Your mom brought you over to the house around 2:30 to spend the afternoon with your dad. Your great aunt Elaine (my sister) was here with her daughters, Jessica and Amanda (your cousins). Shane, Blythe, and Aubrey also came, as well as Great Grandma Cookie and Great Grandpa Dave.

You were adorable as usual. Elaine and the girls were impressed with how smart you were. Your dad tries to get you to say things like you are some trained monkey. Of course, you love the attention. I attempted to stop you from playing with the glass door on the entertainment center, and you gave me this mean, spooky face. I'm probably guilty for teaching them to you when we mug for the mirror in the bathroom.

You and Aubrey are becoming major rivals, fighting over toys, playing tug-of-war with the little keyboard you both love so much, even slapping each other occasionally. You've been known to slap me on occasion, too. It doesn't hurt physically but it damages my ego. You sure love your "Dada." And the latest challenge is that your mom is trying to potty train you. You started pulling down your pants in the living room in front of everyone, so Ian took you to the bathroom to sit on the toilet. After five minutes, he took you off and, standing in the bathroom, you peed on the floor. Oh, well, you'll get it right soon.

I included a place setting your Grandma got off the Internet. I thought you'd like to have it.

Among the many things I am thankful for are my two granddaughters. You make me feel young and appreciated.

12/6/05

For the second time in a little over a month, you have bruises on your body—this time on your face and your buttocks. Once again we have real concerns that you are being mistreated or abused. This is not an easy idea to

*handle. You are not clumsy. You have always been a
wonderful baby. I cannot get the image of your face out of
my head, and it pains me to think that you could be harmed.*

*Friday your dad called and had me come over to look at
you. I brought a camera and took pictures. I also had
Grandpa Jim and Grandma Roberta come by, too. We
tried to call Dr. Legett, but he was not available. His
partner, Dr. Reddy, suggested that we take you to the
emergency room at the hospital to be checked out. Your
dad didn't want to do that because of what difficulty it
would create between your mom and him.*

*That's the dilemma we have all faced. We don't want to
make things difficult for your mom. We can't even be sure
anyone has hurt you. We just want you to be safe.
Someone has to be your advocate since you can't defend
yourself.*

*Your mom said that you slipped on the ice, but your
injuries didn't appear to be caused that way. Still, we
don't know.*

*Your grandma called the Child Abuse Hotline but could
not guarantee her anonymity so did not go through with it.
If your mom found out that we had been responsible for
reporting our suspicions she could make it hard for your
dad and for us to see you anymore. It would just kill us to*

be separated from you. More importantly, though, we'd be willing never to see you again if it meant that you'd be safe.

I don't want to one day upset you as you read this entry for the first time. I wish I could predict what the future will hold. This has taught me to cherish every moment with you even more. You are so precious to me. To us all.

Today, your mom went to the hospital. We don't know why. She called looking for your dad so that he could pick you up at your other grandparents' house. You're spending the night with your dad and Gracie. For one night anyway we know you are safe.

Please understand, Reagan, how tough this has been, not knowing the right thing to do. Any decision we've made has been out of love and concern for you.

Your little soul binds us all together.

12/10/05

Yesterday, your mom called and asked if we could watch you while she went Christmas shopping. Of course, we were delighted! We had a snow day, so we had a chance to do our weekly housecleaning earlier in the day.

Around 5:30, I took your dad to work (he can't drive for a while because of a traffic violation—not paying a ticket, not wearing a seatbelt, having no insurance). When I got back to the house I heard on the other side of the front door a baby wailing and throwing a huge tantrum. This was a side of you I had never seen. Mallory and your grandma couldn't wait for me to get home so that I could comfort you (I'm supposed to have the magic touch when it comes to our little Reagan), but you would have none of it. You kept repeating "No" in blood-curdling screams and even hitting me.

We tried a number of tactics, none successful, then I took you into the bathroom, locked the door, sat on the floor, and waited for you to wear yourself out. About fifteen minutes later, I took you to Grandma, and you promptly stopped and sounded civil again, even pointing to me and saying "Papa" as if I had just shown up and surprised you. The combination of medicine for the cold and cough you have, the nap that was interrupted when your mom dropped you off—well, it appeared that you were having night terrors. I used to have those when I was about 8 or 9.

Well, you slept on Grandma for about the next three hours and then on me for about a half an hour. You looked so tiny asleep in our arms and the flu you've had has resulted in your losing weight. You're too skinny.

When your mom picked you up, you burrowed your head into her shoulder and waved "Bye" to us without looking up.

Is it the beginning of the Terrible Twos? I hope not. I could not take the rejection.

12/14/05

You went to the hospital two days ago with a stomach virus. You were terribly dehydrated. Your mom and dad took you in to Dr. Legett, and he had you admitted. Yesterday, I stayed home from school in the morning, and Grandma and I came to visit. Ryan was there with you; your mom had gone home to change.

You were sleeping but woke up for a little while before throwing up some bile. You haven't been eating because you haven't been able to keep food down. You looked so tiny, so fragile and helpless. One arm had an IV in it. It was taped up with a board—almost looked like a broken arm.

After you got sick, the nurse came in to change the bedding. Your grandma held you and you began to whimper about every five seconds. We passed you on to

your mom when she got back to the room and you
continued to whimper in her arms.

Last evening, Bailey and I went up to visit and your
mom was able to go down to the cafeteria for some supper.
We were encouraged that you had eaten Jello. Again you
had been sleeping a lot and, as soon as you woke up, you
threw up twice—to the left and right. Bright red. And all
over your clothes and the bed.

Bailey and I cleaned you up the best we could, and
another nurse came in to change your bedding. I held you.
You were reluctant at first but then you snuggled with me.
I was so afraid I was going to break you since you seemed
so brittle—like a porcelain doll.

This evening, Mal, Flyn, Bailey, and I visited. You had
just been sick again on the floor and on your mom's clothes
while she was holding you. You were sleepy again. I don't
even know if you realized we were all there.

We are all upset about your being so sick. Mallory
broke down and cried tonight she was so worried. And we
prayed for you during our praise band practice.

I want my Reagan back. I would gladly give up every
Christmas present to have you well again.

12/20/05

*Friday night I went up to the hospital and sat with you
for a couple of hours. Your dad was working at Sears;
your mom went to a Christmas party. When I arrived you
were just finishing up some apple sauce and some
chocolate pudding, and the tube in your arm had been
removed. For really the first time all week you seemed
happy to see me, greeting me with "Papa" and a big, goofy
smile.*

*When everyone left, you settled down for a nap and slept
off and on in the dark, quiet room for a little over an hour.
I watched holiday cooking shows and then A Charlie
Brown Christmas. You woke up, and, for some reason, I
began fake sneezing for you so you'd laugh. Then you
started pretending to sneeze, too—more of a "Whew"
sound. At least you were smiling and laughing again.*

*Your dad came to stay with you about 7:45. After I left,
I guess things got really wild. A nurse brought in a
miniature wheelchair, and your dad rolled you up and
down the corridors much to your delight. I guess you had a
ball!*

*Christmas is approaching with all the anticipation of
opening presents and being with family. Christmas
celebrates the birth of Jesus, but this year I am celebrating*

the rebirth of our very own Christmas babe—our "Little
Christmas" present, Reagan Emery.

Welcome back, my precious one.

12/26/05

Your second Christmas. You came by early Christmas
afternoon and opened some presents from Aunt Heather
and your dad and Gracie. When your mom picked you up,
you cried. She took you to a family Christmas in
Hoopeston and then brought you back in the evening. You
and Aubrey opened presents from us—including a
keyboard and a huge pop-up house. You were so loving to
everyone. Your vocabulary is growing, too. "Ho Ho" was
Santa. When someone would kid with you and say you
were bad, you'd reply "I'm not bad" (and truer words
were never spoken). You say "Papa," "Bay" for Bailey,
"Mal" for Mallory, "Dada," "Mama," "Tay" for Bronte.
You also impersonate a dog, a cat, a duck, a cow, a sheep,
a horse, and a monkey. And you make a monster sound
when you do your mean face. You love to perform, too—
not surprising considering your dad's family.

I enjoyed my time with you as much as anything I did over Christmas. In fact, in your eyes I see Christmas anew. That's the gift you gave me.

1/9/06

Your 2nd birthday was last Thursday. We had a party for you yesterday—Sunday. Your dad and Gracie brought you. They say you'd been asking for "Papa" for several days. I gave you a big hug and then pointed out where the Christmas tree had been in the dining room. You hadn't really noticed it was gone, but, when I told you we took it down, you frowned then looked around the room for it. I took you to the front door and showed you the discarded tree lying in the yard near the curb. There was a sense of awe in your eyes and then loss. For a brief moment, you seemed wiser than your years.

Every time you spotted your birthday cake on the kitchen counter you'd put your hand to your mouth, almost like sign language.

And when Blythe, Shane, and Aubrey joined us, well, the jealousy began. Aubrey is starting to catch on to the charm act so she was all over me. And you weren't happy.

While opening your presents, Aubrey would naturally reach for each thing you unwrapped. You'd scream and yell "mine!" You didn't hit each other this time—in fact, you even hugged and kissed one another. But the two of you are a real pair. The yin and yang of granddaughters. You're so wiry. She's so solid. You were an early achiever. She's been a late bloomer.

You have a sweet voice. Hers is husky. You have a sense of humor. She's just goofy.

Each visit is more rewarding because you are learning how to communicate better. I so look forward to our time together.

Happy birthday, Reagan.

2/5/06

Your cousin, Aubrey, up to this point has never been much of a cuddler; you, on the other hand, got cuddling down at an early age.

The other night we had rehearsal for <u>Working</u>. You stayed here with the girls. When we got home, you ran to me, climbed up in my lap, burrowed your head in my stomach, and closed your eyes. Suggestions of having to get bundled up to leave and go home were met with "No," *head shakes, and more burrowing. It makes me wonder why you are often reluctant to go home. Do you like it here that much? Do you dislike whatever is waiting for you at home? Am I such a prize as your Papa? Are you just contrary?*

Whatever it is, the cuddling is nice, especially now when my own children are grown. So I hope you keep the cuddling coming for a while.

2/25/06

Your Great-Great Grandma Thelma Williams died last night at the age of 96. I spent yesterday with her at the nursing home in Paris. Great Grandpa Jim was there, too. We took a 5 generations picture for both the Danville and Paris papers when you were a baby. She was proud of you. She was the last of her generation. You were the first of yours. Here I am today, her grandson and your grandfather, feeling an overwhelming sense of loss. I know you'll never know of her except through pictures and videos, but she was a part of you, a part of your heritage.

4/18/06

Two days ago, on Easter Sunday, you came to church with Grandma. Mallory, Flyn, and your dad were all there. Blythe and Aubrey and Great Grandma Sharon and Great Grandpa Earl were also there. In the middle of the service, I had to step out and go to the restroom. As I passed by, you whispered "Papa." Soon your dad brought you out because you were restless, and I suggested you look at the turtles in the garth. We found a small turtle right away, and then your dad discovered a big one, and I heard you say, "Mama...baby." What a smart little girl you are.

Later in the front yard of the house we tried to get pictures of you and Aubrey in your Easter dressed, but you were both determined to run off in opposite directions. What a little scamp you can be.

5/6/06

It's Saturday. In a few hours you'll be leaving to go to your other grandparents' house. We've had you here since Wednesday night. Your mom was in the hospital for her C-section and the birth of your half-brother. We've enjoyed having you around. You are such a sweet little girl, and your vocabulary has really increased.

Of course, you still say "Papa." Grandma Marsha is "Dah." Mallory is "Dal." You can say your Ms in words like "Mama," "milk," and "moo," but you can't manage the M in "Mal." Flyn is "Din." Blythe is "Bi." Book is "bik." You add the word "too" to just about every sentence. From the show <u>Dora the Explorer</u>, you say "Dah" for Dora, "Bee-oots" for Boots, "Baa-paa" for Backpack. From Maisy, you say "Me" for Maisy. You constantly ask where something is—"Where shoes at?"

Each night you have slept between Grandma and me. I've taken you to bed, read 3 books to you, and then sung my repertoire of songs—"You Are My Sunshine," "Tell Me Why," "Twinkle, Twinkle Little Star," and the Barney song. You're a very good sleeper, which is great for your weary grandparents.

You do a whole face routine—sad, angry, scared, and a thinking face, complete with hand to chin and a thoughtful "Hmm."

Last night, at dinner, when Mallory brought her glass of apple juice to the table, you asked, "Where my juice?" just as clear as anything? You are truly amazing sometimes. A smart little girl.

We will miss you when you go.

5/27/06

It's Saturday. Your grandma and the girls are shopping in Champaign. I'm sitting in the dining room writing in this journal and preparing to do some bills. You are playing in the living room with Bailey's huge playhouse—a toy that has been relegated to the basement for some time now since Bailey has gotten too old for it but has found a new companion in you.

Earlier this week your mom called your dad and said that he needed to take you for a couple of weeks because it was not safe for you at her house with Ryan. We didn't get much else in the way of specifics so we were naturally concerned for your safety. Since you dad is living on a couch of a friend who's taken him in, and the apartment they share is so small, we decided to keep you here.

At first you were very withdrawn—quiet, not making eye contact. On your first morning here you even curled up in the fetal position on the kitchen rug. You threw up several times, too. Your grandma thinks it's from stress, not a virus.

After some time you began to relax and get into the groove of our family and the old Reagan emerged. You've been relaxed, playful, and secure ever since.

I wrote some time ago about our fears that you were being physically abused and how difficult it has been for us, caught between wanting to guarantee your safety and being afraid of losing access to you. It seems like we're right back there again. This time we think you've witnessed more than your share of domestic violence. Putting you in a living situation where people are physically fighting in front of you is a type of abuse. Ryan has been aggressive with his former girlfriend. Your mom has been in a fight with a girl Ryan was seeing. Now the latest—Ryan and his brother (who's on probation) got into a physical fight earlier in the week while he was supposed to be watching you. You've been afraid of him since then.

Oh, what you must have witnessed. And what emotional damage that could leave.

We are again willing to call the abuse hotline to report this latest incident because our main goal is to keep you safe and secure.

We love you so much.

------

12 Teach us to realize the brevity of life, so that we may grow in wisdom.--Psalm 90: 12

(NLT)

7/2/06

I will forever be haunted by the last clear memory I have of you, my precious one. I was in the den on Father's Day two weeks ago, trying to get away from all the chaos in the house, when I heard tiny footsteps and then an inquisitive "Papa?" I want to hear it again and hug you and sing to you—"Because God made you, that's why I love you."

You died today although we don't know how or why. And Little Christmas will never be the same and Independence Day will always hold this memory. Tell me, what am I to do?

I love you, God's newest angel. I can die now knowing that you will be there waiting for me. Don't forget your Papa. I'll bring this journal along.

7/4/06

We found out yesterday that you were shaken, and that caused brain trauma. I'm sorry. I'm so sorry, my baby. We didn't take you out of there.

I remember another memory—when I saw you last. I took you back. I hugged you for so long. I should have kept driving toward some safe place. Father's Day will always be your day.

Finger to eye, crossed hands, point to you.

---

*4 He will wipe every tear from their eyes, and
there will be no more death or sorrow or
crying or pain. All these things are gone
forever.--Revelation 21: 4 (NLT)*

7/7/06

*Today is your funeral. It will be a difficult day for us
all. I feel more at peace because I saw your little body in
the casket yesterday with your dad and Great Grandpa Jim.
You looked like a porcelain doll, so beautiful, so peaceful.
You wore your yellow Easter dress, and you were covered
by a yellow blanket, just like you were sleeping. We had
your hair fixed better so it would look like how you wore it.*

*I knelt next to you and sang "Tell Me Why." I could
barely get a line out without sobbing. I apologized for
what I wasn't able to do to save you. I'm sorry, my angel.*

*I had them place half of a small medallion around your
neck. I will wear the other half the rest of my life. It says,*

"The Lord watch between me and thee when we are absent one from another." Gen. 31: 49.

We've decided to buy burial plots next to you so your Papa and Da will be with you always.

7/8/06

Yesterday, in the cemetery we released balloons for you. They floated straight up and into the sun until they were specks and we couldn't see them again.

Today, wherever I turn, I see your tiny face, so loving and so trusting. And I cry and say "Papa?" because you can't. Please remember me. I promise to come to you.

7/9/06

So many thoughts flood my brain—some painful, which keep me up at night or keep me from falling back asleep in the morning. Other thoughts sustain me if only for a short time. Some comforting thoughts came from catalogues in the mail, the ideas seemingly placed there for me to read.

Time is too slow for those who wait

Too swift for those who fear

Too long for those who grieve

Too short for those who rejoice

But for those who love—time is eternity.

--Henry Van Dyke

Life is not measured by the amount of breaths we take

but by the moments that take our breath away.

And if I go while you're still here…

Know that I still live on

Vibrating to a different measure

behind a thin veil you cannot see through.

You will not see me,

So you must have faith.

I wait the time when we can soar together again,

both aware of each other.

Until then, live your life to the fullest

And when you need me

just whisper my name in your heart

…I will be there.

If love could have saved you,
You would have lived forever.

Last night, as I sat on the front porch, the lightning bugs came out. I'm sorry, Reagan, that we never got to catch them and put them in jars. It was one of my summer plans for you.

Later today we want to go up to the cemetery to visit.

I'm thinking of you, my little angel. I'll always be your Papa.

7/11/06

Memories come back to me. They bring me comfort and horrible pain. My light has gone out. There is a hollow place in my chest. I don't want to forget.

When I would tell you "Papa loves Reagan," you would ask, "Daddy, too?" but your "too" would sound like "te-oo." I've repeated that sound, had conversations with you being both me and you. "Daddy, te-oo?" "Yes, Daddy, too." "Da, te-oo?" "Da, too." "Bay, te-oo?" "Yes, Bay, too." And so on.

I was the last in our family to see you alive and the last to see you before they closed the casket. I would have crawled in if I could. I bumped heads with you and said, "Boomp." We always did that.

I am so tired, so empty, so lonely for my little Reagan. I miss you so much.

7/15/06

Yesterday evening I took a camp stool and two of your favorite books up to the cemetery and sat by your grave and read to you. It was the Where's Maisy? *book and the touch and feel book with the bear on front.*

I am still challenging God to give me a sign that you are safe in Jesus' arms. If God could show up in a burning bush or a pillar of fire, why can't he help me? In this, my faith is not enough.

Your Grandma Marsha still thinks that you've shown up in the Barbie boom box that beeped and played in the rain last week on its own. Also, Mallory's cell phone beeped the other night for a text message when it was set to vibrate only.

Is that you, Reagan?

7/16/06

I'm sitting beside your grave wondering if you can hear me, wanting to know for sure that you are here standing by me. That's all I ask of God.

I brought <u>Dinosaur's Binkit</u> to read. I even did it in my dinosaur voice.

I want to cry—everyday. I'm afraid if I stop crying that I will not honor you anymore. Even when tears don't come, the emptiness in my heart is still heavy and painful. There is no joy in the world.

7/17/06

Today, Grandma Marsha, Great Uncle Shawn, and I came to see you. I cleaned off your grave, got rid of all the old dried out flowers. Then Grandma and Shawn put new flowers on your spot. There are two Doras, a pinwheel, an arrangement of silk flowers, and two butterflies, so others have been visiting you. I also read your <u>Count with Dora!</u> book to you—one of your favorites.

7/23/06

Yesterday, we went to Charleston to see Mallory perform at their show choir camp. The junior high group sang "For Good" from the musical <u>Wicked</u>. There, in the middle of the audience, I began to cry because the words reminded me of your impact on my life.

> *I've heard it said*
> *That people come into our lives for a reason*
> *Bringing something we must learn*
> *And we are led*
> *To those who help us most to grow*
> *If we let them*
> *And we help them in return*
> *Well, I don't know if I believe that's true*
> *But I know I'm who I am today*
> *Because I knew you...*
>
> *Like a comet pulled from orbit*
> *As it passes a sun*
> *Like a stream that meets a boulder*
> *Halfway through the wood*
> *Who can say if I've been changed for the better?*
> *But because I knew you*
> *I have been changed for good.*

It well may be

That we will never meet again

In this lifetime

So let me say before we part

So much of me

Is made from what I learned from you

You'll be with me

Like a handprint on my heart

And now whatever way our stories end

I know you have re-written mine

By being my friend...

Like a ship blown from its mooring

By a wind off the sea

Like a seed dropped by a skybird

In a distant wood

Who can say if I've been changed for the better?

But because I knew you

I have been changed for good.

*Reagan, I have been changed for the better because I knew
you. We are all better because of your short but significant
life. It won't be long for you (though an eternity for me)
before we are together. I look forward to that day.*

7/28/06

The month is almost over Reagan. Soon we'll think of the 2nd of every month as a reminder and every Sunday morning and, of course, Jan. 5, your birthday.

We are trying to cope, but we want to see you so that we know you are okay.

We've lost our little girl but we want to turn your memory into a great cause as a way to honor you and help other children. We're sorry we couldn't help you.

8/12/06

The other night, while starting the dishwasher, a good memory came back to me. You used to push the buttons on the dishwasher, sometimes just to see how I would react. You loved it when I pretended to be angry. You would laugh, then slowly put your finger up to a button and watch my facial expression change.

In one of the bottom drawers in the kitchen there was a contraption for steaming vegetables that you would open and close like leaves or petals of a flower. You loved playing with that, too—your favorite kitchen utensil, I think.

8/18/06

Hello, baby girl. A teacher I work with was concerned about me yesterday. She heard me say that I had to drink some wine most evenings and take some Tylenol PM to get to sleep, and she was worried where that might lead. Then she asked me an important question—"If Reagan could talk to you, what would she say?" Oh, if only you could talk to me. I've prayed to God, asking for that. But I couldn't answer right away. Now, a day later, I've given it some thought.

What would my perceptive and beautiful granddaughter say to me if she had a chance?

I hope she would tell me that she loved us and felt safe here. I think she would want us to be good and kind and funny whenever possible. I think she would want us to love her Daddy as much as we could. Maybe she would want us to still celebrate her birthday and her life. Most of all, I hope she would tell us that she'll wait for us in Heaven.

Reagan, I may need to put this journal aside for a time and hide it in a safe place. I'll write in it again when I can. Finger to eye, crossed hands, point to you. I am and will always be your Papa.

8/25/06

Your daddy moved out of the apartment he was sharing with his friend, Dan, and he brought all his belongings to our house. Some of the things he brought were yours—the new keyboard we got you for Christmas, your tricycle with a secret compartment under the seat where I found a giraffe puzzle piece you put there, a little shirt that says I ♥ Daddy, and your toy box. When I went through all of your toys, imagining that you were the last to place them there, I sank to my knees and cried over all of your possessions. The pain I feel, the loneliness for you, is as strong now as it was that terrible week in July.

Two years ago, we took a five generation picture and now the oldest and youngest generations are gone. My grandma and my granddaughter. I am not a grandson anymore, and I'm not your Papa.

Tomorrow, your daddy, my grown up little boy is leaving to work in Colorado for a least a few months. And now, though I think it is best that he go, I feel like I'm losing my son, too. Though he won't be near where you are buried, maybe you could fly to him to let him know that you still love him.

Oh, Reagan, please come to your Papa and Da, especially your Da. Your Grandma Marsha misses you so.

She cries and cries for her little baby. She makes a place for you in our bed. She sometimes wants to die so she can be with you. I do, too. But we have work to do—in your memory. We want to make our corner of the world a safer place so that you will live on.

Believe me, we would rather have you.

9/3/06

Yesterday was two months since you left us. The pain has not left, but being busy at school has helped us focus on something else for a while.

Today, we went to church for the first time in a while. Mallory, your grandma, and I performed with the praise band. People at church were happy to see us.

In these last few weeks, thoughts have come to me. I want to write them down so that they'll be preserved.

I was getting ready for church this morning, trying to shave and cut my hair. I noticed a deep furrow in the upper bridge of my nose almost between the brows. I realized it is from crying for two months. When my face contorts while I cry, that wrinkle is especially pronounced. Now I notice it—like a scar from a terrible accident.

I watch C-Span or C-Span 2 and search for the date in the upright corner of the screen when someone is giving a speech, a lecture, or a book reading. If it says 6/30/06 or earlier, I momentarily bargain for another chance or pretend that it is that date and you are still alive. Seeing a 7 or 8 for the month makes me sad.

I don't know what to say when people ask how I'm doing. For a while, I've said, "We're hanging in there," or "One day at a time." I don't know if people want to know how I'm doing. Maybe they're just making conversation. But we're definitely not "Fine." We never will be.

Your grandma is very sad when she leaves work late at night and has to drive through Tilton to go home. She can see the road we used to take to drive you home. She comes in with her eyes red because she's been crying. I wish I could make it all better. She was so proud of you, so good to you. She leaves a place for you in the middle of our bed. That's where you slept when you stayed with us.

We live each day in anticipation of seeing you again or being visited by you. We've read books about that happening. If you don't come today, then we'll look for you tomorrow.

Aunt Heather called a few weeks ago and said that, while driving, she had a clear vision unlike anything she had ever experienced before. She saw you sitting on Jesus' lap and you were both laughing and laughing.

I hope that's how it is, my Sunshine. You'll make Heaven brighter.

9/7/06

Why do I keep writing to you, Reagan? For a brief moment, even a second, I forget that you are gone. Maybe I hope you can read over my shoulder and know my sorrow and, more importantly, know my love for you.

I found a quote from Garrison Keillor who said: "We need to write, otherwise nobody will know who we are." I need to write, otherwise nobody will know who you were, Reagan, or who I was with you and without you.

A couple of weeks ago I had a dream about you, the only one I've had. In the dream, I was carrying you around a house, telling people that you were sick but assuring them that if we could only get to a doctor that you would be fine, that you hadn't died yet but that time was running out. Sadly, no one would listen to me. All my pleas fell on deaf ears. It was only the alarm going off that kept me from dreaming what was probably the inevitable.

I woke up and started the day heartbroken.

Maybe because you are constantly on my mind do I not dream about you—there is so little unfinished to think about, to dwell over.

On Wednesday nights, I drive to Hoopeston to teach my college class. I talk to you all the way up and back. I even reach out my hand to the second seat where you used to sit in the car seat we had for you, hoping that I'll feel tiny fingers or hear a soft "Papa," your way of letting me know that you live on. Please be at the end of my reach, please speak in the stillness of the van. Please, little girl, come to us.

9/10/06

Today was Grandparents' Day. I could have used a hug from you. Am I still your Papa? Are you Papa's girl? Are we connected by more than mere memory? Are you with me in whatever I do?

9/12/06

I have two pictures of you that are favorites. One is from Easter. You and Aubrey are sitting in the front yard. Your knees are drawn up. You look like a little philosopher. The other is of you lying on your daddy's chest. You are staring right at the camera.

When I look at that picture long enough, it seems like you begin to move. I look into your brown eyes and through them, entering a world of goodness and innocence and love. You stare at me from that photograph and you seem to say "This is what was meant to be, Papa." Your wisdom gives me strength.

When I was a boy, there was a movie entitled <u>Doctor Doolittle</u> starring Rex Harrison, with music and lyrics by Leslie Bricusse. In one scene the doctor says goodbye to a seal named Sophie before throwing her off a cliff to be reunited with her mate. The song he sings has always been a favorite moment of mine. Now the lyrics remind me of you and my favorite photograph.

> *When I look in your eyes*
> *I see the wisdom of the world in your eyes*
> *I see the sadness of a thousand goodbyes*
> *when I look in your eyes*
>
> *And it is no surprise*
> *to see the softness of the moon in your eyes*
> *the gentle sparkle of the stars in the skies*

when I look in your eyes

In your eyes
I see the deepness of the sea
I see the deepness of the love
the love I feel you feel for me

Autumn comes summer dies
I see the passing of the years in your eyes
and when we part there'll be no tears,
no goodbyes
I'll just look in your eyes

Those eyes so wise, so warm, so real
how I love the world your eyes reveal

Reagan, I will measure what time I have left—weeks,
months, years—by those eyes. I will continue to look in
your eyes, for there I find a doorway to you.

9/15/06
    There's a song by the Christian artist Chris Rice called
"Smile." Though it's about being impatient for Heaven

and looking forward to seeing God, I think of you when I hear it. You see, when I go to Heaven and see God, I'll get to see you, too. Some of the lyrics are:

> *So where are you now*
> *You're all I have, You're all I've known*
> *Your breath is breathing in my soul*
> *Still I am gasping, aching, asking*
> *Where are you now?*

> *'Cause I just want to be with You*
> *I just want this waiting to be over*
> *I just want to be with You*
> *And it helps to know the Day is getting closer*
> *But every minute takes an hour*
> *Every inch feels like a mile*
> *Till I won't have to imagine*
> *And I finally get to see You smile*

> *My journey's here, but my heart is There*
> *So I dream and wait, and keep the faith, while You*
>   *prepare*
> *Our destiny, till You come back for me*
> *Oh, please make it soon!*

Every afternoon in my empty classroom I play another song by Chris Rice called "Untitled Hymn (Come to Jesus)." I hold your photo close and peer into your eyes, and the tears come quickly. Every afternoon I wonder How far are you? How close am I?

Are you here in this room? Comforting me, whispering "Papa." I need to hear it, little girl

9/20/06

This past Sunday I preached at Great Grandpa Jim's church and used, as my text, a passage from Deuteronomy 30. It is a favorite of mine as it promotes living life fully. Like so many things now, I understand it anew. I interpret it through grief, anger, and doubt.

Verse 15 says "See, I set before you today life and prosperity, death and destruction." I always thought that meant live life fully, try to prosper, don't do anything which might lead to death and destruction.

I was wrong in that interpretation. There is so much more. The passage continues with verse 16: "For I command you today to love the Lord your God, to walk in his ways, and to keep his commands, decrees and laws; then you will live and increase, and the Lord your God will

[72]

bless you in the land you are entering to possess. But if your heart turns away and you are not obedient, and if you are drawn away to bow down to other gods and worship them, I declare to you this day that you will certainly be destroyed. You will not live long in the land you are crossing the Jordan to enter and possess."

By sinning, did I anger God? Did we all? Did we forsake God's commands, decrees, and laws? Because we weren't always obedient, did we bring about your death, Reagan?

We have affirmed our faith in God, believed He did not cause this to happen.

But did He?

We are destroyed. The happiness we hoped to possess when we beheld you is lost to us. Was this our punishment, our curse? Were we not good enough for God or for you, our sweet angel?

10 A final word: Be strong in the Lord and in his mighty power. 11 Put on all of God's armor so that you will be able to stand firm against all strategies of the devil. 12 For we are not fighting against flesh-and-blood enemies, but against evil rulers and authorities of the unseen world, against mighty powers in this dark world, and against evil spirits in the heavenly places. 13 Therefore, put on every piece of God's armor so you will be able to resist the enemy in the time of evil. Then after the battle you will still be standing firm. 14 Stand your ground, putting on the belt of truth and the body armor of God's righteousness. 15 For shoes, put on the peace that comes from Good News so that you will be fully prepared. 16 In addition to all of these, hold up the shield of faith to stop the fiery arrows of the devil. 17 Put on salvation as your helmet, and take the sword of the Spirit, which is the word of God.

18 Pray in the Spirit at all times and on every occasion. Stay alert and be persistent in your prayers for all believers everywhere.-- Ephesians 6: 10-18 (NLT)

9/27/06

Yesterday, Da and I met with a therapist for the first time to deal with our overwhelming grief. We talked about how much we loved (and love) you. We talked about all the terrible things that happened to you. We talked about how we miss you so much. The counselor, Debbie, is going to meet mostly with your grandma because she is having the hardest time. I have put a lot of my energy into helping with the case in any way I can and in working to hold DCFS accountable. I also want to educate people about SBS. Debbie says that I need to be a warrior and not a victim. I liked how she put that. I want to be a warrior for you, Reagan. Please fill my heart with courage and conviction. Please fly over my shoulder as I try to do all these things.

I'm scared. I'm lonely for you. I want to hear your voice. Can you put a word in to God to help? I don't know if He hears me anymore.

10/1/06

Another Sunday morning and another first of the month and so the tears have come easily today. After church, I visited the cemetery and discarded some faded flowers on your grave.

This evening I was sitting in the darkened den watching the last ten minutes of <u>The Green Mile</u> *when Great Grandpa Jim came in and sat down. The film was showing an old man who has outlived his loved ones and who wants to die. When the credits began to roll, Grandpa said quietly, "Strange that I should come in on a scene about death." Then he said, "Your Uncle Frank died this morning."*

I cried again for him, for Aunt Gin—my favorite people in the world—, for our family, for me, and even for you, Reagan Emery. I hope you'll get to know your Uncle Frank. They never had children of their own but they were the most loving and generous people I ever knew. Uncle Frank was 94. Take him by the hand and love him dearly,

Reagan. He was your Great Great Great uncle, and he was a great soul.

10/9/06

On Saturday, Da and Papa drove down to Pigeon Forge, Tennessee with our friends, George and Erin. We made these plans two weeks before you died. In early June, our family and the Halls family vacationed here for a week. It is hard to look at pictures of our trip and not think about you and what would happen only a month later. And during this trip, we have found so many things remind us of you. There is where I stood and talked to your daddy about finding daycare for you. There is where we bought the bear that was later buried with you. There is where we stayed when we should have been spending every precious moment with you.

One of our favorite stores is the Christmas Place. I wanted to find a Christmas ornament for you and Aubrey to add to our tree and to the other family ornaments we have. Your grandma had to leave the store; she couldn't stand to be in there because the thought of Christmas doesn't bring to mind a baby's birth but our baby's absence. How can

[77]

we celebrate your birthday or the Christ child's birthday when our pain is too great?

Will all those rituals we have celebrated now be tainted? We see you in everything we do, even in the activities you were not a part of. Can we anticipate the first day of Christmas without dreading the twelfth day? Will this far off vacation destination where you never visited be ruined because you are no longer in our world?

We need peace. We need a glimpse of you.

10/10/06

We got a real taste of the Smokies this morning. Between Knoxville and the Kentucky state line, early morning mist nestled down in the valleys between the mountain ridges. Each peak looked like a tree-covered island floating in the sea. For a moment, depression set in, and I began to think about your missing beauty like this— and then all the things you'd miss.

Your first visit from the Tooth Fairy, preschool programs, your first day of Kindergarten, catching lightning bugs and putting them in empty jars, your first trip to Disney World, 5th grade graduation, middle school, camp, high school, rituals of teenage years like dances and dating and games and getting a driver's license and graduation, the first kiss, college, the first job, engagement, marriage, your daddy walking you down the aisle, your mama crying, a first child...

Then I noticed something about the mountains around me. The misty scenery, the sun's light playing on the orange, red, and yellow leaves, our looking down into the shrouded valleys—it was a perfect moment of grace. Soon, however, we drove into the fog and the scene turned gloomy. We were socked in for a while and I realized—

From where we were, the earth was depressing and gray, but above us, where you were, it was clear and beautiful.

I hope you're looking down on us in the darkness, knowing there is still light above.

10/11/06

Last night, Da and Papa attended a candlelight vigil at Your Family Resource Connection. I brought along your 2 year old picture and clutched it closely during the program. Toward the end, three candles were lit—one for survivors of abuse, one for those going through abuse now, and one for those who died because of it. When that candle began to glow, Da and I wept for you, little Reagan, because we miss you so much and because you should have been spared.

How could anyone have wanted to hurt our baby?

[NOTE: See the section of the book beginning on page 461 entitled Social Media on the many reactions and opinions of area residents regarding the ongoing and often stalled investigation]

10/20/06

Reagan, we are doing so much on your behalf—to bring honor to your memory and to make up for the mistakes we made, the fears we had, the facts we thought we knew.

We rarely spoke to your Papa Gary and Da Becky. Now, we all wish we had, for together we might have been able to save you. Now, together, we will work to carry on your name and the legacy you left behind.

I write poetry and music from time to time, and I've been working on lyrics for a song for you. I hope to have our band perform it for your Da around Christmas. Here are the words—

> *At Christmastime, I watched you*
> *As you danced around the tree.*

I caught it all on video—
How happy you could be!
You hid from me behind a door
Then looked up with a smile.
I didn't know you'd have to leave
In such a little while.

But wait at Heaven's door.
One day I'll be there, too.
Until I come
Know you're with me
In everything I do.
Please wait at Heaven's door
Though it may take some years.
Hold me close when I am sad
And wipe away my tears.

Were you an angel sent to us,
A gift from God above.
To touch us with your pensive eyes,
To show us how to love?
And though your time with us was brief
You changed us all for good.
I'd give my life to have you back—

Oh, if I only could.

But wait at Heaven's door.
One day I'll be there, too.
Until I come
Know you're with me
In everything I do.
Please wait at Heaven's door
Though it may take some years.
Hold me close when I am sad
And wipe away my tears.

Hide and seek
Seek and find
Knock and the door will open

The hours are days, the days are weeks,
The weeks drag on like years
But every sunset in the west
Means our reunion nears
So, leave me here, go on ahead
Toward that Day so bright.
I'm in the dark except for this—
You're dancing in His light.

So wait at Heaven's door.

One day I'll be there, too.

Until I come

Know you're with me

In everything I do.

Please wait at Heaven's door

Though it may take some years.

Please calm me down when I am mad,

Please dance with me when I am glad,

Please hold me close when I am sad

And wipe away my tears.

Baby girl, I vow that you will be with me—in my heart—in everything I do.

Papa

10/25/06

Everyday I check out myspace.com for clues or gossip
relating to the case. Sometime, though, I am touched by
what I find. Your mom has kept up your myspace, and
many people who love you write to you there. There's a
big picture of Dora smiling and waving to the screen. How
you would have loved that.

Your former daycare provider, Christina, left a
message—

I was thinking about you today and decided to write. I
had to get an extra cot out today for a new child to sleep on
at nap time. When I pulled it out the name tag
on the side was yours so I put it back. I wasn't ready to
share it with anyone else. So the daycare kids and I got on
to your profile to say how much we miss and love you—

The Daycare

Reagan, I'm sure you will keep appearing—in our
thoughts, our dreams, in the photos we discover buried
under a pile of papers, in a toy left then found, in a name
tag left in storage. Each discovery brings us terrible pain
and a moment of joyful reunion.

[84]

10/31/06

A year ago I wrote about receiving a big hug from both of my precious granddaughters. My cup ran over that evening. Now, a year later, my cup has spilled and all goodness and mercy has run out.

Today is the first of several holidays that you won't be with us. I don't look forward to the next few months. All our joy will be tempered by grief, by loneliness. My God, what are we going to do without you, baby girl?

11/3/06

We donated copies of the book <u>The Fall of Freddie the Leaf</u> by Leo Buscaglia to both the DHS and Edison libraries in your memory along with bookmarks which had your obituary printed on them. The book is a profound grown up children's story about a leaf who passes through the seasons and then gently dies. It is about accepting death, something we cannot do nor, I suppose, will we ever be able to do when it comes to you.

We have been sad these past weeks, as sad as we ever have been. We dread Thanksgiving and Christmas coming because of our missing granddaughter. We've even talked about not decorating although we know that is not possible.

Life must go on. It must. But we find it difficult to come up with a reason.

We ordered Christmas ornaments for you and Aubrey. Yours is an angel sitting on a cloud and the word Joy— what you brought us and what we've lost. Aubrey's is a child hanging over a swing and holding on to a garland— so animated, so Aubrey. We never bought you and Aubrey ornaments before this, and we should have. We meant to. Just like we meant to do a lot of things with the long life you had before you. Maybe we should banish the words "meant to" and "ought" and "should have" from the vocabulary since they result in wasted time and lost chances.

That brings me back to Freddie the leaf. Great Grandpa Jim read that book at Uncle Frank's burial service. He was buried next to his parents and near his brother Emory (that's the correct spelling according to the tombstone even though I've seen it spelled with an e, like we spelled your middle name). Grandpa Jim had an old copy from 1982. Da and I purchased 20th Anniversary editions which came out after the author died. In a postscript in the back of the book I gave to the Edison library today, I found that the day after Leo Buscaglia died, a sheet of paper was found in his typewriter which read

"Every moment spent in unhappiness is a moment of happiness lost." I sat on a tiny chair in the library and began to cry. Maybe it was a message from Papa's girl reminding her lonely and grieving Papa not to lose happiness. Not to lose Christmas. Not to lose her birthday. Not to lose joy.

I'll try, Reagan. I'll try to do my best even though my best is not enough.

11/6/06

Yesterday was All Saints' Day at Central Christian. Papa and Da, Mallory, Flyn, Blythe, and Shane were there along with your mom and Papa Green. The service was about gathering around the throne of God, being in the presence of Jesus. We know you are there now, and, one day, we will join you.

At one point names of deceased church members were read aloud and names appeared on the screen in the order that people passed away. As March, April, May, and June went by, I wanted to stop the progression and, miraculously, have you with us. Then July 2 came and your name. Papa Green, Blythe, Mallory, Da, and I went up to light your candle. I offered to let your other Papa

[87]

light the candle, but, in his typical gentle way, he insisted that I do it.

We all cried. Our friends in the congregation cried. I think they felt, like us, that older people die of natural causes, and that is the cycle of life and death, but that your death was a tragedy because you were so innocent. A child, a trusting, loving child. Our loss was our own, but it was a loss shared by our church family.

During communion, Don played a video of the song "Untitled Hymn (Come to Jesus)" by Chris Rice, a song I listen to in my empty classroom every workday, one over which I cry when I hear it. Don didn't know this, I'm sure, but in the verse which talks about dancing with Jesus, I always picture you twirling about barely able to contain your joy. On the video was a child of about 10 or so twirling about. I couldn't help but think of you, picturing you at 10 still dancing with joy, regretting that I wouldn't see my oldest granddaughter dance anymore.

Are you dancing in Heaven? Will you one bright and never ending day dance again for me?

11/10/06

I had to go up to the cemetery this afternoon and take down all the decorations and gifts that people have left at your grave. Sunset is getting ready for winter. We left the solar lamp and the angel as a marker. I brought home a Dora holding a star, another Dora with a purple brush, a My Little Pony with a white brush, four Dora hair ties, a pair of pink, plastic dress up shoes, a soft lamb, a pink butterfly decoration, a pretty stained glass butterfly decoration, and three purple and silver windmills. I wanted so much to believe that those windmills spun around when I spoke to you because your little spirit was blowing them. They have dirt on the tips where they were stuck in the ground—dirt from your grave, from beneath the surface of the grass, down close to you. I don't know what to do with these things except to bag them up and store them away. They're just sitting here now on the floor of the den waiting for a little girl to come and play with them—a little girl who won't be coming anymore.

11/11/06

Tonight, we watched <u>The Polar Express</u>. There was a moment when I felt your presence very strongly, and it *brought just a moment of peace. When the film was over, I found the book. It begins much like the movie's narration—*

On Christmas Eve, many years ago, I lay quietly in bed. I did not rustle the sheets.

I breathed slowly and silently. I was listening for a sound...

I thought of the many nights I have lain quietly in bed, breathing slowly and silently, listening for the sound of your voice whispering my name.

The Polar Express is about the first gift of Christmas, a silver bell from the harness of Santa's sleigh. Only if one believes can he hear that bell ring. Then another Christmas movie comes to mind—It's a Wonderful Life— and a famous line—"Every time a bell rings an angel gets his wings." So I'm hoping to hear the sound of a special bell this Christmas. I will know then that my little Reagan has made it.

At one time most of my friends could hear the bell, but as years passed, it fell silent for all of them... Though

I've grown old, the bell still rings for me as it does for all who truly believe.

11/16/06

Your great aunt Elaine sent an e-mail to me today, a forward from Oprah's Mission Calendar. The quote, from the Gospel of Thomas, read "If you bring forth what is within you, what you bring forth will save you."

I don't know what is within me anymore. As I look over these pages since you died, I discover a mixture of emotions, a muddled mess. From the depths of depression and fatalism to the heights of hope, from loneliness and pain to peace and the promise of Heaven. What is in me is anger and confusion and regret and fear but also resolve and determination and, strangely, a clarity I've not had before. You, little girl, will somehow have to save me. Your home movie images or your photographs or your pilgrim spirit. You are within me and upon me and around me. Reagan, you will need to save your Papa.

11/19/06

Today was Thanksgiving Sunday. Don encouraged us to be thankful as a way to worship God. How can I rejoice for my many blessings when my one blessing—you, Reagan—was taken away?

I sat there listening and numb while he spoke about gratitude, words that at any other time in my life I would have gladly accepted, wholeheartedly agreed with. And during communion tears ran down my face. At first they weren't tears of thanksgiving but of sadness that your chair would be empty this coming Thursday and then again next month when we gathered to open presents.

For some reason, though, I thought, first, of sending a Thanksgiving card to your other Papa and Da, inviting them to church. Then I wondered what I would say to them, and the idea came to me. Maybe we were all meant to come together in this fundraising effort because we were strong enough to do it. Maybe our families were chosen for this tragedy because we could handle it and respond positively.

After the service, Don asked how I was doing, and I shared with him my...well, not a belief because I don't know if I believe it totally, so maybe my...speculation that

God gave us what we could handle. He referenced a
scripture passage—I Corinthians 10:13.

No test or temptation that comes your way is
beyond the course of what others have had to face. All you
need to remember is that God will never let you be
pushed past your limit; he'll always be there to help you
come through it.

11/21/06

Tonight, we watched <u>Meet Me in St. Louis</u>. It is usually
the first Christmas movie we play because there is a
Halloween section and then a Christmas part. I think
we've avoided the film this long because of one lovely but
now haunting song—"Have Yourself a Merry Little
Christmas," particularly these lyrics:

> *Someday soon we all will be together*
> *If the fates allow*
> *Until then we'll have to muddle through somehow*
> *So have yourself a merry little Christmas now*

Last year, after your first injury, visit to the emergency
room, and x-ray, I think I had my first doubts about safety

[93]

and security. Now with you gone I see the fates didn't allow us another year, another Christmas, and we are left to muddle through.

But someday, and soon I hope, we all will be together. Until then, I'll miss you, Reagan, more than I ever knew was possible.

11/23/06

Thanksgiving. This morning I went out to the grocery store to get an anniversary card for Shane and Blythe, a newspaper, some Coke, a loaf of bread, and flowers for your grave. I wanted to spend some quiet time with you. The sky was very blue, with a few wisps of clouds. The temperature was very mild. I set up one of our collapsible chairs next to you and had a long chat.

Later, in the afternoon, when it was time for dinner, I couldn't say a prayer. I had actually been dreading that moment, not wanting to get too emotional or upset others.

Had we gone around the table and shared what we were thankful for, I would have said, in this order, "Reagan and the time we had with her and how much she is in our hearts; my family because they are strong and I love them; finally, tears which everyday help me deal with my sadness and prove that my grief is still present and my emotions still strong."

Shane, Blythe, and Aubrey were here. Aubrey still talks about you. She kept us laughing. She still plays hard to get. Not like you. You never hesitated to love or hug me.

WITY started playing Christmas music. Once in the background I heard "Christmastime is Here" from <u>A Charlie Brown Christmas</u>. I remembered sitting in the hospital room last December when you were sick and watching that program while you slept in the bed beside me. Hearing it made me sad.

There's some news in the family. Blythe is pregnant. And your daddy is coming home soon. I know he is homesick. We miss him, too. Still, I dread his returning to Danville. I don't think he'll be safe. I'm worried for him like I was worried for you.

11/27/06

When I started writing this journal I thought I'd write about important moments in your life, the kind we preserve with photographs. Since July, I seem to write about many topics in one entry. Because of who I am, what I'm like, and what I do for a living, I get discouraged at the lack of focus. My thoughts come in a whirlwind, flying about me and chaotic. Sometimes the thoughts, coupled with just living day-to-day, come at me relentlessly, like ocean waves against which I'm trying to tread water and keep my head up.

I'm more forgetful these days from too much thinking and not enough focusing.

So here are my latest ideas—

I was watching an episode of <u>Inside the Actors' Studio</u> *when the host, James Lipton, asked his usual list of questions. The last one brought tears to my eyes because I thought of how I'd answer. Lipton asked, "If Heaven exists, what do you want to hear God say when you enter the gates?"*

"Here's Reagan" would be my response.

Don's sermons have so accurately reflected my struggles these past few weeks.

He talked about Jonah and the consequences of running from God.

He talked about Esther and the power of one individual who can and must make a difference.

Yesterday, he talked about Zechariah, the priest, and his barren but blameless wife, Elizabeth. For years the couple prayed for a child, but none came as if the prayers had fallen on deaf ears. One day, when Zechariah is in the temple, expecting no miracle, the angel Gabriel appears to tell him that she would deliver a son who would become the great prophet, John the Baptist. Since Zechariah does not believe, he is struck dumb.

I felt a little like that old man. Are my prayers just "therapeutic soliloquies?" Do I think God isn't listening because I haven't seen you yet? Is there that little bit of doubt keeping me from having faith? Maybe God will answer, is answering, my prayers even now.

We continue to see wristbands. I was interviewed for and appeared on Channel 15 WICD twice on Sunday and a couple of times this morning to promote the cause. I also did a spot for Channel One. They played "You Are My Sunshine" underneath a picture of you surrounded by bracelets. I hope we can get people talking and understanding.

Da put up the Christmas houses last night. Please come and see them. She did it for you, baby girl. In case you are able to stop by...

Several months ago, I ordered a shipment of storybooks by Dr. Seuss and other authors. These are books I would have gotten you, and so, in your name, I placed an order, thinking that I would donate them to other children or Your Family Resource Connection. I forgot about the books until they came in October addressed to the Parents of Reagan Williams. Today, I got another two books, along with a form letter. The letter stated, among other things: "This month, and every month you and Reagan will enjoy hours of fun from great storybooks by Dr. Seuss and His Friends." I didn't know about the letters, that the company would refer to you. I went ahead and cancelled the account. I don't think I could deal with that every month.

Oh, I miss you so.

11/28/06

Two weeks ago I subscribed to an Internet service called Grief Share. A new daily devotion is sent to me each morning. Today's topic was on experiencing joy again. The scripture that was referenced today was the text I used for a sermon just weeks before you passed away.

In John 16, Jesus says: "I tell you the truth, you will weep and mourn while the world rejoices. You will grieve, but your grief will turn to joy...Now is your time of grief,

*but I will see you again and you will rejoice, and no one
will take away your joy."*

*Is it a coincidence that I revisit that scripture now or
that I read it from the pulpit before you went away? Was I
being prepared for losing you?*

*Joy is what I lost when you died. Joy is the word on the
angel which hangs from a branch of our Christmas tree.
Jesus promises that God will restore the joy I have not felt
since the morning of July 2. Reagan, will you see me
again? Will I see you and rejoice?*

12/3/06

*Five months yesterday have passed since you died and
still no arrest. The last time I spoke with Frank Young, the
State's Attorney, I came away with a better understanding
of his strategy. Patience, trust, and not enough
aggressiveness on our part led to your death, but maybe
patiently waiting is what we will need to do during the
investigation. And trusting in justice and in God's plan.*

*I found a saying in a catalogue from Mary Anne
Radmacher which suggested "Courage doesn't always
roar. Sometimes courage is the quiet voice at the end of*

the day saying 'I will try again tomorrow.'" Perhaps being quietly persistent is what is necessary now.

I have so many thoughts on this cold weekend. Your other Papa and Da purchased an evergreen spray for your grave. It looked so pretty and fresh. Sometimes the sprays are called blankets. I thought of you warm under that evergreen blanket, protected from the harsh winter winds, and then I cried. We let you down. We didn't protect you. You didn't have a chance against the monster that did this to you. You should be caught up in the lights and the carols, anticipating the arrival of Santa. You should...

We should...

They should...

Yesterday, a small box arrived and inside an ornament from Karolyn Grimes, the former child actress, who played Zuzu in It's a Wonderful Life and Debbie in The Bishop's Wife, two favorite Christmas movies. On the ornament is a photo of Karolyn with Cary Grant who plays Dudley, the angel. He tells the little girl about a shepherd boy whose flock is endangered by a lion. When the danger has passed, he writes a song, the Twenty-third Psalm, which begins "The Lord is my shepherd, I shall not want."

I asked that Karolyn inscribe the back of the ornament with "He restoreth my soul" and her signature, but she added *"In memory of Reagan."* Both Papa and Da cried when we looked at it together. We will treasure the ornament always.

Life is so fragile. Last night, on the way back from seeing a movie, we nearly hit a deer that jumped in front of the car. Da and I were both touching the rosary which hangs from the rearview mirror, trying to adjust it. It almost seemed like we went through the deer, which looked to me like a white blur, but there was no contact. We could have been killed. That's how close we were to seeing you again. And I wasn't afraid.

12/7/06

I was in the principal's office today when an emergency call came in from Shane. I was afraid that something had happened to Aubrey or that Blythe had lost the baby or that your daddy had been hurt.

Shane said that Ian had been arrested. He flew home yesterday from Colorado. A friend picked him up at the airport but got tired during the drive home, so your daddy drove, went too fast through Milford, got pulled over and, when the police found out there were outstanding fines, was *arrested. The police from the Sheriff's department in Vermilion County were supposed to drive up to get him and bring him back. I suppose about now he is sitting in jail at the Public Safety Building.*

As his father, I want to set things right, but I don't think that is the best action to take. Reagan, I love your daddy, but so many decisions he has made have caused heartache for the rest of us.

He shouldn't have been with your mom, but then we wouldn't have known you, but then we wouldn't have lost you, either. And given the choice of never knowing you or being touched by your life for two and a half years, I would selfishly choose to know you.

You died because conditions were created by your parents who were too young, too naïve, too stupid, and, in your daddy's case, too lazy to deserve you.

Your daddy ran into the back of a car. He got a ticket but didn't pay it—even though we told him to. Last year, on the day after Thanksgiving, he was arrested for driving without a seatbelt, for having no insurance, and for not paying his fine. In court, he was given time to pay a larger fine, but he lost his license. And now, a year later, that first accident results in more jail time and an even larger fine. And we can't bail him out this time. We won't bail him out.

It's going to be so difficult not to run to save my little boy.
I imagine him alone, scared, ashamed, perhaps even hating
himself for his stubbornness and stupidity. Maybe if he had
stayed in Colorado until his contract ran out, he could have
avoided this somehow, but he did it his way.

Will these events lead to more tragedy? Will it ever
end?

I thought losing his little girl would somehow straighten
him out, but he only digs himself a deeper hole.

I'm sorry, Reagan, for writing about this. He needs you
now to direct his life. In fact, we all need you.

12/9/06

Because your Great Grandpa Jim has such a huge heart
and because he wants things to go well for his family, he
bailed your daddy out of jail yesterday. Our reunion with
your daddy didn't go well. A lot of anger and frustration
and disappointment led your Papa and Da to say things
that were hurtful. Even though he doesn't need reminding,
I told your daddy again how his actions led to your death in
an indirect way. I told him, too, how much his family was
still hurting. I also told him that we loved him and feared
for his safety, but, after what was said earlier, I don't know

how easy it was to believe me. Later, after he left, I realized I hadn't even hugged him, and I began to wonder if you were there in the den taking part in this reunion, hugging us, pulling on us to make peace.

I'm sorry, Reagan, for any mean things I said to your daddy. How selfish I was. Please forgive me.

I did call your daddy later to apologize. He was with his friends eating dinner at the truck stop, a favorite spot of his. I told him again that I loved him.

---

9 Two people are better off than one, for they can help each other succeed. 10 If one person falls, the other can reach out and help. But someone who falls alone is in real trouble. 11 Likewise, two people lying close together can keep each other warm. But how can one be warm alone? 12 A person standing alone can be attacked and defeated, but two can stand back-to-back and conquer. Three are even better, for a triple-braided cord is not easily broken.--
Ecclesiastes 4: 9-12 (NLT)

12/10/06

Today, during church, when Don told us that Mary and Elizabeth both saw their children die before them, your Da began to cry. Eventually, she had to leave and go outside for some fresh air. She wasn't sure why she had this panic attack but it frightened us both.

Because you came and stayed with us in May and slept between us we think of you at bedtime. You're there with us, and we can't be intimate.

I bought Da a Christmas card. There was a passage from Philippians 2: 2—"Make my joy complete by being of the same mind, maintaining the same love, united in spirit, intent on one purpose." Maintaining love has been a challenge.

Here's what I wrote in Da's card—

Marsha,

Since July, I've looked at the rest of the world through a screen door. Sometimes I've focused on the wire, and the world beyond has been blurred. Sometimes I've looked through the door to the outside; what I've seen has been almost clear but still altered and not quite right. Reagan is the screen. I think of her alone sometimes; at other times I

see life through her. She never entirely goes away.
Especially at night.

For several months I didn't even think of making love.
For the last two months, I think about it a lot and wonder
how we can be together again. The nights are hard
because we're left with thoughts and silence, but I want you
to know that I love you and that, when you're ready, I'm
ready. Let it be our gift to each other.

G

I pray that losing you won't result in losing everything else.
You did show us how to love—that's what I wrote in your
song. Maybe you can help us here.

12/11/06

I realized some weeks ago that I had not sung publicly
since July except for two occasions—auditions for a
musical and Bailey's birthday. No songs in church, no
singing along to the radio. I didn't intend to stop singing,
but now not singing has become intentional. I don't have
much of a song in my heart except as it relates to you. I
have sung privately—beside your grave. I have also sung
the melody line for your song. Just like I need to cry for

you every day, I need to keep from singing. I've sung for joy, and joy is gone.

12/12/06

On Channel One, reporters have been asking students what they want for Christmas. Cell phones, cars, vacations all seem to be the popular answers. If I were interviewed I would say, "I want a time machine."

12/13/06

Tonight, on the way to teaching my night class in Hoopeston, I had a breakdown. I haven't made sounds like that since that first few days after you died and I wept when listening to "You Are My Sunshine." I remember being cradled in Da's arms. I recall wailing "They took my Sunshine away" over and over. Tonight was like that. While driving sixty-five miles an hour, trying to see the road through a blur of tears, I yelled out "I'm sorry, baby girl. I'm so sorry. We couldn't save you. We couldn't save you." I yelled it over and over and, for a brief moment, thought of accelerating until I lost control of the car. But then I thought of Bailey, and I couldn't go any faster. She still needs me.

The wailing sounds I made scared me. It's a dark place. I don't think I can go there again.

The dried tears left my eyes red and puffy and my cheeks tight. I'm also feeling very lonely for my family right now.

12/15/06

Oh, Reagan, I miss you so much, especially during this time. I keep going back to read entries I wrote when you were alive and wonder for a moment if the ending will be different. And it won't. It never will. I'm trying to cling to the air.

On Wednesday, after I had written the previous entry, I was astonished by the generosity of a DACC student. She asked for a bracelet, asked who to make the check out to, put the check in an envelope, and gave it to me before leaving class. When I opened the envelope there was a check for $100. She didn't know you personally but she was touched by your story and by our fundraising efforts. Her name was Deena, and she's similar to so many people in this area who've been so concerned, compassionate, and generous.

Today in the DHS library, a boy, Miles, gave me a ten dollar bill. Others have bought bracelets in bulk or given a five dollar bill and said to keep the wristband and sell it to someone else. Your great aunt Barb sent a fifty dollar check so that she could give bracelets to her family. Each time people approach we are so touched by their kindness.

People also ask about the delay in the arrest. We are not alone, but both your Papas and Das are so lonely for you.

We look to Aubrey to fill some of the void but her personality is still so unpredictable. She has moments of great warmth, great love, but then she runs away or has a kicking, screaming tantrum. She's not you, and maybe we're unfair to wish her more like you. We probably try too hard with her. There was never any need for trying with you. You were a perfect fit all along, maybe the one perfect fit of my life. And because you will not have a chance to grow up and lose innocence and, perhaps, grow distant, our perfect love will always remain. I hope you like the poem. You are now our Everlasting Child and Love's pure and holy Light.

How bright it must be in Heaven.

12/20/06

A year ago I wrote that you had recuperated from your stay in the hospital. "Welcome back, my precious one," I wrote. And now, this year, I just want you back. You've gone to a distant place I can't reach. And life doesn't seem fair.

Tonight, we were trying to find a song for your daddy to sing at Great Grandpa Jim's church on Christmas Eve. Da found a song by Amy Grant called "Christmas Lullaby (I Will Lead You Home)." The lyrics are so appropriate for those women and their children from the shelter who will be at the church at Great grandpa Jim's invitation.

Are you far away from home
This dark and lonely night
Tell me what best would help
To ease your mind
Someone to give
Direction for this unfamiliar road
Or one who says, "Follow me and
I will lead you home."

How beautiful
How precious

The Savior of old

To love so

Completely

The loneliest soul

How gently

How tenderly

He says to one and all,

"Child you can follow Me

And I will lead you home…"

As Da sang through the song for your daddy, she came to the verse from "Away in a Manger," words we know but, like so many songs, words which have new and painful meaning:

Be near me, Lord Jesus

I ask Thee to stay

Close by me forever

And love me I pray

Bless all the dear children

In Thy tender care

And take us to Heaven

To live with Thee there.

Da stopped before the last line and cried, "I guess that's another one I can't sing."

From our point of view on Earth, God didn't bless you. Maybe, when He took you to heaven to live with Him, that was the greatest gift of all. It's just hard to believe that when there are no small arms about my neck. Why couldn't God have protected you?

An elderly member of our church, Everett Meeker, died this past Monday just months after his wife of sixty years passed away. In his grief, Everett always found the time to ask how we were doing. I guess this past Sunday he was heard to say that Christmas was his wife's favorite time of year and that he wanted more than anything to see her face and that of his Lord's. The next day he was gone.

I hope he got his wish.

If it were only that simple for me.

12/24/06

Christmas Eve—my favorite night of the year when I try, if only for a moment, to steal away outside and look at the stars and a say "a prayer to the close and holy darkness."

This evening was difficult because I felt your absence strongly. Through the 7 p.m. candlelight service (where your Aunt Bailey sang so simply and beautifully) to opening presents with Great Grandpa Jim and Great Grandma Roberta. I held the tears back, but I don't think I was very convincing.

After everyone left, I drove up to your grave. I wrote "Merry Christmas, Reagan" on your Dora Magna Doodle. I sang your two favorite songs, voice cracking from emotion and my nose running from a combination of crying and the cold I have.

Before I left I asked that you send us a sign, and then I slowly turned around, looking off in the distance, hoping to see you approaching me. Suddenly, I saw three deer staring at me, standing between me and the mausoleum which was all lit up. I really only saw their silhouettes, but they just stared silently and serenely. After a minute the largest one snorted, and they ran off. As I drove out of the cemetery, I looked for them, but they were gone.

Thank you, Reagan. I had a feeling of peace and, somehow, certainty that these three represented the Trinity in whom I have to place my faith.

Thank you for your special Christmas gift.

12/29/06

I haven't done very well at the four Christmas gatherings we've had this year—on December 22 with Great Grandma Sharon and Great Grandpa Earl, on Christmas Eve with Great Grandpa Jim and Great Grandma Roberta, on Christmas morning with Da, your daddy, and your aunts (Mallory, Flyn, and Bailey), and today with Great Grandma Cookie and Great Grandpa Dave. On each occasion I have found myself choking back tears and missing you so much. When I am most lonely for you, I am probably at my most selfish. Because I don't think I ever had as loving and as uncomplicated a relationship with anyone as I did—and do—with you, I sometimes feel like I'm the only one truly grieving.

I saw pictures today of you from last Christmas that I had never seen before, and I cried. One was of you and Aubrey sitting together on a chair and wearing antlers. One was a close up of you. Another was you on my lap. We are effortless in our love, and the photo shows two people at ease with each other.

Well-meaning family and friends will suggest that I need to move on and accept what has happened, but I can't. I acknowledge what happened, but I can't accept that that's

how it had to happen. I'm not ready to get on with my life,
yet I know that that may be what you need.

I've been reading a book by psychic Allison DuBois
entitled <u>We Are Their Heaven</u>. She believes that our
deceased loved ones share in our lives and want us to be
happy so that they can share in that happiness. She writes:

"Your loved ones don't want you to suffer for the rest of
your life, paying homage to them through your tears. They
sit there with you while you cry, and the harder you cry, the
louder you get. But of you are drowning them out with
your sobs, then how can they be heard? Allow peace to
enter your heart…and ask them to let you know they're
with you. They will find a way."

Allison goes on to say that, since hugs and kisses are not
possible anymore, those who grieve should talk to the
deceased, eat their favorite food, or find a picture that
draws them in.

"Remember, they can hear you and touch you still, so
it's a matter of your learning how to reach them again.
You're playing catch-up with them. They've been trying to
reach you since the day they died."

I know that she is right, but it is still so hard to let you
go.

1/1/07

We said goodbye to a terrible year last night with the hope that better days are ahead. You made the front page of The Commercial News yearend review of top stories. Inside, the editor mentioned your loss at the hands of your abuser. We have several albums of clippings about the many accomplishments of our family but I've included none of the articles about your death and its aftermath. Maybe one day I'll take those clippings I've saved and put them together in one special album. Not now, though.

Because of Allison DuBois's book, I've started thinking again about signs. Why did I hug you a second time the last day I saw you alive? Why did I feel compelled to do that? Did I know you weren't long for this world?

What about the deer that jumped over the car on the interstate or the three deer in the cemetery on Christmas Eve? Why, when I turned on the Tournament of Roses Parade this morning, was the band beginning to play "You Are My Sunshine"?

Now I look in every corner, in your little rocking chair, on the bench in the dining room, and I smile, hoping that you are there. I look at your pictures in the hallway and see them staying the same while your cousin Aubrey's pictures change and age.

Was this truly how your life was supposed to end? That,
ultimately, we couldn't change the inevitable. Is there a
bigger picture? Is there a larger plan?

1/2/07

Six months today.

I watched the Memorial Service for President Gerald
Ford and so many moments brought back feelings from that
terrible first week of July.

Today, we're going to Walmart to fill the Women's
Shelter Wish List. We're also stopping to order flowers for
church on Sunday in your memory.

And we're going to find balloons to release on Friday.

---

8 I have sent him to you for this very
purpose—to let you know how we are doing
and to encourage you.--Colossians 4: 8 (NLT)

1/3/07

*I returned to school this morning after a two-week
Christmas break to find a package and a card for me in the
mail. The package, the book 90 Minutes in Heaven, came
from Cheryl Rhodes, former associate pastor at Central
Christian Church. She had been in Australia until recently
and only heard of your death and our circumstances on
Dec. 26. In a letter she wrote "I trust that in reading this,
you will find peace, knowing that your grand-baby is safe—
safe in the final, unfailing, eternal meaning of safe. I also
pray you will find joy, realizing the inexpressible glory in
which she dwells."*

*There's that reference to joy, the one positive emotion
we've lost. Odd that she should focus on it. She also
mentioned King David who "Found comfort in knowing
that he would go to his child." I requested David's story
be included in your service, remember?*

*The letter I received, along with a Christmas card, was
from my former high school American Lit. teacher, Joyce
Alexander, whose wisdom and kindness I have come to hold
especially dear.*

*She wrote: "As you started with Frost, I will close with
a favorite Frost mini:*

We dance in a ring and suppose, but the Secret sits in the middle and knows

Frost capitalized secret.   I think the Secret is Love; God is Love, so the Secret is God. If that is true, then, although Reagan is greatly missed, her family will be reunited with her at a very special time in the future."

Reagan, you know that last night, as darkness descended, my spirits sank dangerously low. I broke down and cried while sitting on the living room couch and your Da began to cry, too. I missed you so. For some reason I saw the front door repeatedly open in my mind and you come through wearing your winter coat. When I realized that was never going to happen, I broke down and sobbed from the very depths of despair.

Coming back to school, these gifts from concerned friends/teachers helped my wounded spirit. And the blessings continued.

Track coach Steve Luke, Erin Halls's cousin, contacted me about naming the first track meet of the season the Reagan Williams Invitational, with proceeds going to Reagan's Rescue. He's even hoping to bring a sponsor on board.

And both newspapers want to do follow up stories.

We're grateful for the interest but we'd rather have you back. I know that sounds trite, but it is a fervent wish.

As I look over these entries I realize how selfish my loss is. I am not grieving alone. The Williams family is not grieving alone, and there are people in this community who are not relatives of yours at all who cry at the mere mention of your name. I still feel sometimes, however, that I suffer more than anyone. I also know that that is neither correct nor fair. I suppose, little girl, it is a reflection of the hold you had on me. The hold you still have.

1/4/07

Sitting here this afternoon in my darkened classroom like I often do, I began talking to you and then wondered if you were kept busy by the many people who think about you and converse with you. I figure I monopolize quite a lot of your time, but then I'm sure you are in the thoughts of your mommy and daddy and your Das and your other Papa, too. Can you be in more places than one, or are you moving back and forth between each of us? I'm sure you are thought of most of the time.

Last night, while reading <u>We Are Their Heaven</u>, I came across this paragraph:

The word P-A-I-N can never sum up what it feels like to lose someone. There's no word in any language that can fully describe the loss of one's self when someone dies…Every moment that you take a step forward by making it through another day, no matter how good or bad you feel, you can't run fast enough or far enough to escape loss. This is because you can never leave behind the love inside your heart. It moves with you. It moves with you because the person who died stands beside you.

I reacted so strongly to that passage because Allison DuBois understood what we're going through. It also gave me some peace that you were really moving with us.

I know when I started this journal it was not meant to be about living with grief. It was supposed to be about your life. There are still memories of your two and a half years that are happy. Those memories come to me occasionally in snapshots in my head.

You standing next to me in the bathroom making faces in the mirror. You sliding down the stairs on your butt.

You gathering teddy bears and carrying them around. Nothing earth shattering but now worth all the world to me.

Great Grandma Cookie sent a note today and included a check for some bracelets. In it she shared "My happy memory for the day is remembering a picnic here and just watching her eat grapes! (You had to be here)"

Yep, nothing earth shattering but now worth all the world.

1/6/07

Yesterday would have been your third birthday. It was a day we had dreaded. Your Papa Gary even said, "This isn't how we should have been spending this day."

Around 4 p.m., we stopped at Berry's Garden Center to pick up 10 pink balloons we had ordered. When I asked what we owed, the sales clerk said, "No charge." We were really touched by that gesture.

We drove to the cemetery, attached messages we had written to the strings, and gathered around your grave. Great Grandpa Jim brought three pink candles, put them in the soft ground, and lit them. I said a few words and then we let the balloons go (nine of them as Aunt Bailey accidentally let one go when we got there). It was an overcast day, not like the sunny day of your funeral, but I reminded everyone that just above the gray clouds, the sun was shining brightly, something I remembered from our last trip to Tennessee.

The balloons all stayed together, at one point forming a cross and then looking almost like an angel hovering in the sky. After about two or three minutes they were swallowed up by the mist and were found, I hope, by our little angel.

Your daddy, your Da, your aunts, Great Grandpa Jim and Great Grandma Roberta, and your Papa, of course, all had tears in our eyes. It was hardest on Bailey because in all our visits to the cemetery, she has always stayed in the van.

Aubrey recognized your picture on the marker and said, "Reagan." She delighted in jumping from marker to marker and even slid in the wet grass and mud occasionally so that her clothes were a mess. She was fascinated by the candles and balloons and kept calling out "Happy birthday."

After your Papa Gary arrived and we stood around your marker waiting for the last pink birthday candle to go out, the solar lamp came on and cast little rays of light over your picture. It reminded me of the little baby on <u>Teletubbies</u> *you used to love to hear giggle. I was*

surprised that the lamp worked at all since it was so
overcast yesterday and the day before.

Maybe you were sending out your sunshine to all of us.

1/7/07

Today, we took supplies and a check to Your Family
Resource Connection for the Women's Shelter. Don also
had a short dedication ceremony. A passage from Isaiah
was read about his vision for a peaceful world—

The wolf will live with the lamb, the leopard will lie
down with the goat, the calf and the lion and the yearling
together; and a little child will lead them. The cow will
feed with the bear, their young will lie down together, and
the lion will eat straw like the ox. The infant will play near
the hole of the cobra, and the young child put his hand into
the viper's nest. They will neither harm nor destroy on all
my holy mountain, for the earth will be full of the
knowledge of the Lord as the waters cover the sea. (Isaiah
11: 6-9)

In the work that our church members have done to fill
the wish list of the Women's Shelter and to raise money for

a room, it has been your image, little girl, and your memory that led us. You once played near the hole of a cobra; you put your trust in a viper's nest, and you were harmed. Now, perhaps, since you are not capable of being harmed, you will lead us to help others.

In this difficult week of anniversary and birthday, leading up to this presentation today, I've been reading the final chapters of <u>We Are Their Heaven</u>. Allison Du Bois's ideas have been so relevant, so accurate, that I must believe I was meant to read them now.

"There are circumstances," she writes, "where the death of one person would serve to change many lives through inspiring change for the better and serves as a powerful, positive rippling effect that moves more people than could be moved by the living…we don't always see the many reasons to have faith in a 'bigger plan.'"

She goes on to explain that those who pass don't want their deaths to define their lives, and that one grieving family reaching out to support another family brings joy to the victim. We've tried hard to do this with the Greens because we are in this forever.

What we share are the terrible images of what you went through, what you suffered, Reagan—or what we envision happened to you based on what limited knowledge we have—especially in those last moments. Allison pleads: "I hope you can look through my eyes, to know that the ones taken from you were surrounded with the arms of unbreakable love as soon as they crossed." We cling to that image, too, the peace you found when you entered Heaven—what made Sister Joanne share with me that she fell in love with that beautiful little girl on the gurney when she laid eyes on her for a brief moment.

"Remember," Allison writes, "that every day forward is a day closer to your reunion with the ones who await you."

Remember, Reagan, every sunset in the west means our reunion nears.

At the Women's Shelter, we all read from the prayer of St. Francis, beautiful words but in our grief and anger difficult to reconcile. Though we are trying to be instruments of peace, the rest of the criteria still challenges even though I've always found this prayer to be so beautiful and inspirational.

Love instead of hatred. Faith instead of doubt. Hope instead of despair. Joy instead of sadness. Always the conflict of darkness vs. light. And I can't pardon for what injury was done to you, little girl, or to us.

We've tried to console while being consoled. We've tried to understand and love. We've given because it felt *like the only thing we could do in light of so many blessings, so many prayers, and so much concern.*

And we have struggled to believe, even at our darkest, that "it is in dying that we are born to eternal life."

I pray that we do what we do not for our recuperation but to perpetuate your memory, Reagan. I pray that we never mix the two motives up.

1/12/07

Two evenings ago, your Da and I stopped off at your grave for a visit, something I'll find any excuse to do. We discovered that some of the Mylar balloons that were brought on your birthday had rubbed off onto your marker leaving little shiny flecks. We managed to get some of the flecks off, but they were stubborn.

I realized that as I approached your grave I began to tear up, like I normally do, not just because of grief but because I look forward to this time together, time to visit you and see your face. As soon as we were involved in the task of restoring your marker to its original condition, I stopped crying. I'm sure part of it was also the bone-numbing wind that turned my skin purple and blue. The task we had to perform helped keep our tears in check.

Until we were preparing to leave. When we stood up from cleaning, discovering I had a round patch of wet mud on my knee from kneeling on the soft ground around your grave, we turned to your face looking up at us, just like on your birthday, rays of light poured out of the solar lamp and framed your innocent smile in sunshine.

"She is our sunshine," I said softly. I felt like you were thanking us for our hard work.

We didn't plan on leaving just at the moment those rays appeared, but, for the second time in a week, it worked out that way. Is it mere coincidence, or are you sending us messages?

This week I read <u>A Grief Observed</u> by C. S. Lewis, his journal written after his wife's death as a way of surviving "mad midnight moments." We've had those midnight moments of madness. They've kept us up at night. They've made us fear falling asleep. Not sleeping but trying to get to sleep because we're left with silence and darkness and thoughts of you. Da and I sleep with the television on now as a nightlight and as company.

As I read Lewis's reflections, I found validation for what we've gone through. He was born over sixty years before me and died when I was three, but I discovered a kindred spirit.

Lewis's stepson, Douglas Gresham, in his introduction described the book as "the passionate result of a brave man turning to face his agony and examine it in order that he might further understand what is required of us in living this life in which we have to expect the pain and sorry of the loss of those whom we love." He adds that Lewis "attempts to come to grips with and in the end defeat the emotional paralysis of the most shattering grief of his life." Gresham suggests, "the greater the love the greater the grief," concluding with these words: "It almost seems cruel that her death was delayed long enough for him to grow to love her so completely that she filled his world as the greatest gift that God had ever given him, and then she died and left him alone in a place that her presence in his life had created for him." That description could have been written about me after you died.

Then Lewis's journal begins. He talks about "the laziness of grief," loathing the slightest effort. Since July I've stopped walking. I've rarely completed a crossword puzzle or sudoku page. I can tell there have been changes in me. I feel achier, older. The most mundane of household chores is a bother.

Lewis's anger is mine, and some of it is directed at God. If you praise Him, He will welcome you "with open arms.

But go to Him when your need is desperate, when all other help is vain, and what do you find? A door slammed in your face and a sound of bolting and double bolting on the inside."

There is the door again—the door you hid behind, the door which separates us, the door I ask you to wait at in the song.

All that I have written about and analyzed these six months is an example of what Lewis says: "I not only live each endless day in grief, but live each day thinking about living each day in grief." I can do nothing but live each day in grief; I can't avoid thinking about how I live each day grieving, so clear is your image before me.

Lewis fears that, after only a month, the memory of his wife is changing, becoming less her and more his recollections of a more and more imaginary woman. In that I have the advantage. We have DVDs of your life. I can see you and hear you. I have the early pages of this journal, too. Lewis describes the loss as being like snow-flakes—"little flakes of me, my impressions, my selections, are settling down on the image of her." He rails at those who offer advice: "What pitiable cant to say, 'She will live forever in my memory!' Live? That is exactly what she won't do." I, too, have resented this suggestion, however well-intentioned.

Lewis is somewhat ashamed to admit that the prayers he has said for the other dead have seemed strong but were not, in fact, altogether sincere; however, he thought he meant them. I have discovered that I have never truly grieved until I lost you. Felt bad, yes. Thought I meant the prayers I prayed, certainly. But I never knew ultimate loss until you left us.

Like Lewis, I want "the happy past restored." Like Lewis, that's why I cry at night, why I fear falling asleep, why I speak your name to the darkness, why I long for you to appear, why I wait for you each night, why I can't wait for our reunion.

"And grief still feels like fear. Perhaps, more strictly, like suspense. Or like waiting; just hanging about waiting for something to happen. It gives life a permanently provisional feeling."

And when the agonies begin to subside, what replaces them? The "dead flatness" of apathy? "Does grief finally subside into boredom tinged by faint nausea?"

Lewis reaches a point that I still fear to reach. I have cried every day since you died. He ultimately reaches a place of understanding where it becomes clear that one *must accept a loss of a loved one and embrace joy once more in order to be truly reunited with that loved one.*

His teaching here is so much like what Allison DuBois says. I plead for you to come back, Reagan, only to make myself feel better. Do I cry selfishly? Do I miss you selfishly?

Doesn't my faith tell me you are in Heaven and that nothing can compare with that perfect place? Or is my faith just "a house of cards" so easily knocked down on that terrible Sunday in July?

Must I let you go to find you? Lewis remembers his wife clearly but unexpectedly only when he mourned her less, "as if the lifting of the sorrow removed a barrier."

He instructs "You can't see anything properly while your eyes are blurred with tears. You can't, in most things, get what you want if you want too desperately."

And then, startlingly, he returns to the door metaphor once again, and this was when I finally decided Truth was being presented to me when I needed it.

"'Knock and it shall be opened.' But does knocking mean hammering and kicking the door like a maniac?...You must have a capacity to receive, or even omnipotence can't give. Perhaps your own passion temporarily destroys the capacity."

Is my hammering keeping you from perfect peace? Am I too busy trying to get in to see you that I'm not allowing you to come out? Am I just trying to prove what a tragic hero I am by continuing to count and take pride in how many days I've cried?

Maybe Claudius was right about Hamlet when he said that "to persever/In obstinate condolement is a course/Of impious stubbornness, 'tis unmanly grief,/It shows a will most incorrect to heaven,/A heart unfortified, a mind impatient."

Is my grief incorrect to heaven? Is my heart so weak, my head so restless?

Though I fear letting my grief go, I also know I will have to reach that moment and turn to you "as often as possible in gladness."

Like Lewis's wife, you took so much with you when you left us. You took my past for I connect with you so many things now that once had no connection to you. You took what we'll never share. You took your hugs and your smell and your forehead bumping against mine and the funny faces in the mirror I never caught on tape.

I want you back—not words in a journal. Not photographs or DVDs.

1/13/07

Today is my 47th birthday, but I might as well be 67 for how old I feel. My one birthday wish I can't have.

I'm proud that we shared January birthdays. I'm sure I'll always feel the same regrets, the same old age, and the same connection to you.

I am one more year closer to seeing you again.

1/15/07

Tennessee. In this tranquil mountain setting and unseasonably warm weather, your Da and I found some momentary peace. In another time zone and in a bedroom not our own we were finally together. And the image I had of you was not before my eyes, reminding me of my grief, but standing next to the bed and looking at us with happiness that we could love this way again.

I don't know what a return home today will do, but at least we've made an important start.

I'm still not good in shops. Yesterday afternoon I wandered through some stores and found the melancholy mood descend on me again as I looked at racks of name tags, buttons, door signs, and other personalized items. I didn't find the name Reagan among them, but the fact that I looked in vain anyway was telling. I'd never be able to buy you these things or bring home souvenirs from trips.

Despite what I wrote earlier, things aren't entirely healed I guess.

1/18/07

For days now I have obsessed about one particular phrase from your funeral service. Don called you "our bright, shining star, Reagan." For some inexplicable reason I have heard him say that in my head over and over. And when I couldn't stand hearing it, I began to say it aloud repeatedly.

"Our bright, shining star, Reagan."

"Our bright, shining star, Reagan."

"Our bright, shining star, Reagan."

Over and over.

Why?

1/19/07

I'm so afraid to stop crying every day. I started crying the afternoon of July 2 when your Da told me that you were gone. I've cried every day since. It's a connection I have between now and that horrible then. What if that link of daily tears is broken?

1/21/07

We went to a show choir competition in Aurora, Indiana, yesterday. Both Mallory and Flyn did very well. Attending marching band and show choir competitions makes me sad, though, because I invariably think of you and what might have been. We were planning on taking you along to these this year. We were sure you would become a singer and dancer with so much musical talent in your family. Now I watch kids perform and know I will never be your proud Papa sitting in the bleachers and applauding you.

Today, Da and I went up to your grave, the first time it's been covered by snow. We cleared your marker, wiped snow away from the angel statue, threw out some wilted flowers. We felt discouraged that more has not been done, afraid that people may forget. It was a moment of loneliness, isolation. We have them from time to time.

As if to soothe our troubled minds, a woman approached us in the grocery store. She was wearing a bracelet and offered support. It was the first time we had seen a stranger with a wristband on. After a conversation, the lady left, and the cashier nearby asked, "Are you the grandparents?" When I said yes, she, too, offered support—someone would be punished, she vowed, and then she added, "God bless you."

Later, when I got home, I found an e-mail from a former pastor, Phillip Hayes, just letting us know that he and his wife, Dorothy, were thinking of us.

I have to believe that these three encounters were meant to happen, meant to keep us going.

1/25/07

The other night, before going to bed, I looked under the stack of books on the nightstand and found some pamphlets from a funeral home which Great Grandma Sharon brought me last summer. One of then called "Handling the Heartbreak of a Child's Death" included a short poem by David Ray. I read it and found an accurate description of grief.

> There will come a day
> When you would have lived your life
> All the way through.
> Mine long gone.

And peace will descend then.

Such a great peace, like a breath

Moving those pines, moving

Even the stone.

And then, then I can let go.

The poem was written following the death of his son. I know it goes against all the advice I've read recently about letting go to find one again. Right now it captures the depths of sadness I experience every day as well as the possibility that I'll never be able to let go until I see you again.

I found David Ray's website and other poems he's written. One was called "The Snapshots."

> *Had we known*
> *these few images*
> *were all we'd have of you*
> *we'd have been taking*
> *pictures all the time.*
> *The one I need to forget*
> *—to stop weeping, to live—*
> *is the one in my mind*
> *without looking.*

We often regret not taking more pictures and videos of you, Reagan, because we assumed, foolishly it seems, that you would always be there.

I sent an e-mail to David Ray and told him about you. He wrote back and suggested that one day we'd meet. I've also ordered a book of his poetry—<u>Sam's Book</u>, after his son.

How your loss has connected us to so many people in so many places.

2/13/07

A snow day today so no school. Time to write to you, Reagan, on a date that I've anticipated for some time now. Today, your cousin Aubrey is the exact age you were the day you died. We had photos taken of her at Sears last evening, so those shots will always remind me of you.

I haven't written for a while which frightens me. Does this mean I am getting used to your being gone? Is this what healing feels like? If so, I don't want to heal. All I feel recently is cold and numb. It may be the temperature outside, so different from those summer evenings when we sat on the porch in shock and despair. It may be because of how this case has seemed stalled for months. I find myself having to force tears someday by watching the funeral service again, by listening to certain songs, or by reading through this journal, especially the early pages. I don't know if that's cheating. I just know I am not able to let you go and get on with life.

Yesterday afternoon your grandma was upset. We received a book offer from Scholastic which mentioned you by name several times and referred to your preparing for school. I had to call Scholastic and beg them to take us off the mailing list. I said you were "deceased," the "victim of a homicide," that we "couldn't take this" painful reminder of our loss of hope. Your loss, really, not ours. But for a half a second I could somehow believe that you would one day attend school. Then I remembered, and you were cruelly pulled away from me once more. No preschool. No Kindergarten. No hugs from Papa's girl.

I often stare at your rocking chair and wonder if you sit there and watch us. If you are that close to us, why do I feel so far away from you? Oh, I miss you so much, little girl.

2/15/07

Yesterday was Valentine's Day, but my heart was broken. When you were a baby, I asked you to be mine and you agreed. For a time we were a pair, an item. People noticed, and it made me so proud.

You still hold my heart, little girl. But I'm afraid only death can mend it.

2/18/07

Today, another unexpected connection and a painful memory.

As we sat in church and watched the mission trip video, I thought of my granddaughter, Reagan, and what might have been. The group from church left on New Year's Eve for Juarez, Mexico. They built a 3 room house for a couple in their 70s who had been living in a bus under very impoverished conditions. On Friday, January 5, they presented the keys to a new home—a home with electricity, doors, windows, insulation, a roof. The couple were so grateful—for God above and for the Central Christian team before them. The mission team exemplified Christ's definition of believers—loving God and helping neighbors.

*As I watched keys pass from Don to this Mexican family,
I remembered what we were doing on that day—gathering
around your grave top release balloons on what would
have been your third birthday. In that flash of memory, I
also saw you as a teenager helping others on a mission
trip. It was another example of what you won't be able to
experience. Then I hoped that, as we share your fund with
those at-risk or less fortunate (and how can anyone be less
fortunate who still has life and a future?), you will be there
not just in our memories but in spirit, hovering on the edge
of the scene or, maybe, beside us.*

*Yes, unexpectedly and through the pain of regret, I
thought of my granddaughter today.*

2/22/07

*Last night, while visiting your grave, like I do every
Wednesday after class, I brushed away snow, gathered up
the stems of now budless white roses, and looked at your
face peering from behind the lamplight. As I spoke to you
and rubbed your features on the marker, I realized that
your likeness is raised up from the background. I could
feel the outline of your fingers, your arms, your head, even
your teeth. It wasn't like holding you, but it was better than*

[142]

touching glass that separates your image from my
fingertips. You almost emerge from that bronze, and so,
with imagination I could feel you. It's not enough but it is
better than flatness.

Will we be able to hug in Heaven?

2/23/07

Another day. Another edition of the newspaper.
Another front page story. The same familiar words—"the
waiting game continues," "a coroner's jury declared her
death a homicide," "No arrests have been made," "no
charges filed," "only two people were with the toddler,"
"they have a suspect in the case." All I can feel is
emptiness, numb. The same small picture from your 2nd
birthday photo is used. It's grainy and distant like you're
yesterday's news or someone else's granddaughter, a
stranger unrelated.

I don't want to feel that way. I don't want my tears to
dry up. What's wrong with me?

What's wrong with all of it?

3/2/07

Another month has come and gone. In that time, crimes have been committed, arrests made, sadness and grief felt, victims buried, headlines and lead stories announcing them all. Still no arrest in your homicide.

Like the very human being that I am, I want resolution. I want an explanation from a God I'm not too happy with right now.

"Suffer the little children to come unto me." Why our little girl? We tried so many times to prevent your leaving us. We didn't want you to go to Jesus. We needed you here.

I don't feel like going to church, especially in the weeks leading up to Easter and the image of your pretty pale yellow Easter dress we'd bury you in. I want to hold out, go on strike, until we have some positive breakthrough in the case.

I wish you could let us know how you are doing. How do you spend your time? Who have you met? Do you get to play and laugh? Do you get to see us?

You know, Aubrey refers to our house as Grandma's. That makes me jealous. You always called it Papa's.

You spoiled me, Reagan. I can't imagine ever having a closer relationship with anyone. All grandchildren will be judged by your example. I doubt I'll be so lucky and blessed ever again.

3/6/07

For such a long stretch, I was writing in this almost every day. My contributions have recently slowed down. I don't know if this is a sign of healing for I don't feel any better. If anything, all the emotions sort of run together into a kind of gray field, a nonexistence, a phantom zone.

I have felt heaviness in my chest in this last week. I assume it is from stress. I don't really care much about my health except how it would affect the family—especially Bailey.

Two local educators have recently died from heart attacks. I sometimes envision a third headline about me. How glorious a reunion I would have with you, my Papa's girl. But I think my dying now would be a hardship for your Da and your aunts and daddy. I just don't want to exist in the gray. And for how long will this go on?

I received an e-mail from the pastor of your Great Aunt Heather and Great Uncle Mark's church. He included a recent sermon about God's Timing. There are two kinds of time in the Bible—Chronos, measured by hours, days, weeks, months, and years, and Kairos, which translates as "in the fullness of time" or "moment of God's opportunity."

He encourages us to live on Kairos time for then, anything is possible. Trying to live on Chronos time is frustrating and powerless.

"Perhaps you are at a crossroads in your life, a momentous decision awaits you. What you need is to seek Kairos time, the moment of opportunity when God opens the door and all you need to do is walk through it."

There's that door again, but I haven't felt close to God, certainly haven't felt His guidance or presence. Just grayness, directionless and alone.

So I'm standing and knocking. Why doesn't He answer?

3/10/07

I continue to be surprised at how often you are a part of our daily lives. Today at the Watseka Show Choir competition, I saw my former high school choral director, Jim Rimington. He teaches at Pekin High School, and, over the years, we've managed to run into each other and catch up on numerous occasions and in several places.

He asked if I was performing anywhere, and I told him that I was taking a break. I felt I needed to explain, so I told him about losing you and how I've lost my desire to sing or act. Tears welled up in his eyes as he shared that he was the grandfather of three. Our relationship spans thirty-two years. We were once teacher and student; now we were two grandfathers with a deep, abiding love for our grandchildren. I was touched by his compassion; it certainly changed—strengthened—our bond.

Aunt Mallory sang a song for solo contest entitled "I Remember." The last lines of the song so aptly express my desire—

> *And the bluest ink*
> *Isn't really sky,*
> *And at times I think*
> *I would gladly die*
> *For a day of sky.*

The clearest photo or a video which lingers on your face isn't really you. Certainly, there are times I think I would gladly die for a day of you.

3/13/07

Little girl, I bet you're tired of hearing your Papa say how much he loves you and misses you. If I could put it another way, I would, but those are the only words I know for sure.

I never thought I'd be wearing a pink and purple wristband with your name on it. I never thought I'd see your second birthday photo on the news or the front page. I never thought I'd have a regular Wednesday night date by moonlight with you week after week. I never thought I'd stop singing "You Are My Sunshine" or "Tell Me Why" or that the silence would go unnoticed for so long. I never knew that one little girl could mean the world to me.

This past weekend at a show choir competition in Watseka, the Danville Delegation gathered before a performance to hold hands in a circle and pray. One of my students and your Aunt Mallory's friend, Alex Bates, quoted Paul—"My grace is sufficient for you, for my power is made perfect in weakness" 2 Corinthians 12: 9. Weakness is power in Christ. I guess that means a 2 ½ year old girl—or the memory of her—can move mountains.

Alex went on to quote a line from "The Color Purple," a song from the musical of the same name—"Like a drop of water keeps the river high." He was trying to convince every performer in that room that he or she was not only important but vital.

As I stood in the back of the group in the corner, I thought of you, Reagan. You were a drop of water, a skinny, little thing, but you kept us flowing and high instead of stagnant and shallow.

I can't do much these days but wait and wait some more. I grow stagnant. My resentment is deep, my pain is deep, my frustration is deep—but I feel shallow and lifeless. I feel no power or perfection in weakness, only anguish.

What can I do? It wasn't just you that died; it was a future, posterity, a part of my body and mind and spirit. It was all the days and years, all the gatherings and celebrations and rituals, all the bear hug hellos and the squeezes and waves of goodbye. All the hopes and dreams.

There was awesome power in little you. I pray you know that.

3/22/07

There's so much going on in your memory and on your behalf, little girl. This Saturday the DHS track team will host the first annual Reagan Williams Invitational as a fundraiser for Reagan's Rescue. Coach Steve Luke, the

Witzels who own McDonald's, and many volunteers are joining in this cause.

There have been stories in both local newspapers and reports on area television stations. Your picture has appeared in print and on screen. I am grateful for the interest and for the messages that will get out to the public—about Shaken Baby Syndrome, about community, about generosity, about what an angel you were and are.

We also keep working with attorneys even though that process is agonizingly slow.

I talked to your Papa Gary on the phone once and in person twice in recent days. How sad he looks sometimes, how often on the verge of tears. He seems smaller every time we meet, but then I have changed, too. My beard is grayer, almost white in places. Your Da often comments about how pained I now look on a regular basis.

In the stillness of my empty classroom or at home in the bedroom or (now that it's warmer) on the front porch, I long to feel your hugs, your hands clutching my neck. I want to pick you up and hold you aloft after you've run into my arms.

These projects, the media attention, the meetings and planning—they give us something to do; they keep us busy and our minds focused on a goal so that we can forget long enough to feel whole, but they also move us closer to July 2nd, 2006, not farther away. When the projects end, we're right back to that Sunday when we lost so much.

3/25/07

Yesterday, at the Invitational, we raised $950.76 with the promise of more to come. Focusing on you so much makes us miss you even more, but at least our little Reagan continues to exist and to matter.

I hope you were there in the bleachers or in the hallway where your two Papas sat together and talked and sold wristbands and t-shirts. Both television stations came, too, and had reports on the news that night. Your mommy and daddy, your Papas and Das, and all your aunts and uncles were there along with Aubrey. We've all come together, Sweetheart, because of how special you are.

People came out who were friends, and sometimes strangers, approached us and said, "God bless you."

I'm grateful for this further proof of "the community of Reagan" but I still wonder why you had to be sacrificed.

Whether right or wrong, I continue my protest by not going to church. I've asked for answers or guidance or assurance or glimpses of you, but all I've received is *silence. If messages have been sent, I've missed them. If answers to prayer have come they weren't clear enough.*

I see generosity around me but it seems to be coming from human goodness, not Godness. In moments of doubt like this, I begin to question eternity, question Heaven. If it doesn't exist, then Reagan is simply asleep with no consciousness and no memory of pain. Maybe no memory of pain is what Heaven is. If, however, this is so, then this writing is fiction, and no little girl looks on or receives my thoughts.

So I must trust that your spirit lingers, that you are, somehow, with us. Right now that trust is all I really have, all that keeps me going.

3/26/07

Yesterday turned out to be an emotional time. While shaving in the morning, I had the radio on, and the Titanic song, "My Heart Will Go On," began playing. I gazed in the mirror, saw a blurry, reddish reflection, and realized I was crying, the lyrics touching me in a new and unexpected way.

> *Near, Far*
> *Wherever you are*

I believe that the heart does go on

Once more, you opened the door

And you're here in my heart,

and my heart will go on and on.

Love can touch us one time

and last for a lifetime

And never let go till we're gone

And then, at the end

You're here, there's nothing I fear

And I know that my heart will go on.

We'll stay forever this way

You are safe in my heart

And my heart will go on and on.

You did open a door, Reagan, and now a door separates us. You are so very near and so very far at the same time. You touched me once, and that touch will last a lifetime, and you will forever be Papa's girl.

As I write this, I once again gaze into your eyes which look on from the photograph on my desk. I realize while staring at you that your eyes reflect back a feeling of contentment and peace and security. Your expression tells me that you knew you were loved as it assures me that we were loved, too.

Last night, Mallory needed help practicing a song for this week's Cabaret performance, the last show choir gathering of the year. As I played her solo, "How Could I Ever Know?" from The Secret Garden, *I heard the lyrics as if they were a message from you.*

How could I know I would have to leave you?
How could I know I would hurt you so?
You were the one I was born to love,
Oh, how could I ever know?

How can I say to go on without me?
How, when I know you still need me so?
How can I say not to dream about me?
How could I ever know?

Forgive me,
Can you forgive me,
And hold me in your heart?
And find some new way to love me,
Now that we're apart?
How could I know I would never hold you?
Never again in this world, but oh,
Sure as you breathe, I am there inside you,
How could I ever know?

How could I ever know?

The speaker of these words takes some blame for her
passing away, and I don't want you to think I blame you,
Reagan. I know you couldn't help having to leave. As we
continue to cry, I don't want you to feel the need to ask
forgiveness. I hope that, if you can be near us, you will
know just how much we miss you, and I hope that fact isn't
a surprise to you, either. How could we ever fully
acknowledge what you meant to us, what indescribable joy
you brought into this world? No lyric, no poem could ever
capture the blessing of our little girl.

Papa and Da lay in bed last night and cried. Da regrets
all the times she didn't take you for walks or to the park.
Having feelings like that is normal, but we compound them
with guilt, our regretting what we couldn't do to save you.
We talked about priorities—Is it more important that the
girls sing together than pick up their rooms?—and
discipline—Should we say "yes" more than "no"?

I told Da that trying to negotiate grief in a marriage is a
challenge. When Da is up, I'm down. When I'm okay, Da
may not be. Then she and I grieve alone and in silence,
hiding out in some corner of the house or driving in the car
or visiting your grave. Silence means we drift apart.

I held her close and said, "The only thing I'm really sure about anymore is that I love you."

That's how our emotional day ended—with tear-streaked faces and reaches across the bed to the other.

"I never thought we'd ever have to deal with anything like this," Da whispered.

"I didn't either," I responded, and sleep finally came.

4/4/07

Today, I got a tattoo in Pigeon Forge, something I've been planning on doing for several months now. The time and place just had to be right, and all the pieces seemed to fall into place quickly and decisively.

Yesterday morning, we stopped for gas across the street from a tattoo parlor, the parlor next door to a medical clinic and across the street from a Christian theatre. On impulse, I asked the gas attendant, who had tattoos himself, if he knew about this business, and he assured me that they did good work there.

Later in the afternoon, I stopped off to make an appointment with JR. When they asked what I wanted, and I responded with "Dora," they pulled out a color with paints book from under the counter—not exactly the reaction I counted on. And when I found the ideal drawing—Dora walking away with her head looking back over her shoulder at the viewer—I knew this was meant to be.

This morning, I also asked for a halo, and JR drew a kind of sunburst which so reminded me of you, Reagan—our sunshine—and of the solar light which casts rays over your likeness. I knew that this was absolutely right.

JR asked about the significance of the image, and I told him all about losing you nine months ago. He shared that he lost a baby sister to violence when she was about two. He also told me about his difficulties in Indiana and his incarceration. He even lent his future support if I ever needed it.

So I have Dora permanently on my right arm, a symbol of our little explorer who has gone on ahead of us—Reagan forever in my heart and forever on my arm.

4/11/07

I've nearly reached the end of this first journal, and I dread each page I fill and turn over. Had you lived, Reagan, I wouldn't have written so much by now. I know, too, that I would have filled up many books anyway before

[157]

giving them all to you on your 18th birthday. Because you are constantly on my mind, and emotions come so quickly and strongly, I will continue to write to you—in another book and then another, hoping that you are reading over my shoulder and are receiving my gift every time I write.

I guess I am sad about reaching the last pages because it means something is coming to an end as if you are dying all over again. I had such hopes for you and for this project, this history, your history. And it has all been taken away in a moment. We are left with archives— photographs, video, clothing, fingerprints, favorite toys, and cherished books. We are also left with what is valuable about history—the lessons it provides.

If we had only…

If we had just called…

If we had been more…

Your Great Grandma Roberta wants to paint your portrait and asked for a favorite photo. Mine sits on my desk at school. It's the picture I stare at. It's you and your daddy. It's your brown eyes mostly looking back at me.

I told your Da of Roberta's plan and of my suggestion of that photograph. Your Da began to cry, reluctant to tell me what was wrong at first. Then she said that she didn't like that picture because it was the day your mom brought you to our house to stay the week. She blames herself for not taking you to the doctor. You threw up several times, but your Da thought it was from stress and not a stomach virus. Still, she waited.

And so this picture of you, my favorite, brings me peace and brings your Da only sadness, guilt, and regret. She didn't want to tell me because she knew how much I like the photo. Whenever she discussed not liking it, I always assumed it was because of the composition of the picture. I didn't know it triggered such terrible memories for her.

I guess negotiating our grief goes on. Nine months later we haven't really made much progress in our coping with the loss of our baby girl.

When people suggest that God needed you in Heaven, I first resented that view. Now, I realize that you just may have been too good for this world, too precious for us to deserve. How did we let you slip through our fingers?

Volume Two

Today, I begin a second journal. This one feels different, colder. As difficult as it was to read sometimes, the early pages of the first journal were about your life. You were a breathing, laughing, dancing, singing, hugging, and playing little girl then, and we never imagined our fears would become terrible reality. What I wrote about were everyday occurrences, the mundane events that we don't take pictures of or write down in calendars or celebrate. What losing you has taught me is that there are no unimportant events in the life of a precious little girl. That watching you from another room play with Bailey's doll house or getting down on the floor with you and, side by side, setting up house is what life is really about.

There is so much I believed but didn't really live. Wasn't Emily in <u>Our Town</u> supposed to relive an unimportant day because it would be important enough? Didn't I always think that passage was true and beautiful? Haven't I always taught students to "seize the day"? I certainly believed but I didn't really live it until you lost your life.

Didn't I begin every sermon I ever delivered with "Have thine own way, Lord"? Don't I still believe that God is the Potter and I just clay?

Even weeks before you died I requested George sing "Praise You in the Storm" because I believed that was the healthy and hopeful Christian way to face tragedy, hardship, and setbacks. Was I just effectively acting? Did I learn how to touch others but leave my soul untouched?

I haven't been to church for about five weeks now. I wanted...I want...to hold out until an arrest is made. I just don't feel worshipful. I can't live up to how I should be. With thunder in my brain and more than rain falling down around me, I can't raise my hands and praise the God who gives and takes away. Why did God's way have to include ignoring my little girl? Why hasn't God whispered "I'm with you" to me or any of us?

And still, in loss we try to gain. Your Da and I visited Your Family Resource Connection this afternoon to get some idea of what the playrooms will look like and where they'll be in the Women's Shelter. One is being built with funds donated to YFRC soon after you died. The other is being sponsored by Central Christian.

We got an idea of what toys are needed. We want to go out and look for a Dora kitchen set. All of us—both Papas and both Das, your whole family—will forever associate Dora with you and you with Dora, so it is only right that Dora should be in the design.

When those rooms are finished, they will be an important tribute to you. Children will get to play there and, perhaps, for a time, forget violence and evil.

Oh, Reagan, I miss playing with you. I miss the unimportant. What I wouldn't give for one day to rock you gently in my lap or make faces in the mirror or sit beside you on the floor, arranging life inside Bailey's doll house.

4/17/07

Today, Papa and Da had to meet with two investigators from the Office of Inspector General for the Department of Children and Family Services. They are finishing up their investigation of the local DCFS office, trying to determine whether mistakes were made which lead to your death. Da and I don't need any investigation to confirm what we've felt all along—that, in addition to our ignorance of and trust in the system, people who work for DCFS didn't take reports seriously or wouldn't listen at all.

I told Lisa Coronato and Karyn Rosman about the only dream I've had of you in which I carried you in my arms

[163]

looking for someone who would save you before it was too late. I then showed them a DVD of you in our living room when, at about eight months, you hugged your Tickle-Me-Elmo. I also showed them clips of Christmas 2005 with another Elmo, this one a dancer, and of you and Aubrey playing hide and seek at Great Grandma Sharon's—the last video I have of you and the moment that inspired the song I wrote. I wanted them to know that you were not just a case number or a statistic but our beloved granddaughter, a little person I cherished above all others. I hope they understood.

Da and I then related all of our concerns and attempts to get help while our attorney, Charlie Hall, sat with us. Your Da broke down in tears many times. I shared with the two investigators my regrets that I didn't drive the car through the front door of the DCFS office to get some attention and that I didn't whisk you off to a safe and faraway place on Father's Day.

When the meeting was over, Charlie encouraged us to let go of our guilt, to let you enjoy your new home in Heaven, and to put our energies into remembering your name and your life through our charity work.

For a brief moment, as he spoke, I almost saw a new hope for us, like a door opening and a glowing light beyond it.

The best I can do now it to believe in almost.

4/20/07

A busy week has come to an end. Last night, I presented several workshops at Your Family Resource Connection on Shaken Baby Syndrome, using materials I've gathered from various state and national child abuse organizations. I had pamphlets, a video, a poster, plenty of bracelets for sale, and an example of the Reagan's Rescue t-shirts. I spoke to small groups of women about how your Great Great Grandma Konold used to warn me never to shake our baby when Blythe was a newborn. She continued to remind me of that through all five children. Even in 1982, she was warning against SBS. And then, last summer, as a new grandfather, I lost you because of a violent streak, a fiery temper, and ignorance. No matter what, no matter how much crying, no matter how stressed you are, you never shake a baby. That's what I shared with those small groups. I told them about grief and about having to live on and bringing some possible good out of our tragedy. I looked into their eyes and saw tears reflected back. And they said, "God bless you for what your family is doing." I didn't expect that.

I was okay during these presentations. I held it together, partly because Great Grandpa Jim was there and Great Grandma Roberta. Only once did I tear up. While watching the video of a mother gently rocking her baby up and down while swaying back and forth, I remembered getting you to sleep that way—and one night in particular.

You were probably eight or nine months old. I babysat you. You were a little fussy so I took you upstairs, turned the TV on, found the movie <u>A Mighty Wind</u>, a comedy about folk singers of all things. I swayed to the beat, bounced you lightly up and down, and for about an hour and a half, we danced together to music. It was just an insignificant evening of walking back and forth in our bedroom, but I cherish that night as one of my happiest memories of you. I didn't feel sore. I didn't want to lay you down. I just wanted to hold you and nuzzle and nibble on your tiny ear lobe and dip you and pray that we could always be this close. I'll keep that long ago evening in my heart always.

After the workshop was over, I visited your grave, sat there in my folding chair, and recounted that date night we shared dancing to folk music. In the trees around me, the birds sang of spring. Occasionally, a pair of geese would fly by overhead, honking to each other or maybe to me. Cars driving by on the nearby road are an intrusion. The drivers must think I'm pretty pathetic sitting next to a grave, but then they didn't know you, did they? They never appeared on your dance card.

In this afternoon's paper, there's a story about the child abuse workshop, pretty much all focused on my booth. Well, I'll take the publicity if it does some good.

4/21/07

"When someone you love becomes a memory, that memory becomes your priceless treasure. It also drives your passion, becomes your cause, and leads you to action!"

I found those words on a website for the Shaken Baby Alliance and felt, at least for the time it took to read them, less alone.

In these past couple of weeks while I've continued my protest against God, I've asked for answers, hoping, I guess, to witness or at least hear God directly. Maybe I'm expecting special effects from <u>The Ten Commandments</u>. Maybe just a small voice, even a whisper. But I've heard nothing so direct, and I am beginning to wonder if God has continued to send me messages all along, and I've just missed them or didn't realize they were from Him.

I ran into Alice Cowan, a neighbor, a Christian, a dear friend and member of Central, my touchstone in matters of faith. Alice teared up as she said how she understands anger toward God. She also referenced Rabbi Harold Kushner and his best-selling book <u>When Bad Things Happen to Good People</u>, suggesting I read it when I'm able to. Then, whether meaning to or not, she challenged me not to give up my music if only for the sake of the girls.

"They need you to sing," she said.

For nine months now, I haven't sung and, selfish as it is, I'm glad that someone noticed. I am also somewhat ashamed that, after losing you, Reagan, I've also lost those passions which drove me and which helped me contribute— theatre and music. I can easily give up acting, but music runs through me like blood. Giving it up takes effort.

Still…is this what you would want for your Papa? And do you know if my chance meeting in the hallway at Danville High School with Alice was actually by design? Is that how God works it?

My good friend, George, sent me an e-mail attachment, something he rarely does by his own admission. It was a

story of a boy in need of major heart surgery who
confidently tells his doctor that, when his heart is open,
Jesus will be found there. The doctor argues with the boy
and then himself and then the Lord until Jesus tells the
surgeon, "The boy, my lamb, was not meant for your flock
for long, for he is a part of My flock, and will forever be.
Here, in My flock, he will feel no pain, and will be
comforted as you cannot imagine. His parents will one day
join him here, and they will know peace…"

The surgeon, in anger, asks why God created a life to be
taken so young. The Lord answers, "The boy, My lamb,
shall return to My flock, for he has done his duty: I did not
put My lamb with your flock to lose him, but to retrieve
another lost lamb."

Were you, indeed, an angel sent to us, a gift from God,
to touch us, to show us how to love? Was that your duty?

And was George's highly irregular forwarding of this e-
mail story just a whim or another message?

Even in an early page of a book Great Grandma Sharon
sent called The Miraculous Journey of Edward Tulane
about a china rabbit whose complacency is challenged
when he is lost at sea, there seemed to be a clear message.

The heart breaks and breaks
and lives by breaking.

It is necessary to go
through dark and deeper dark
and not to turn.
--from "The Testing-Tree," by Stanley Kunitz

Is God telling me that we live—really live—by heartache, that we must travel through the dark and not surrender to temptation and bitterness?

Is the peace I find at your graveside a foretaste of glory divine?

Am I missing what has been in front of me all along?

4/24/07

Last night, as I read some chapters of The Miraculous Journey of Edward Tulane *to your Aunt Bailey, I was, for some unknown reason, struck by a number which appears in the book. Without warning or preparation, Edward, the China rabbit, is tossed overboard from an ocean liner and descends to the bottom of the sea, there to stay until the 297th day when a storm disrupts the waves and flings Edward into a fisherman's net. From the depths and darkness and starless loneliness to rescue and salvation.*

[170]

After putting the book away, I got a calendar and a calculator out and added up how many days had gone by. The sum was 296. Today, then, is 297.

Is it a coincidence, or does it suggest that rescue is at hand, that once again I will know the stars?

I was especially depressed yesterday because I was told that the investigation has been in the same place now for the last five weeks or so. The medical expert in Chicago is still waiting on a nearby hospital to send a set of X-rays. The assistant State's Attorney's explanation that "Well, you know hospital red tape" hurt deeply, my recent hopes crushed. What should I do? Reagan, what should I do?

Is Christ, who fished for people, throwing out his net to catch me, lost and adrift? Is it a sign, like the others I've recently written about, or just chance?

4/27/07

More signs…or coincidences. I want to believe in the first rather than settle for the latter.

One of my assistant principals, Sharon, quoted Dr. Seuss to me today. She was referring to another matter but I immediately thought of my little girl.

"Don't cry because it's over. Smile because it happened."

The advice from Grief Share this week was very similar. Focus on a positive mental image of the child you lost rather than an image that brings you pain.

It's not as simple as all this—all these words, all this advice. I do understand, however, the importance of celebrating a life rather than mourning a life lost. I understand why smiling is preferable to crying.

So I'm smiling, Reagan, because you happened.

Please try to forgive me when I cry too much.

4/29/07

This weekend, your Aunt Flyn played the Baker's Wife in <u>Into the Woods</u>, a musical I have known and enjoyed for nearly twenty years but, because of you, now hear differently and at a deeply personal level.

I think about your daddy and all the advice he ignored.

> *No matter what you say*
> *Children won't listen.*
> *No matter what you know,*
> *Children refuse*
> *To learn.*

[172]

Guide them along the way,

Still they won't listen.

Children can only grow

From something you love

To something you lose…

And then those children, beyond your control, lose their children, too.

Running away—go to it.

Where did you have in mind?

Have to take care:

Unless there's a "where,"

You'll only be wandering blind.

Just more questions,

Different kind.

Where are we to go?

Where are we ever to go?

Running away—we'll do it.

Why sit around, resigned?

Trouble is, son,

The farther you run,

The more you feel undefined

For what you have left undone

And, more, what you've left behind.

and then

How do you ignore
All the witches,
All the curses,
All the wolves, all the lies,
The false hopes, the goodbyes, the reverses,
All the wondering what even worse is
Still in store?

and

Sometimes people leave you
Halfway through the wood.
Others may deceive you,
You decide what's good.
You decide alone.
But no one is alone.

and

You move just a finger
Say the slightest word,
Something's bound to linger,
Be heard.

and

Hard to see the light now
Just don't let it go.
Things will come out right now.
We can make it so.

[174]

and, finally, from your Aunt Flyn

> *Sometimes people leave you*
>
> *Halfway through the wood.*
>
> *Do not let it grieve you,*
>
> *No one leaves for good.*
>
> *You are not alone.*
>
> *No one is alone.*
>
> *Hold him to the light now,*
>
> *Let him see the glow.*
>
> *Things will be all right now.*
>
> *Tell him what you know…*

Your Papa and Da sat in the audience and watched and cried and, in the empty seat beside us, you sat there with us in the dark staring at the light from the stage. No one is alone.

5/2/07

Ten months (although missing you makes the time that has passed seem like ten years).

Last night, as I read aloud a few chapters of The Miraculous Journey of Edward Tulane *involving a little girl named Sarah Ruth who finally dies from a prolonged illness, your Aunt Bailey began to cry. I put my arm*

[175]

around her to comfort her but also to be comforted for I was crying by then.

I loved her and now she is gone. How could this be? he wondered. How could he bear to live in a world without Sarah Ruth?

Without Reagan Emery. Wiping her tears and rubbing her forehead and hair, I told her that I was so lucky to have her in my life, that I didn't know what I'd do without her. This story shows that, along life's journey, there are bad people and good people. It also gives us hope that, even though we may get separated from those we love, one day we'll be reunited with them.

Then I told your Aunt Bailey that I loved her and promised that the rest of the book would be happier. I wish I could promise the same about life.

I went to school today very down—it is the 2nd of the month after all. When I needed something positive the most, an e-mail appeared from a former student I have not seen for twenty-two years. Erin McBride Lounsberry, Pleasant Valley High School class of 1988, wrote to tell me of my influence in her life. In her letter, she quoted from a card she received from a student who appeared in a

[176]

production of <u>The King & I</u> she directed at Moline High School. "Success is measured not only in achievements...but in lessons learned, lives touched, moments shared along the way." I guess in my roles as teacher and director I've been a success for lessons were learned, lives touched, and moments shared. But Reagan, you were, and continue to be, a success, too. We learned so much through your eyes. You touched so many. We shared priceless moments, priceless memories. You didn't get to achieve greatness, but you were still a success.

This afternoon State Representative Chapin Rose called to thank me for my offer of help in a fight to get HR0228 passed. The resolution urges the State Board of Education to develop a curriculum for implementing Shaken Baby Syndrome prevention and awareness programs for junior high and senior high students. I want to help bring that about.

A year ago you came to stay with us for part of a week while your mom went to the hospital to have your baby brother. A year ago you were a big sister.

But our journey brought us to unexpected places and introduced us to unexpected people—police officers, reporters, politicians, prosecutors, concerned strangers— all because of the miracle that was you.

More than ever my journey is here, but my heart lies
with you, Reagan.

5/3/07

Erin Lounsberry sent another e-mail, sharing that her
birthday is July 2 and that she would always think of the
little girl we lost on that day of celebration for herself.
Another connection. Another surprise that surprises me
not very much at all.

5/9/07

It has been harder to cry for you recently, and I am
afraid of having the day end with no tears shed. It hasn't
even been a year. Why should I have trouble crying when I
miss you more each day, not less?

My wristband is still intact though others have snapped,
including your Aunt Mallory's. Each time that happens I
feel pain akin to stabbing. Losing a bracelet is like losing a
piece of you all over. And now the chain on my Mizpah
necklace has rusted. Da says that I have to get a better
quality silver necklace, but it feels like a betrayal. A new

chain won't be from the original box where the two coin halves came from.

Well, Reagan, that's your Papa. I've lost my granddaughter, but I'm hung up about something so material and trivial.

Papa Gary brought photos of you from the Green household. Despite Ryan's cruelty, you were loved and adored by your mama's family. There is one picture—my favorite—of you on a riding lawnmower, looking like you're steering and shifting gears. There's no baby or toddler about you but a hint of the young woman you would have become. So mature and so focused in pretending.

There's skinny you with a wide-brimmed hat and sandals. You sitting on a Dora couch. You on Christmas morning. You at the zoo. You loved. You loving. You. Love.

When I first looked at those photos—reluctantly, after avoiding the envelope in which they came—I wept, cherishing each new moment, each new second I was discovering, like having thirty extra seconds to spend with you. Now, with not even a week gone by, I look at those same photos like they are history, detached and distant.

Perhaps I am used to the idea that you are gone. Maybe I've reached the stage of grief known as acceptance. Then

again maybe the tears are there deep down in a well of
anguish and shock and the pump just needs primed.

Pictures and videos have primed the pump. Sounds of
your laughter or crying or your voice have primed the
pump.

Maybe it's that, with time, I've forgotten how you
smelled. The sense of smell is most closely associated with
memory, I've always maintained. I don't know what you
smelled like.

When I bend down and kiss Aubrey on the forehead, I
always get the scent of shampoo. Blythe does a good job of
keeping your cousin clean. There's always a soapy smell, a
fresh scent.

How did you smell, Reagan?

I can, thankfully, still remember how you felt, especially
when we bumped heads—as you left our house or, for the
last time, when I bent over your tiny coffin and said
"Boomp" before the lid was closed and sealed.

Maybe I can't cry as easily because of my anger toward
State's Attorney Frank Young. For a while, I felt like his
caution was justified and the time the case was taking
reasonable, but now I'm not convinced. Through
peristence, I was able to track down Dr. Soter last week at
John Stroger Jr. Hospital in Chicago. We had a lengthy

phone conversation. She told me what evidence she was waiting for (films, pediatric records, and hospitalization records from your October 2005 catscan and your December 2005 weeklong hospital stay when you were suffering from dehydration and a stomach virus). She also confided, off the record, that we should sue DCFS. Unfortunately, I think that opportunity has passed.

Today is a Wednesday. Since last Friday, I have left a message every day with Frank Young's secretary (he's always out of the office, in court, or unavailable). I also sent an e-mail to which he has not replied.

I don't know how to proceed. I don't want to damage the case. I don't want to make an enemy of him, thereby jeopardizing the investigation. I believe he is playing on our trusting nature. I don't want to be used.

Dave Matthews sang:

> *I am no superman.*
> *I have no answers for you.*
> *I am no hero, aww that's for sure.*
> *But I do know one thing:*
> *Where you are is where I belong.*
> *I do know, where you go is where I wanna be.*

I just reread this entry, Reagan.
And I cried.

5/17/07

For a while, when I was a boy, I feared the Bogeyman under my bed. I feared long, bony fingers reaching out from under the bed, grabbing my ankles, and pulling me into the darkness below. For a while, I countered that threat by taking a running start and leaping into the bed so that the evil could not grab for me.

Sleep brings its similar fears, not of the Bogeyman but of the curse of dwelling too much on disturbing images as I attempt to drift off. I want my head to hit the pillow and sleep to come instantly.

Falling asleep is that mysterious space under the bed; images of you being hurt or being wheeled out on a gurney or being snatched from Life by a monster is the Bogeyman; my leap onto the mattress are the pills I take to help me fall asleep faster and the tears I shed as I whisper "Good night, little girl. I love you, Reagan Emery" and the alcohol I consume to seal the deal.

The other morning I woke up, and my first conscious thought was "My Reagan was murdered." Why, after over ten months, does that seem a surprise somehow? I've used that word before in describing what happened to you. I've gone past "shaken to death" or "the victim of a homicide" or "killed." The word "murder" implies intent, and I use it intentionally.

This morning I woke up to the word "traumatophilia," a phrase I learned years ago from researching the book _Seize the Day_ by Saul Bellow. What was running through my mind was the mental health of your mama. Did she have a masochistic need to fail, to be destroyed at the hands of a manipulative bully in order, under the terms of the masochist commitment, to retain his love?

Then I wondered why she didn't move out last spring when she had the chance and both the money and support from your Da and Papa Green.

I wake and feel the fell of dark, not day. That's a phrase I recently ran across in a book I am reading by Joan Didion, her _The Year of Magical Thinking_, about the sudden loss of her husband and the grief that followed. She cites Eric Lindemann, chief of psychiatry at Massachusetts General, who interviewed families of the 1942 Cocoanut Grove fire. He lists among the many attributes of grief "sensations of somatic distress occurring in waves lasting from twenty minutes to an hour at a time…need for sighing…empty feeling in the abdomen…tension or mental pain."

The need for sighing has been the most prevalent with Da and me. Sighing along with crying and drinking. The popping of a beer can tab at regular intervals each night means Da is attempting to cope. The need to be alone on the front porch. The chance to talk to you in whispers so others can't hear.

We're just trying to get a running start before we leap into bed, afraid of the dark and afraid of the dark.

5/26/07

Yesterday, I felt a heartbeat away from you. Your papa had to tell a senior in high school that he wasn't going to pass my class and that he wouldn't be able to graduate with his peers. He was upset—maybe at me, maybe at himself. Later, he ripped up a final exam in someone else's class.

This was a young man for whom I had written a letter of recommendation so that he could get into the Marines. I had had him in another course before. When he was suspended from school earlier this spring, I gave him a chance to redo some assignments—assignments that he either turned in late or only partially completed. I felt sorry for him. I understood his frustration, but I didn't

[184]

believe it would be ethical to give him a passing grade when he had put so little effort into passing.

Then I started thinking, due especially to his quiet demeanor and plans for military service, that he might be the one to end my life. What if he went home, got a gun, brought it back to the school, and used it on me. I thought it would make for fascinating copy as well as irony— Teacher helped student get into the Marines, but student killed teacher anyway, or Family struggles with second death.

I was afraid to leave school since he could be waiting for me, a sniper hellbent on revenge.

But then I thought of you. In one shot, I could be meeting you, hugging you, at Heaven's door. I was just one heartbeat away, and my personal safety didn't matter so much. I knew that your Da, your aunts, and your daddy would all be sad, but I would be with my sunshine, and they would be happy for me.

I also thought about what I would say to this boy to encourage him, to help him get through this setback.

"I know you are disappointed. I am disappointed for you as your teacher and as someone who has had your interest at heart for several years. But you get to correct this error. You get a do-over. You have life and time to

right your wrongs. There are those like my granddaughter, Reagan, who won't ever get a second chance. Maybe, one day, all of this will make sense to you. Maybe you'll find peace. But remember how lucky you are. You get a do-over."

Because I am a mere heartbeat away from you, I will recommit to living in a way that will guarantee our reunion.

It's now after midnight and so May 27. One year ago I sat at the dining room stable paying some bills and watching you play with Bailey's dollhouse in the living room. We even got down on the floor together and played. Later on, your mama came to pick you up and I told her that if she ever needed to bring you here to stay, if it wasn't safe or she was stressed or she needed some time to herself, we would always gladly watch you. I don't know if she understood. I don't know whether I was too subtle or too afraid to say what I really wanted to say—that we feared for your life, and we wanted to raise you in our home.

June came and our vacation trip to Tennessee with the Halls family. Father's Day came when I saw you alive for the last time.

In my journal for you I told you that we wanted to keep you safe and secure. I told you that we loved you so much.

The next entry was dated July 2, 2006.

Tomorrow is Memorial Day, and, for the first time in my life, I will have a grave to visit.

I'll say it again, little girl, trusting you can hear me—We love you so much.

6/6/07

Last Wednesday, after taking your Aunt Mallory to the airport, I heard the song "Somewhere Out There" on the radio. I soon realized it is another lyric which has personal meaning because of losing you. As I listened I was afraid to glance at Da for fear that she might be crying. Luckily, she had dozed off, and so I continued to think about the words and about you.

> *Somewhere out there beneath the pale moonlight*
> *Someone's thinking of me and loving me tonight*
> *Somewhere out there someone's saying a prayer*
> *That we'll find one another in that big somewhere*
> > *out there*

> *And even though I know how very far apart we are*

It helps to think we might be wishing on the same
bright star
And when the night wind starts to sing a lonesome
lullaby
It helps to think we're sleeping underneath the same
big sky

And, finally,

Somewhere out there if love can see us through
Then we'll be together somewhere out there
Out where dreams come true

Reagan, I don't know for sure, but I have to cling to the tiny hope that you do think of me and you do still love me. I have to count on the two of us finding each other and that, in the meantime, we are still connected. I don't know whether you are in the stars or looking up at them from next to me. I know there is an ever-widening gulf between me and God as July 2, 2006, grows more distant. Each day I feel that much more removed from you, my Sunshine.

Maybe my dreams will come true and we will be together but it all seems so impossible sometimes. I guess I need another sign—another three deer, maybe.

I haven't written in a while because all my thoughts have been jumbled up. I don't want to ramble, but, like summer weather, my moods change, often in a moment. No one has been held responsible for your death, but I must trust the system. I miss you so horribly, but I believe in Heaven. I want to live and be a husband and a dad and a grandpa for other children, but I could easily die knowing my grief would end and we could see each other. I sit on the porch and appreciate the simplicity of lingering, but I miss you sitting in the backseat of your mom's car as she brings you over for a visit. I feel so dead, so numb, but I also feel alive and in tune to creation around me.

I'm sitting in a chair next to your grave as I write this. It is a beautiful evening. Birds are providing melodies of late spring. There's a gentle breeze caressing this hillside. Everything is green and grayish blue. A perfect night but so imperfect and flawed by human standards. We should be able to go for walks hand-in-hand on evenings like this. We should be able to stretch a blanket out on the ground and read from your favorite books. I should be spraying you with Off and wiping away that long strand of hair from your forehead instead of wiping your grave marker with Armor All and staring at the same bright and shining pose—my Reagan, smiling, surrounded by butterflies.

I had a growth, a lesion, removed at the doctor's office the other day. Turns out it was skin cancer. One more sign, I suppose, of my getting older and feeling older. But I have no fear in hearing the report because I don't fear dying. Somewhere out there is where I want to be, not in the condition I am in now, not in the place I am now.

I'm thinking of you, Reagan Emery. Are you thinking of me?

6/16/07

Tomorrow is Father's Day, and, naturally, I think about a year ago and the last day we spent together. I had welcomed my author friend, David Van Deusen, to Danville and took him to all the sights associated with Dick Van Dyke—Red Mask, WDAN, old houses, the Fischer Theatre. We took in a Danville Dans baseball game. We had a book signing at the public library with a call-in interview with both Dick and Rose Marie. We met Bob Hackman, one of Dick's closest friends, and listened to stories of Dick, the Burfords, and Bob's nephew, Gene. We had a delicious and leisurely dinner at the Heron Restaurant. I dropped him off at the airport in Indianapolis on Sunday, Father's Day, and I looked forward to spending the afternoon with my family—especially with my granddaughters.

I didn't know, you see, that that afternoon would be the last time I saw you alive. I didn't know, or I would have changed the world for you. You were so happy when you found out Papa was going to drive you home. We had a fine talk, you and I, but I don't remember what it was about. I remember vividly how we parted. One hug. Then a second as if one wasn't enough. It turns out two weren't enough, either.

I had everything I could hope for. I was carefree. I took happiness and safety for granted.

Two weeks later you left us.

Nearly a year has gone by, and we wait for an arrest. The Commercial-News has helped in prodding the State's Attorney along. A medical expert, Dr. Demetra Soter, is supposed to finish her report soon. We are trying to get a copy of the report from the Office of Inspector General concerning the mistakes that DCFS made with your case. Both sets of your grandparents continue to raise money for Reagan's Rescue. If there is no arrest made by July 2, we will hold a candlelight vigil in your memory. These are all the things we do. All the things we do. We've become so many action verbs—calling, writing, interviewing, planning, crying, remembering.

Truth is, my favorite memories of you were about just being. No activity—just being together in each other's company. Kind of like writing in this journal.

We now have the solar lamp and the reading angel at the corner of our backyard patio. Sunset Funeral Home asked that all decorations be taken down. Even though we paid an extra fee to have decorations around your marker, I took ours down and brought them home so they weren't discarded by the groundskeepers. Your marker looks so bare that I went out and bought another solar lamp and stuck it in the ground. It's identical to the original, but it doesn't have the strong sentimental value of the first. I don't think I could bear losing the angel and the lamp because they made your grave somehow alive. Now you are as close as the backyard or the bathroom window. I've spent many nights this week sitting out back staring at that angel and talking to you. Crying, of course.

Give us the strength to face these next two weeks, little girl. We are all hurting and dreading the coming anniversary.

6/21/07

Since last July well-meaning friends have told us that the heartache will soon fade and we'll be able to get on with our lives. Recent days and moments of unexpected emotions seem to suggest otherwise.

I told you a while back how hard it was to cry sometimes as if I have shed all the tears allotted to me. Then there are days when the tears flow with no prompting. Most days are like that.

When I enjoy your cousin Aubrey's company—her humor, her stubbornness, her melodramatic flare, her love of movie musicals—I feel sad because I've taken a real shine to another little granddaughter and felt happiness for a time until I feel guilty for seeming to leave you behind. Then I cry.

When the light of my life went out and I can't get elected officials to return a call, I cry.

When, on Memorial Day, your Papa and Da Green and your mama published a picture of you in the newspaper and these perfect words—"Perhaps they are not stars in the sky but rather openings in heaven where our loved ones shine down to let us know they are happy"—I was able to cry.

When, on Father's Day, I suddenly felt so sorry for my little boy, your daddy, because last year he was honored on Father's Day, and this year he wasn't a daddy anymore so he had no card, no hug, and I couldn't find the words—I was able to cry.

I still cry easily. Easily at a horrible, unthinkable price.

Tonight, I was answering an e-mail from my friend and reporter Barbara Greenberg. She needed me to verify some information, and I had copies of hospital records from when you were first injured and taken to the Emergency Room in October of 2005. Your Da walked by and peered over my shoulder and, when she saw the accident reports, went out onto the porch to cry. I worry so much for her.

Please, Baby Girl, pay her a visit. Let her know that she's forgiven for what she feels she didn't do to save you. Let her know you are, indeed, happy and shining in Heaven. She cries a lot, too.

6/22/07

Inspiration, small lessons, connections, continue to come our way. Although I have had doubts about my faith in recent months, I must believe that these moments are not coincidence.

Last night, Da and I watched a film called <u>Infamous</u> in which the author Truman Capote interviewed members of a community still reeling from a grisly murder. Standing in the middle of a field, a farmer and friend of one of the victims speaks poignantly about how fragile life is.

And I've always believed that whenever you do something right it gives you a little bit of weight so that you come to feel rooted to this earth, you know? Solid. Secure. Now what scares me is that...well, sometimes, out of nowhere a bad wind blows up. Now it could be cancer, could be drink, could be some woman that don't belong to you. And despite the weight that's holding you to the ground when that wind comes, it picks you up light as a leaf and it takes you to where it wants. We're in control until we're not. Then we're helpless.

I used to feel rooted. Solid. Secure. Stable. Then that big wind hit.

Cut to almost three years ago, sometime in the fall, I believe. A night we spent together—a first date I like to think of it when we went slow dancing. I babysat you, and *we ended up in Papa and Da's bedroom watching the movie <u>A Mighty Wind</u>. The gentleness of the folk music depicted in that film and our closeness resulted in my swaying back and forth to the songs, you resting your head on my chest.*

The love song from the movie manages to resonate so deeply with me now that I once again slow dance with my little girl.

Oh when the veil of dreams has lifted,
And the fairy tales have all been told,
There's a kiss at the end of the rainbow;
More precious than a pot of gold.

In tales of ancient glory,
Every knight and maiden fair shall be joined when
*   the quest is over,*
And a kiss is the oath that they swear.

My sweet, my dear, my darling, you're so far away
*   from me.*
Though an ocean of tears divides us,
Let the bridge of our love span the sea.
There's a kiss at the end of the rainbow,

More precious than a pot of gold.

I live with one ultimate goal—to find you at the end of my life and to feel a kiss more precious than a pot of gold.

Cut to this afternoon. While searching for footage of the real Truman Capote, awestruck by how uncannily similar Toby Jones's portrayal was to the author, I found a clip of Capote singing "You Are My Sunshine."

Connections. Uncanny and precious.

6/26/07

Your cousin, Ainsley Grace Allison, was born yesterday. Today, as we prepared to leave the hospital after our second trip to Lafayette in as many days, I reached into her bed where, wrapped up tightly in a blanket, she lay sleeping. I gently rubbed her cheek with my right forefinger then rubbed her forehead with my thumb, whispering, "Bye bye, Baby" to her.

I was suddenly transported back to the afternoon of July 7, 2006, your funeral, when I did and said the same to you as you lay in your coffin. Then I touched my forehead to yours, said "Boomp," and nodded to the funeral directors to seal the lid.

[197]

I can't look at Ainsley and know that she's guaranteed a long, happy, and healthy life.

"We're in control until we're not. Then we're helpless."

Losing you, Baby Girl, has taught me to cherish each moment I have with Ainsley, Aubrey, my own children, my wife. It's hard to live that because we are so rushed, but it's a goal worth shooting for.

One other thought—

As I watched Aubrey hold Ainsley, poking her, handling her too roughly because she doesn't know, I wondered what type of big sister you were. You didn't have much of a chance to practice it. I suspect you were as gentle as you were in everything else you did. Or did we only see the gentle side?

7/2/07

Rituals—repeated patterns of meaningful acts. We had ours—singing together our favorite songs, reading favorite books, arrivals when you'd hug us and then head straight for the toy box, partings when we'd bump heads, and everything in between—dancing, silly faces, chasing you up the stairs, animal sounds, saying "I...love...you" in our special sign language (Finger to eye, crossed hands, point to you), even the mundane of picking a drink or washing up after a meal or changing a diaper ("Legs up...legs down...spread 'em").

Even after only a year, the specific sensory memories of you are starting to fade but knowledge of these rituals remains. What the rituals tell me is that you were so easy to care for.

Today, too, is about a ritual and about my truly unimportant attempt to be here in the cemetery beside your grave at the moment you left this world—or at least when you were pronounced dead.

I've been prepared for several days. Today I brought supplies to clean your marker, fresh flowers, a camp chair, this journal and the first volume, your two favorite books (<u>Where is Maisy?</u>* and <u>Touch and Feel Home</u>), pens to write with, a hat so that I don't get a sunburn on my scalp, the cell phone (to tell the time). I'm wearing my pink dress shirt.*

All morning I've kept track of the time, remembering what I was doing on Sunday morning, July 2, a year ago. At 10, I would have gone to church for praise band practice. At 11, the service would have started. Around 12, Mallory and I would have driven her car to the automotive parts store. Around 12:20 we would have driven home only to hear the usually happy Flyn try to explain to us what your mommy had told her on the phone—that you were not breathing and had been taken to the hospital by paramedics. Your Da was already there and alone. Mal and I drove the familiar route to the hospital hoping that you were okay. I believe that at some point during our drive or walking up to the hospital or getting on the elevator or wandering the halls looking for anyone we knew, it turned 12:25 and the doctors working on you let you go.

It is 12:25 p.m. on July 2, 2007, now. Exactly a year since you died.

And now at 12:26, we begin year two.

Tonight at 9 we're holding a candlelight vigil in your memory to talk about how special you were, to inform those gathered about Shaken Baby Syndrome, to hear about legislation regarding SBS education, to pray, and to light candles as a way to remember you and as a symbol for passing along information. It's ritual to end the day with. Be with us, Baby Girl. For, despite my often waning faith, I still believe your spirit can show itself.

7/4/07

Independence Day. I don't feel much like celebrating. I suppose if you had died at some other time, this particular holiday would not always be a reminder of your loss. As it is, I foresee every July 4th being not so much more than a replay of the first terrible week. Does it get any better? Does the grief go away?

The candlelight vigil was everything we hoped it would be and more. We estimate around 275-300 people were there—neighbors, theatre friends, church members, the Tilton Fire Department, family, close friends, co-workers, people from the area around the church, concerned citizens, even the Chief of Staff of our State Senator, and both reporters from WCIA and WICD along with representatives from both newspapers. The mother of a young man killed in a downtown parking garage gave us a card. A woman gave us a bear with a rainbow-colored crocheted shawl. Your Great Great Aunt Barb gave us a card with $50 in it and a short saying I used at the conclusion of the program—"It matters not how long the star did shine but the brightness with which it shone." You were here for only 2 ½ years but you shone brightly and will continue to shine.

Hours before, as Da and I were returning from Wendy's with some food, we pulled up alongside Ryan who was a passenger in a car. I was just feet from him. When I realized who it was, as their car pulled away, a sharp pain went through my chest. Had I known he was beside us I might have rammed the car with our van. Why, after a year, did I finally see him on the anniversary of your death? I don't believe it was coincidence, but I don't understand the significance of that encounter.

I think we touched many people with our vigil, shared a lot of important information. It was just a beginning. We have much work left to do. Already I see a ripple effect—more postings on myspace, a chance to work with Provena to erect a billboard, an offer for a t-shirt with your image, another offer for a playground in Tilton dedicated in your memory, improved plans for play rooms at Your Family Resource Connection. All of these developments give us hope and provide us with goals. We have to move forward with your memory driving our passion, becoming our cause, leading us to action.

Later...

Celebrations are different now that you're gone. Generally, holidays and birthdays meant celebration and that meant family and family included you.

*Last year, while fireworks went off just blocks away at
the American Legion, Da and I walked hand-in-hand back
from a party which included the Hendersons, the
Woodrows, and Pat Linn. I'm sure others were there, but I
don't remember. I do remember wondering how our
country could celebrate Independence Day when our little
girl was gone. I couldn't "stop all the clocks," no matter
how hard I wished it.*

*Tonight, Da, your Aunt Bailey, and I walked several
blocks over to get a good view of the fireworks display at
the Legion, but it did nothing for me. Each explosion
sounded like gunfire to me, a firing squad, a potential
accident resulting in missing fingers or burnt flesh. The
colorful lights only reminded me of what you'd never be
fascinated by, never "ooo" and "ahh" over. While Bailey
held her ears, I was reminded of how I'd never be able to
protect you or draw you close or whisper "Everything will
be all right; Papa's here now, and you're safe. Hold on to
me. I won't let you go."*

*Last week, during a trip to the Abraham Lincoln
Museum in Springfield, I teared up when reminded of
Lincoln's grief in losing Eddie and then Willie. I also cried
while standing in the middle of the gift shop, children and
child-like adults all around me absorbed in Lincoln*

mythology for sale. I told Da, when she asked if I was
okay, that I think I get blue when I realize all the trips of
discovery and fascination that you'll never be able to take
and we'll never be able to enjoy together. It is one of the
times when I feel this is all so unfair. And I was only one of
your Papas.

I saw your mom at the vigil and spoke to her and
hugged her. I have not seen her as grief-stricken and
lonely for her little girl as I did that night. She seemed to
be in the very depths of despair. I know these last few
weeks especially have been excruciatingly difficult for her
with so many references in newspapers and on television to
her being one of two responsible for your death. I don't
think I've ever truly understood her pain and loss as a
mother until that moment. Her murmurs still echo in my
ear—a sad sound that overshadows even the loudest of
firecrackers.

I watched two patriotic Hollywood musical biographies
today—<u>Stars and Stripes Forever</u> and <u>Yankee Doodle
Dandy</u>. Both provided moments of chilling gooseflesh.
Maybe Sousa's and Cohan's love of country and flag were
of a simpler time when wars seemed just reasons to join a
parade, oblivious to body counts. Except for a few
moments of movie magic, the rest of the day was met with

[204]

numbness. What is there to celebrate when the rest of the week means seeing you in your casket for the first time and seeing your body for the last time? What is there to celebrate when our nation's birth is now linked with my granddaughter's death? What is there to celebrate when we have no life, no liberty, no happiness? How does one celebrate independence when a captive of Hell?

"Self yeast of spirit a dull dough sours"

7/7/07

Today is a last milestone, I guess. It is the one year anniversary of your funeral. It was on that day that I saw you last, that I touched you. And now, a year later, yours is the touch I miss the most. I haven't been able to nestle on the couch with a granddaughter who loved books so. You took to reading so early. Your cousin Aubrey is not there yet although I hold out hope that reading together is one activity we will be able to enjoy eventually.

I didn't want today to go by without your knowing that your papa thought of you—and thinks of you—with love. Oh, my baby, I am so lonely without you. All I can do is to have faith in your ability to read this and to know how I feel. If you are sending signs occasionally, grant me the wisdom to recognize them.

7/10/07

I don't handle crying toddlers very well, children who shriek or sob. If it goes on long enough, I begin to envision what your last hour was like, particularly what violence was done to you. The images drive me insane. I have to concentrate for a long time to clear my mind of these painful pictures.

It happened today in the dentist's office in Lafayette while I sat with Da waiting for your cousin Aubrey to get done with her appointment. Across the room this little girl—probably two—began throwing a tantrum. Anything the mother did to quiet her down resulted in even louder crying, wailing, screaming bloody murder (I don't like using that expression any more). I tried to ignore it. I looked away, but, suddenly, I was in the house in Tilton watching helplessly as your life was shaken away. I think having Ainsley in her carrier resting on my lap gave me something else to focus on—life, hope, serenity.

Soon a trio of young teenage girls sat together comparing braces. Suddenly, I was watching you as a thirteen year old chatting with your teenage friends until I realized (and I find it odd that, for a second, I forgot) you'd never get to gather with giddy, gossipy, grinning girls of thirteen because you only had two and a half years.

The screaming toddler and the chatty teens made me cry in that waiting room. After a year, I am still at the place where I find it unfair. It is difficult, if not impossible sometimes, to find solace in Heaven.

That's why a vision of you would help us all.

7/16/07

I've had moments of deep depression, loss, and loneliness recently—like twinges. They've happened anywhere. In the store, in a restaurant, while driving. I can't find a trigger except, perhaps, in music. I found the CD with the funeral music tucked away in my bookbag, hooked up Bailey's CD player to my car stereo, and began playing the selections whenever I drive across town to the college or back home. I've listened to them before in this past year without the same reaction. The four songs took those at the funeral through a kind of healing faith journey, from your favorite songs "You Are My Sunshine" and "Tell Me Why" (the live baby and then toddler Reagan and the

memories of cuddling and rocking and singing together) to
"It Is Well with My Soul" (somber in tone and then
transcendent, a song written about personal loss and,
despite that loss, trust in God that "faith shall be sight")
and, finally, to "Remembering You" (a Celtic dance-like
tune of the passage of time and enduring memory and the
dead that comes back to life).

I think hearing the music again has connected me in a
very real way to last July. I've fixated on the use of "you"
in the first two songs and in the last because (and I should
not need to be reminded of this) "you" is you, my little
granddaughter who was killed. I think hearing the songs,
especially your favorites, brings us together; for just a brief
moment, you're on my lap again, and you are safe—we are
safe. The tears I shed are both a visible and audible sign
that I haven't forgotten; the tears, the shock, the sense of
loss and loneliness are as real and as strong as a year ago,
probably more so because the numbing surprise has worn
off, and I experience senses and emotions so much more
deeply. Maybe it's like going on a terrifying rollercoaster
for the second time—now there are not only the same fears
and physical responses but the knowledge of what is about
to happen.

I often take comfort in what comfort there is to be had in thinking that you died without fear. A man going to the gallows or the chair would have overwhelming anxiety, even terror. A child would not know to be scared, would not fear for her life. I hope that is what happened. I can't bear to think of the alternative.

I've thought recently, too, about a memory from some thirty-five years ago—really a premonition.

Around 1972 or 1973, I recall, I saw a Billy Graham movie entitled <u>For Pete's Sake</u> about an average working guy whose life is changed when his wife suddenly dies. At the time, I projected myself into the son's role and my mother into the role of the wife who dies. I even remember her doing something like decorating, maybe standing on a ladder, and then suddenly hemorrhaging violently, blood coming out of her nose. I was instantly afraid of my own mother's safety, but I also remember a very strong and, through the years, abiding...knowledge, understanding...that I would one day suffer a similar loss. Over time, I wondered if I would lose my wife and then, one by one, each child. Which would be taken from me early?

I was also aware that I would get through the loss but that it would change me, give me some tragic edge. I knew it would be someone I loved thoroughly. Last July 2, I got my answer—my Reagan.

I've not shared this with anyone. I don't know if I will. I wish the premonition had not come true, but its occurrence makes that distant movie memory complete.

I didn't realize that a tragedy like this makes one relive so much of the past for such an extended time. Maybe it's not to lose hold. Maybe it's to wallow in hindsight and in the regret of missed foresight. Maybe it's to cherish a happier time. We look back so much, more than I've ever done with any other relative who has passed away.

The wise look ahead to see what is coming, but fools deceive themselves.—Proverbs 14: 8.

Dr. Norman Peart has written: "I've seen individuals who are still living in a state of memorial, a state of going back and rehearsing and feeling bad about what has happened and really verging on cursing God and walking away from Him." I am guilty on all counts. I will go back to church, of course, and try to understand God's plan in all of this. I will not look back to the past so much. But, as Don said at the funeral, "We're not there yet."

7/18/07

We begin a new chapter today. We move from familiar emotions of the last few months—emotions repeated over and over—to new experiences, new settings, new challenges and emotional reactions.

Ryan was arrested for your murder today. We were contacted by Investigator Todd Damilano who we met at the hospital the day you died. From then on, the phone became the center of attention. We called relatives; friends and reporters called us. I did five interviews (both papers, WCIA, WICD, and a radio station). One of the reporters suggested that I sounded calm. Didn't I feel anger? Wasn't I overjoyed at the news of the arrest?

Reagan, I hope you know that I am angry, always have been, but I've tried channeling my rage into something productive. Writing poetry, music. Talking to groups. Educating people about SBS. Fundraising.

Though I could have run Ryan over if he had crossed in front of the van, I don't think being angry or violently acting on that anger would solve anything.

Regardless of how pleased we may feel that we've reached this long-awaited point, nothing will bring you back. You lost your life. We lost the lives we knew, too. Ryan selfishly took so much when he took you.

I miss you, Little Girl. I miss you more than any of my words can say.

7/22/07

I've spent this last year marking time by what happened a year earlier. By a year, I don't mean Jan. 1-Dec. 31 but rather July 2-July 1.

And so, in October of 2006, I remembered the first time you were injured, the first time my heart broke, the first time Da and I promised to do anything to help you. In December of 2006, I recalled the bruises which appeared on your body and our frustration with DCFS and your hospitalization. In January of 2007, I looked back at your 2nd birthday—the last—and how thin you were. In April of 2007, I remembered Easter and the baby turtles in the garth at church. In May of 2007, I remembered keeping you for the week while your brother was born and keeping you again at the end of the month because it was not safe at home. In June of 2007, I thought of Father's Day and how little we saw of you the rest of the month—but then it wasn't a concern, a regret, because we had your whole life to spend together.

I thought when I reached July 2, 2007, I would stop telling time by events which occurred a year earlier, but I have continued to reflect on the past. Whether it is stubbornness or unmanly grief or delighting in misery, I still think back. The day we found out you were shaken. The day we saw you in your casket. The day of the funeral. The day Mallory performed at show choir camp. The day my speech class gave me a card of condolence.

July 2 to July 1. How I tell time now. My New Year's Day to New Year's Eve.

"...going back and rehearsing and feeling bad."

---

3 We can rejoice, too, when we run into problems and trials, for we know that they help us develop endurance. 4 And endurance develops strength of character, and character strengthens our confident hope of salvation.--Romans 5: 3-4 (NLT)

7/27/07

Yesterday, Great Grandpa Jim, your daddy, and I traveled to Springfield to meet with the state director of DCFS, Erwin McEwen, to find out about the results of the Office of Inspector General investigation into your death. We didn't know whether he'd even be there to meet with us or whether we'd travel two hours for nothing, but, as it turns out, Mr. McEwen was there, candid, genuinely concerned about our loss, and interested in initiating change in DCFS policy and procedure if possible.

We read the twenty page redacted report, discovering answers to questions we have had and finding out about several incidents that occurred at the house in Tilton, incidents that involved anger and violence and even the police. If we had known some of the facts we were introduced to in the report we would have done all we could to take you somewhere safe. As hard as it was to read the report and its findings, we also feel like we accomplished several goals.

Mr. McEwen told us that, from now on, fathers will be routinely interviewed during a DCFS investigation when the mother is living with a boyfriend. Your daddy was never questioned by the local DCFS caseworker.

I should have been allowed to speak with a caseworker when I took photos of you into the local office. There is even a policy regarding a counselor being available when someone walks in with information about a child in danger.

I pleaded with the director that those answering phones for the abuse hotline take information without the caller having to supply a name or number so that the caller could be contacted later. Your Da and I both regret our decision not to give information to the hotline; we will have regrets until we die.

I gave Mr. McEwen a bracelet and, later, at the conclusion of our meeting, he gave me a $10 donation to Reagan's Rescue.

None of this does anything to bring you back, but, once again, in your memory we can foster change where it needs to occur.

We left the DCFS building feeling a sense of accomplishment and hope and some justice.

Several blocks later, as we walked past a downtown Springfield park, we saw a statue of Abraham Lincoln and, beneath, a plaque which read:

> *Why should there not be a patient confidence in the ultimate justice of the people?*

[215]

Is there any better, or equal hope, in the world?
March 4, 1861

It capped off a stressful day, a day of learning what more
we should have done and learning about what more
happened to you.

7/28/07

Today, we drove as far as Kearney, Nebraska, on our
way to a vacation in Colorado. There's no vacation from
our thoughts of you—the good and, especially, the painful.
Along the interstate there were so many reminders. A car
passed by with the dealership name on the back—Reagan.
A music display in a museum gift shop featured snippets of
selections, including "You Are My Sunshine" at the very
moment I was thinking about you. A thin and pale little girl
about your age broke away from her mother several times
and ran by us, once again reminding me of what we will
not be able to share together.

I have to believe that these are not coincidences but
signs yet I don't know if they are supposed to make me feel
bad or good. Without any direction from Heaven, I am left
feeling worse.

[216]

Are you there with us, Little Girl? Can you let us know?

8/2/07

Today, we met our Great Nephew, Greyson, the son of my sister Elaine's boy, Zachary. Greyson is almost two, a blond-haired, fair-skinned boy with big blue eyes and a temperament similar to yours. Both Da and I noticed how alike you are. Or were. I don't know how to say that.

You were able to play by yourself for long stretches, and Greyson is able to do that, too. He repeated a lot of actions (like pushing a toy truck back and forth across the carpet or turning the fan on and off again and again). When he continued to open and close the sliding screen door to the deck, and Da and I laughed and held our ears with every slam, he giggled, revealing an emerging sense of humor. How we could laugh with you.

We bought Greyson a little board book, Five Little Monkeys, and read it to him several times with as much drama and gesturing and tickling as we could manage until he began to catch on, trying to say the words along with us. That chance to share a book so thoroughly is something we've desperately missed.

When someone put a hair tie on Greyson's head, he looked more like the little girl we lost. And when it was time for him to be taken back home, he hugged and kissed everyone, blew us extra kisses, and waved, a ritual we used to repeat with you every time you left our house.

Besides the book, we gave Greyson a puzzle, too. He gave us much more—a chance to remember you through the five senses and not just through memory. We cried at the realization.

"I haven't broken down like this in a long time," your Da said, adding, "but that's okay." I agree. Each day I spend some time thinking about you, talking to you, crying, even breaking down. It means we still have a connection. That Da and I are experiencing many of the same emotions means we are closer in our grief and, therefore, more understanding of each other.

Tonight, so far away from Aubrey and Ainsley and so separated from you, I'm missing my granddaughters even more than usual.

8/6/07

This evening I visited Whispering Pines Chapel at Snow Mountain Ranch near Granby, Colorado. Eleven years ago, while working as the Chaplain's Assistant here at the Y, I sat down in the chapel one evening and prayed for answers and for guidance in finding a job. I couldn't do it on my own, you see, and so I gave it over to God. His answer came quickly, and I began teaching at Danville High School a month later.

Tonight, I entered that special and holy place lost and hurting and too weak to do it on my own. I came prepared with a CD and a CD player to listen to the music I normally play when I want to feel close to you, but a young man was playing the piano—beautiful playing—and so I let that be the score of my visit.

While walking around the room I found a devotional book for June, July, and August of 2007 called Our Daily Bread. On the front cover was a green, lush mountain scene and these words from Isaiah 32: 18—"My people will dwell in a peaceful habitation, in secure dwellings, and in quiet resting places."

No words could more aptly describe Snow Mountain Ranch.

I looked up the devotion for today about stretching one's muscles to gain full range of motion. I couldn't help but think of my hike up Snow Mountain today and how sore my muscles are right now. The author went on to talk about stretching one's spiritual muscles with God's promise that His strength is made perfect in weakness (2 Corinthians 12: 9).

I was feeling weak, but I wanted to stretch some more. Out of curiosity, I looked at the devotions for several other dates.

June 25 (when Ainsley was born) talked about the ways people deal with stresses in life. Drinking, blaming God, overeating, hiding feelings, all temporary means of escaping problems. Instead we must reach for God. In Psalm 55, David says, "My heart is severely pained within me…Oh, that I had wings like a dove! I would fly away and be at rest." Putting our cares in God's hands will allow peace to dwell in our hearts.

July 2 (when you died) was written by a former high school teacher who imagined lecturing a classroom of students who weren't paying attention. He then compared that to our ignoring God, something I've done too much of by not attending or participating in church.

August 16 (Aubrey's birthday) talked about one of the more precious gifts we have from God—the ability to remember. "Good memories become a treasure chest of priceless reminders of relationships shared and joys experienced," this writer shares. Paul felt the same about the church in Philippi: "I thank my God upon every remembrance of you." I thank God when I remember you.

Finally, August 23 (Da's birthday) talked about the tipping point, a critical juncture, a moment of decision. The devotion encouraged the reader (me, in this case) to surrender his will to God. "Surrender is the tipping point," the author shared. "When we make that choice, God can use us to do great things for Him."

And so, as the young pianist played on, I had confronted my pain, my sins, and my salvation, all through the important dates in my life. Eleven years after my last chapel vigil, I came again to this place I love to seek God's grace—and I found it. I believe you were there in that room, sitting beside me, leading me to answered prayer.

8/7/07

Psalm 19 says: "The heavens declare the glory of God; and the firmament shows His handiwork. Day unto day utters speech, and night unto night reveals knowledge."

This evening, the sunset revealed God's glory, an awe-inspiring coda to last night's revelations. As the rains passed and the sky began to clear, mist settled in the valley around Blue Ridge and ringed both Snow Mountain and Nine Mile.

The western sky turned a golden yellow. When the rays of the setting sun fell over layer after layer of clouds, the result was sunbeams coming out like a crown, much like the beams which emanate from the solar lamp at your grave. For a moment, I could almost see your face in the distant sky. What I did imagine was you running through Heaven, laughing and in pure joy even as my eyes teared up at the sight of God's handiwork. For a moment there was peace.

Was this the direction from Heaven I was searching for over a week ago?

2 Dear brothers and sisters, when troubles of any kind come your way, consider it an opportunity for great joy. 3 For you know that when your faith is tested, your endurance has a chance to grow. 4 So let it grow, for when your endurance is fully developed, you will be perfect and complete, needing nothing.-- James 1: 2-4 (NLT)

8/19/07

Life is filled with dying and resurrecting. Sometimes it is important, like when a sainted grandmother or an innocent child crosses over to glory. Sometimes it demonstrates a natural progression, like when a school heals after some violence or a community rebounds after tragedy. Most of us go through little deaths and resurrections daily or weekly when bad luck comes or setbacks or some unforeseen state. We're sure the world is going to end, but then it doesn't, and we once again realize how blessed we are and how much worse things could be. Everything's relative.

We had a string of bad luck this week—expensive car repairs, the sewer backing up into our basement, and, then, this morning when my key broke off in the ignition of my car as I stopped at Starbucks in Matteson, Illinois, on the way to pick up Dal—your Aunt Mallory—at Midway Airport. I was also locked out of the car with a useless half a key and had to call AAA Motor Club so that they could locate a locksmith. Because help would not arrive for an hour and a half, making me late to pick up Mallory, I called Great Grandma Sharon to drive to Midway while I stayed around for the lockout technician to show up.

During all this, I tried to keep it together and stay positive, but thoughts of losing you began to sap my spirit. Haven't I suffered enough? You take my granddaughter and then give us this expensive week of repair costs and overtime rates? I felt so alone sitting at a corner table reading the Sunday Sun-Times. I felt picked on, singled out, victimized yet again. Then I found salvation. The Family Circus comic strip showed the family lamenting a miserable vacation with bad weather, sickness, and engine trouble. After a near head-on collision, the family gathers in the pouring rain to reaffirm just how lucky they all are. Even the rain looks beautiful.

Everything's relative. Conditions could be worse.

[224]

I made idle conversation with the technician, telling how this key breaking was the latest in a week of calamities. He said he had had a week like that, too, and understood my frustration. Then he shared parts of his life with me. His first wife died of cancer at age 38. His second marriage, to a victim of childhood abuse, was ending in divorce. His brother was in poor health, the bills leaving him nearly penniless. But this technician said how much help his son and daughter-in-law were to him.

"It's only money, Dad," she had said to him as an offer of comfort. And that message made it to my heart through him.

I told him about you, Reagan, and about loss that really matters.

Mallory got picked up on time. I got into my car, and all of us got home safely. The technician even knocked off $25 from his initial rate then encouraged me to make a claim with our auto insurance.

Everything's relative. Things could be a lot worse.

Before I left, I asked his name. Brian. That was also the name of his son for whom he was filling in today. Barb was his daughter-in-law.

He unlocked much more than my car. He allowed me to live again after I died in front of a Starbucks on the way to the airport.

8/30/07

"The sacrifice of praise."

It's a title of a song we've sung in church. It's an idea that praising God, especially in rough seas, demands sacrifice. I had not attended services regularly until this past Sunday. Since March I stayed at home each Sunday morning, enjoying a more leisurely ritual of coffee and several newspapers. I didn't feel like praising, couldn't play the keyboard, couldn't perform praise songs and not think myself a fraud.

Praise seems so out there, so committed, so total, and I was anything but, clinging to the so-so, the average, the neutral, the unsatisfying. Lukewarm. The difference between Starbucks and a pot of coffee which has sat on the same burner for hours. The difference between filet mignon and an inferior cut of meat full of gristle. The difference between a homegrown garden tomato and a hard grocery store imposter, Styrofoam with tomato flavoring.

Last week, my friend, Stefanie, and one of your champions, Reagan, wrote a piece for the newsletter at

[226]

Central Christian. George, as praise team leader, normally fills this page, but his dad died two weeks ago, and he was unable to come up with anything coherent. Stefanie's submission was so beautiful and personally challenging to me. She wrote:

...no matter how happy, sad, angry, confused, or lost I feel, that I should make the effort or "sacrifice" to praise God. I need to give those feelings over to Him so that praise, and possibly joy, may take their place.

She went on to mention three people—George, who would no doubt be offering up sacrifices of praise during worship even though his heart is aching; dear Everett Meeker, who thanked God for all his blessings only a week after his beloved wife, Adeline, passed away; and then you, our little Reagan, who left an angry, broken-hearted congregation to praise God through quivering voices and eyes stinging from tears.

She concluded by reminding us that God knows the pain of sacrifice and that those who are hurting may need others to make the sacrifice for them. I know that, in my time away from Central, many made that sacrifice for me when I couldn't find the faith or the words.

I still can't praise God, but I will try and hope that He'll accept what can only be half-hearted praise at best.

9/8/07

Tonight on <u>John Edward Cross Country</u>, John gave a reading to a mother, father, and brother of a young man, himself a husband and father of three, who was killed while riding his motorcycle, dying alone on a lonely highway. This young man, through John, tried to implore his grieving family to get beyond the thirty seconds of his death and be grateful for the life he led. The accident, after all, had been for him not an exit or an ending but an entrance into a far better level of existence. The young man also appreciated the moments his family members talk to him.

As the program went to a commercial, I told Da that if we took some names, places, and events out and replaced them with references to you, all of John's advice and the messages he translated from the other side could fit our lives this past year.

I wonder again, do you appreciate when I talk to you, when I sing for you, when I write in this journal? Do you, too, want us to get beyond July 2, 2006, to focus instead on your life and the gifts you gave us? I want with all my heart to believe that you are still with us. I would put aside mourning if I had just a little proof beyond faith, beyond hope.

I do know that John Edward spoke to us this evening. That's why I'm writing.

Because of the partnership between Reagan's Rescue and Provena—the billboards, the radio PSAs—an article for Provena's magazine <u>One Life</u> is being written. I was interviewed for the article through e-mail. Perhaps we can reach people beyond the Danville area and not just the general public but hospital officials. I want there to be stricter SBS education given to parents of newborns before they can leave the hospital. If newborns can't leave without proof of a suitable carseat then parents shouldn't take their babies home before being fully trained on the dangers of shaking an infant.

The billboards, the radio spots, the magazine article, the media stories, the wristbands, the vigil—all a part of our lives after you left us.

But as a new pastor Deborah said last week in church, referencing Matthew the tax gatherer, who left his position to follow Jesus, "New occasions teach new duties." We now travel a different road, hoping for, trusting in, God to prepare us.

In closing, two moments today which I never imagined having to experience. Two small but somehow significant moments.

Your wooden rocking chair sits in the dining room. Several weeks ago, Da rearranged the furniture and redistributed the rooster collection. She put a plush rooster on the seat of the chair. Today I moved it to the corner of the seat to make enough room for you to sit there. I want you to visit us whenever you can. That's why I keep the backseat of the car clear, too—for you.

The other moment—seeing your photo on the National Shaken Baby Coalition website, there beside all the other angelic children, survivors and victims. I cried when I saw it even though it is the same picture we have in the den and on my desk at school. I think I cried because I was letting you go to be shared with people all over the country. I also cried because I realized once again how beautiful you were.

Thank you for being in my head and in my heart. "I thank my God every time I remember you."—Philippians 1:3

9/12/07

As time has passed, this journal has been more about my grief and my need for something therapeutic to get me through the darkest of moods. It has been less about you, Reagan, partly because I am losing hold of clear, vivid memories. You become more distant, the glass in the picture frame thicker. How I long for your touch and for the smell of your hair. How much I need a visit.

The radio PSA is done. It will be effective. It contains the voices of Angie Mansfield, Gretchen Wesner, Jordan Worthington, Jessica Valdez, Scott Zercher, and Ted Vacketta. They were all very happy to be involved. They believe in what we're trying to do.

The pride and sense of accomplishment I feel toward this latest venture is balanced by the numbness I battle. I wish I could cry easier; that would make my daily life more bearable.

At church on Sunday, Deborah flashed a slide on the screen which read: GODISNOWHERE.
Her point—how easily we can waiver between "God is nowhere" and "God is now here." Her message accurately reflected my wavering between doubt and despair or faith and hope. My mood seems to coincide with how I feel about your presence—irretrievably lost or closer

than I can even imagine. I must believe you are here, or I will be lost.

Yesterday, your daddy and I both received a summons in the mail for an October court date. I assume that we will both be witnesses in the trial.

This morning there was a motion for exchange of information, and a new hearing date was set for September 18. Bond is to be discussed again and a request for a continuance made.

Legal matters test my faith. The light dims. Hope retreats. You seem pulled farther away. Is this what healing leads to? Numbness, oblivion? Is this emptiness a sign that I am getting better or worse?

9/23/07

When I started keeping a journal for you, Reagan, I intended to record all the important events in the first eighteen years of your life. Since July 2, 2006, I've found it harder to remember that life. The journal has become more about me and my views on all that has happened. Nearly fifteen months have passed, and the only real blessing I can find—a blessing not paired with some struggle or doubt or selfless gesture—is that I am fifteen

[232]

months closer to dying. Dying will mean being reunited with you or oblivion, nothingness. I hope for a reunion, but, if there is no eternal life save in the memories of those we leave behind, oblivion will be acceptable.

I still cry for you every day, and there are long stretches recently when tears have flowed easily. This past week has been especially difficult.

I attended a training workshop in Springfield on Tuesday morning, enabling me to conduct my own workshops and presentations on SBS. Much of the information shared with us I already knew, but I also got to see two videos about children who were killed from being shaken. They were moving, heartwrenching, hard to watch and so powerful tools in SBS awareness and education. Two DCFS employees from Danville attended, and for a while I felt weak, cowardly, ineffective. A joke really. One, Michelle Hernandez, was sympathetic, emotional, when we had a chance to talk during a break. I wanted to confirm with her what I was told by DCFS State Director McEwen in July, that, when I showed up with photographs at the Danville office that December day, there should have been someone to counsel me, a designated caseworker for walk-ins. Unfortunately, that employee had left the Danville office and had not been replaced. Bad luck. Bad timing.

Fate. The will of God? I don't know. I only know how pathetic I was, am. Michelle volunteered to collaborate with me on presentations to school boards. I recognized the other employee but could not remember her name. She seemed smug, amused at my pathetic life, but then it was probably my imagination.

I drove back to Danville just in time for what we were led to believe would be a routine hearing at the County Courthouse. Two hours later, bond for Ryan was set at a mere $150,000. We couldn't help but equate that amount with the perceived value of your life. Don Vanzant said yours was a short but significant life. The law suggested otherwise. Bond was set because Frank Young and Larry Mills failed to draw up murder charges correctly, according to the judge. They also failed to make a motion to consider Ryan a threat and a flight risk. We sat there helpless as the charges unraveled. Weak. Pathetic. Guilty of something. Of not understanding violence and ignorance. Of not tolerating incompetency. I tried to confront Frank and Larry after the hearing concluded. All I got was a smile from Frank and an excuse from Larry.

"Maybe this happened for a reason," I whispered into Da's ear while Ryan's family was celebrating. I don't like

admitting this, but I wish some kind of vigilante would kill him.

You see, I can't because I'm weak, pathetic, cowardly, afraid to hurt my family any more than they've already been damaged. If I were a real man, I'd hunt him down. But then there's your Aunt Bailey who still needs me, at least for a few more years.

Please, please, Sunshine, come to us. If we could be certain of your eternal life, certain of a reunion one day, we could go on. We could live confidently again. I know that's not acting in faith, but it's all I'm capable of.

There is good news of a kind, hopeful news. Plans are underway for a Second Annual Reagan Williams Invitational at DHS. And this Wednesday I go before the school board to ask for SBS education in the middle schools and at the high school.

At home I've begun putting together a website for Reagan's Rescue. It is a donation from my stepbrother, Gary.

We're doing what we can, Reagan, but our efforts will never be enough. If I can manage to leave this life and not overstay my welcome, then, finally, I'll be a success.

An hour later…

I received an e-mail from former praise team leader, Melany Jackson. I uttered no specific prayer, but maybe God heard me anyway, using Melany as His voice.

Hi Greg,

I know it's been awhile since I've been in touch. I was so thankful to finally see the arrest. And now I see that just yesterday he was released on bail and there have been more mistakes by the state's attorney. This has to be very tough for you and Marsha and your family.

Every time new news would come out in the investigation of my friend Karyn's murder, we would all hope this would be the time for the arrest. And then there would be more waiting. The arrest in her case took more than 5 years, while all the time the murderer was raising her precious son and brainwashing him about his mother, erasing her from his mind. I still struggle with everything that happened in her case. I can only imagine what this must be like for you.

I do think of you often and pray for you and for the case to be fairly resolved.

Please email or pick up the phone anytime day or night…I'd love to hear from you.

Dear God, thank you for being holy and omnipotent.
We rest in your powerful arms. God, we continue to pray
for justice to be served. Please work through all of the red
tape and mistakes in the legal system. I pray that Reagan's
memory will live on and that those who hear about her will
think twice and stop before shaking a baby or toddler.
Please strengthen Greg tonight. Shower him with your
love and peace. Continue to bring believers into his life to
encourage him and stand with him. Thank you for using
him in the lives of so many. Bring him joy, Father. Thank
you. In the holy and precious name of our Lord and our
Savior, Jesus Christ, Amen.

10/2/07

Another 2nd of the month though I didn't think
about the date or the significance until this evening. I
guess that's a sign of healing, but I don't know for sure.
Recently, I've begun to feel like I was splitting in two. The
highs are about the same. Not really highs but manageable
moments of distraction—teaching, conversations, TV. The
lows, however, seem lower. I feel depressed, like I'm
losing hold.

Others have noticed. They are concerned. My friend, Angie Mansfield, who provided a voice for the radio spot, sent a packet of music to me and a CD. "Take this for what you will and again, remember that I have the best of intentions," she wrote. The songs were from show tunes mostly. Two of the songs brought a flood of tears when I heard them.

One was from the movie <u>Camp</u>, a song entitled "I Sing for You." I never thought about how closely the lyrics matched my own emotions about you, but, once again, losing you has made me see things in a different light.

I sing for you and only you
Wherever I go I find you
You're in the sound of every hello
In everything I do
You're the song I was destined to know
And I only sing for you

You went away. I should have known
You leave so many dreams behind you
Thought I'd be fine just being alone
I didn't have a clue
But my heart had a mind of its own

[238]

And would only sing for you

You're in the sound of the rain
Clouds in a winter sky
In a thousand unsaid words
In a thousand crazy reasons why
You were meant to fly

So fly for me and day by day
I'll keep hoping your heart reminds you
Nothing but love can stand in our way
But love can see us through
Maybe that's all I wanted to say
I will always sing for you
I will always sing for you

The other song, from a film called <u>Joseph</u>, is a plea to God.

I thought I did what's right
I thought I had the answers
I thought I chose the surest road
But that road brought me here

So I put up a fight

And told you how to help me

Now just when I have given up

The truth is coming clear

You know better than I

You know the way

I've let go the need to know why

For you know better than I

If this has been a test

I cannot see the reason

But maybe knowing I don't know

Is part of getting through

I try to do what's best

And faith has made it easy

To see the best thing I can do

Is put my trust in you

For You know better than I

You know the way

I've let go the need to know why

For you know better than I

I saw one cloud and thought it was a sky

I saw a bird and thought that I could follow

But it was you who taught that bird to fly

If I let you reach me will you teach me

For You know better than I

You know the way

I've let go the need to know why

I'll take what answers you supply

You know better than I

I am lucky to have such caring friends, lucky, too, that they challenge me not to give up. One day, maybe I'll believe wholeheartedly that God knows better than I. For now, I can't sing for Him. I can only sing for you, little girl.

---

4 He comforts us in all our troubles so that we can comfort others. When they are troubled, we will be able to give them the same comfort God has given us.--2 Corinthians 1: 4 (NLT)

10/17/07

I haven't written to you in over two weeks. I've wanted to. I've had so much on my mind, but I couldn't put it into the right words. I don't like not being able to communicate with you because then you seem impossibly far away, farther than just a thin veil.

Da and I have watched John Edward in the last month. At first, I avoided the show because I didn't want to see your Da cry. Sometimes the stories of loss are very emotional, but they also bring us peace. Maybe you sit between us. I wish we knew.

I finished the Reagan's Rescue website, and the response has been very positive. I used a lot of photos of you. I hope you don't mind. Your Papa shamelessly tells your story or shares your picture whenever I can get an emotional response from people.

Last night, I read some of my poetry and a few from David Ray at a Library Club Poetry Reading in the courtyard of the Java Hut. I made some people cry.

Then I spoke at the candlelight service at Your Family Resource Connection. Da, Great Grandpa Jim and Great Grandma Roberta were there, along with our friend, Barb. I talked about you and the Maisy book, about the week we lost you, about Reagan's Rescue and SBS and hope. I used

the quote "When God closes a door, somewhere He opens
a window." Afterwards, I met the family of Kimberly Gray.
They hugged us tightly. I think we felt a strong bond
because of losing a loved one and dealing with an often
inept justice system. Their names were Barbara and
Michael Wombles.

I'm sorry I can't write more, Reagan, or write more
eloquently. Pouring so much energy into speeches and
poems and websites and non-profit forms and business
cards and school board presentations leaves me little room
for feeling. I do still feel, Sweetheart. When I watch a
program about a little girl pulled from a well and I see that
girl hug her daddy, put her arms tightly around his neck, I
so long for your touch. I wonder, then, if people can hug in
Heaven. When I drive in my car and glance back at the
spot where we used to keep your carseat, I feel your loss
deeply. My loneliness hurts. The right words, like my
tears, don't flow so readily. Please know I still miss you.
Please know that I am still your Papa.

10/26/07
  Always blessings
  Never losses

11/1/07

When I wrote the previous entry there was nothing else I could add at the time. The words were at once simple and profound. Your Da and I watched an episode of John Edward which featured the grieving parents of a four year old boy who had died from natural causes. The father had harbored a great deal of resentment while the mother had come to terms with the death of her son, her sunshine (just like you, Reagan). She told John by phone, "Always blessings. Never losses." John had to pause and choke back tears, commenting that those words, and the faith that they revealed, would continue to touch viewers for years to come. I know they touched us, taking us to a new place in our grief. We had 2 ½ years of blessings. You're in Heaven now, and so you are not lost.

I still miss you, Sunshine. Last night as Da and I waited for the neighborhood Halloween parade to begin, we both teared up, remembering you as a bee when you were nearly one and as a pumpkin when you were almost two. So many children passed by on the sidewalk—some the age you would have been, some the age you were when you last joined the parade, some the age you were going to be the next year and the next and the next as we marked the passing of time by this Walnut Street ritual. I prayed that, as we gathered as a family, you would be there.

Papa just found out last week that a Reagan Emery Bear from Boyd's Bears will be coming out in the spring/summer of 2008. I've seen the picture online, and I've talked to representatives of the company. Now I have to wait and keep my secret until they are available.

I told you in the car the other day that I wanted two of them—one for Da's collection and one to sleep with like you used to sleep with us. I am no older than a boy in this, often lost and frightened like a child. Like a little boy— perhaps like the boy I once was—I believed in this project, and my wish came true.

Not all wishes do, you know. Or maybe not all wishes come true now. Maybe some have to wait—like hugging you.

11/4/07

A new month means another 2nd of that month. There have now been sixteen. Sixteen anniversaries. And today another time to pause and reflect as it was All Saints' Sunday at church. I went alone this time, and I felt abandoned.

I realized, though, that sometimes I must seem selfish in my grief. I sat in church, waiting for the service to start, with a furrowed brow, enough of an expression to illicit a few questions regarding my welfare. I wanted all the laughter and chitchat to stop—all the clocks, too, if I had my way—so people could join me in my mourning. Then it struck me that I was surrounded by grief. My good friend, George, lost his dad just a month ago. The Cannadys lost a stillborn grandson. Their tears were real. They had reason to cry, too.

Maybe losing a parent to cancer or losing a grandchild one has never met is easier than having a beloved 2 ½ year old granddaughter whose life is taken away. Maybe I can still justify the tears I shed as I lit a candle for you, Reagan. Time has not healed my wounds.

I only know that I do not grieve for you alone, and I do not experience grief alone. Knowing that, however, only helps for a short time.

As I sat in the pew anticipating the candlelighting ritual, I envisioned you with Uncle Frank and Grandma Williams. Are you together and happy? Are you meeting other family who never met you?

11/23/07

On this day after Thanksgiving, I have so much for which to be grateful. Family, friends, and co-workers continue to be supportive and concerned. I have a job which allows me to pay my bills, buy groceries, and keep the light and heat on. We live in a house in a friendly neighborhood in my hometown. I have a dog and two cats who need me and who give love in return. I have my health.

What I don't have are small arms to hug me. What I don't have is my granddaughter to hold. As the holidays have approached, that moment of greeting—that hug of reunion—has played over and over in my mind. I know I will never have that hug in my lifetime, so I look forward to our reunion in Heaven. Will we be allowed to touch?

I visited your grave yesterday—cleaned off the leaves, polished up the marker, told you how thankful I was for you, and again cried because I would not have that hug at our front door. I sobbed, really, out of loneliness for you and for gathering with family without you there.

A few moments ago I saw the end of <u>Home Alone</u> when, on Christmas morning, Kevin is reunited with his mother and family. Then he spots his neighbor, the scary hermit played by Roberts Blossom, who has a reunion of his own *with his estranged son and his granddaughter. I always cry at this scene, but now I cry harder because I see a grandfather who has a hug from a little girl he has missed, one he adores. Is that indescribable joy what awaits us?*

I often comment on how time moves so much faster the older I get. The one advantage is that I will be with you sooner than I know.

November has certainly passed by quickly. I had another article written about Reagan's Rescue. I spoke at school board meetings in Hoopeston and Bismarck about Shaken Baby education. A Christmas tree called Angels on Earth was on display at the Festival of Trees a couple of weeks ago. Julia Megan Sullivan designed it. Originally, she was going to have pictures of you on it, but she decided to create a tree you would have loved, and you would have loved this tree—with its Doras, butterflies, stars, and Reagan bracelets. It's now in the den, and so when I light it and sit in here and gaze at it, I can almost see you standing there in a nightgown looking up at it with your mouth open in awe.

People ask me if things are better this year. They're not. Only farther away...and then a little bit closer.

11/25/07

I woke this morning and shaved to the sounds of a Sunday morning service on the radio. The pastor spoke about thankfulness even when life does not go well. We are to be grateful in all things for it is stated in Romans 8:28. "And we know that in all things God works for the good of those who love him, who have been called according to his purpose." I have found it difficult, almost impossible, to believe there is a greater good in your death, Reagan, and yet Reagan's Rescue has reached out to the community, something we wouldn't have done were it not for losing you. God is working for good.

In the comic strip <u>Mutts</u> today, a quote from Meister Eckhart was the only caption for pictures of a man walking his dog and staring at the sunset: "If the only prayer you say in your life is thank you, that would suffice."

Though recent entries have gone back and forth between despair and hope, I am trying to remain thankful for the blessing of 2 ½ years with you. I need God to help me in this struggle. I need you to help, too, Little Girl. Remind me of our reunion.

Thank you, Lord, for Reagan.

11/27/07

I picked up photos of Aubrey and Ainsley at Sears last evening, updating the 8 X 10 we have of Aubrey. Several feet away is the picture of you holding on to the giant 2. It never changes. You never age. I haven't really noticed this before or paid much attention. Aubrey is getting taller, losing the baby look. She now looks older than you—and that doesn't seem to make sense.

Tonight, <u>A Charlie Brown Christmas</u> is being broadcast on TV. I can't watch it. Too painful. I remember a hospital room and a very sick little girl and the quiet, the hush of winter right outside the window. That's an image that won't change, either.

12/9/07

This past Friday evening, while your Da was at work and your Aunts Mallory, Flyn, and Bailey had a night out, I drove up to the cemetery to visit your grave. The sun had already set so the solar lamp was shining. Snow had fallen a couple of days earlier, and I expected that grave markers and grave blankets would have been covered, the snow on the ground pristine and untrodden. What I found both broke my heart and gave me strength. The children's section was crisscrossed with footprints. It seemed every grave had been visited, the snow wiped away from markers. I found your face smiling up at me and lit by the solar lamp.

The footprints meant that those in the Garden of Innocence are not forgotten but are still very much a part of the lives of those family members left to grieve. So many footsteps. So much sorrow. So many lost hopes. And so much faith in that last great hope—a reunion in Heaven.

As I stood there in the cold and the dark I felt sadness for my fellow grandparents and the parents and siblings of children all around me. I felt something else—a kinship, a sense of belonging to a group that knows what I know, that hurts like me, that cries like me, that makes this routine pilgrimage like I do. Sometimes I can only manage my despair by remembering others grieve and have grieved besides me. The footsteps in the snow meant I am not alone. The numbing drive I take north on Vermilion, the right turn into Sunset, past the pond, the swans, the gazebo, then our crest of the hill, is the drive others take. We all grieve differently, but I bet there are things we can agree on.

12/17/07

Today, on the way back from standing in line to mail Christmas packages to Aunt Heather and Aunt Elaine, with snow on the ground, the sun beginning to set, and a chill running through me, I thought about what time we waste waiting, how hectic our lives are during the holidays. Then I thought about you in Heaven. How do you spend your day? What is a day like in Heaven?

I wonder if you find yourself sitting on Uncle Frank's knee or visiting with your great great grandparents. I'd like to believe that you can visit with them or be with us and so you are surrounded by family all the time as we are enveloped by your love, your light, and your memory.

12/24/07

Last night, we attended a Christmas candlelight service at your Great Grandpa Jim's church, held to honor very special guests—women and children from Your Family Resource Connection shelters. Your aunts Mallory and Bailey sang Amy Grant's "A Christmas Lullaby," perfect for those displaced families in attendance. Bailey's part included words from "Away in a Manger":

> *Bless all the dear children*
> *in Thy tender care,*

And take us to Heaven to

    live with Thee there.

Whenever I hear those words, I think of you in Jesus'
tender arms. Mallory also sang "Some Children See Him"
by Alfred Burt, so children—especially one special child,
you—were on my mind. The service was about Jesus' light.
Again, I thought of our Sunshine, the light that went out,
and the light that keeps burning.

    When, by candlelight, the congregation sang "Silent
Night," I wept openly there in the pew. Every time I've
heard that song played since, I've done the same. Into a
night when all is calm and bright, I've placed all my
sorrow and all my hopes.

    Today, Christmas Eve, I visited your grave and read a
brand new lift-the-flap book, Dora's Christmas Adventure.
I hope you stood by me to listen and discover hidden
pictures behind each flap. One flap, behind the smiling full
moon, revealed, surprisingly, three Christmas Explorer
Stars, each wearing Santa hats. You are our Explorer Star,
gone on ahead to prepare the way for us. I'll come back
tonight, my Papa's Girl.

    Merry Christmas, my angel.

12/26/07

I went to Berry's Garden Center this afternoon to order a floral arrangement for worship on January 6 and to line up a dozen balloons to let off on your birthday. While roaming around the store I came across a plaque which read, "Those we have held in our arms for a little while, we hold in our hearts forever." As I look ahead to what time I have left (and I certainly wish, sometimes, that it were sooner than later), I can't imagine a day that I won't hold you tight in my heart—my forever 2 ½ year old granddaughter.

I took the Reagan Emery Bear to the Hallmark store downtown to see if the owner would sell them. She was touched by the story of our visit to the Boyd's store in Pigeon Forge, the bear we bought for you, the bear you took everywhere during that last month, the bear you held when we buried you, the bear that still keeps you company today. She said that she would call her rep and get a supply in. One more chance to keep your memory alive.

Your Da cried on Christmas morning when I gave her the Reagan Emery Bear and a necklace which read "Heaven has in store what thou has lost." Then we all cried. You are so very much a part of our lives still.

Like I promised, I returned to the cemetery around 10:30 on Christmas Eve. No deer this time but a moon which seemed to pump streams of bright, heavenly light down on top of us—almost like the Star of Bethlehem as it is so often shown in paintings and TV shows. Maybe a star was able to light one sacred patch of ground.

1/5/08

Happy birthday, Reagan. You would have been four years old today. The day you were born seems like it happened so long ago, much longer that a mere four years, probably because we've gone through so many changes during that time.

Today, we take down the Christmas tree, put away the decorations we've had up since the day after Thanksgiving. Then we'll gather at the cemetery once again to release balloons. We'll all be especially sad today, but, even in our sadness, there is room for celebration and hope even.

We were so blessed yesterday when both newspapers featured stories on the Reagan Emery Bear from Boyd's. Then I received e-mails from the Director of Marketing for Boyd's Bears who asked if they could include a write up about you and a link to our website. She also is sending some extra bears for us to use for our fundraising efforts. Late last night, I received an e-mail from a pediatrician at Carle Hospital in Champaign who volunteered to help in putting us in touch with a statewide pediatrician's organization. I'm going to take her up on the offer so that we can discuss more strict and uniform SBS education in hospitals for parents of newborns.

This is all because of you, Little Girl. Besides the pink balloons we send your way, we offer our commitment and our energy as presents. I love you and miss you, my Angel.

1/16/08

Today, I received two e-mails from Dr. Beck, the pediatrician at Carle Hospital. She is pursuing more specific, stronger SBS awareness in hospitals throughout Illinois. We've just made a start, but it's an important first step.

I came home to find a box from Boyd's Bears with 12 Reagan Emerys. How remarkable. How generous. How touching. A box with 12 bears and a whole lot of love.

And our mail carrier also delivered Provena's magazine <u>One Life</u>*. In it was an article about Reagan's Rescue, the billboards, the PSAs, and SBS.*

Blessings flow down.

I received a letter at school from my former teacher, Joyce Alexander. Although she talked about educational concerns in the community, she also mentioned the bear, adding "What a fitting tribute to have a Reagan Emery bear for a special little girl. Through the bear, Reagan will be loved by many children."

Oddly, I had never thought about children playing with Reagan Emery.

"Fitting" is the right word.

1/24/08

Lately, I've begun to think about what our relationship might have been had you lived. I'm not suggesting that we are better off this way; only time will reveal that, or newfound knowledge in Heaven. But I've written before that I don't think I ever had a closer relationship with anyone as I had with you. You will be our forever 2 ½ year old granddaughter. Our relationship will always be close. Would it have changed if you had grown up to be a teenager and then an adult? Would part of your adolescent rebellion meant turning your back on me or perceiving me as a joke, a fool? Would I one day disappoint you? Would you somehow hurt me?

I'm probably thinking very selfishly now. Unable to know the many roads we may have traveled, the many actions we may have taken, the many consequences we could have been left with, I wonder of the sweetness, the innocence, the perfection we enjoyed, even briefly, is not to be wholly treasured, one tiny—maybe warped—blessing I have left.

Again, I glance at your picture sitting on my desk at school. Your wise, brown marble eyes, your porcelain skin, your coral-colored lips in so content a smile reach out to me from behind the veil to encourage me to go on.

"Go on, Papa. Keep living. Keep working. I'm here to watch over you. I know all that you don't. One day, you'll know, too."

1/30/08

Today, we dedicated a playroom at the YFRC in your memory. Both of your Papas and Das were there. Your daddy, Aunt Kelsey, Uncle Cory. Great Grandma Roberta painted a portrait of you which your daddy and I hung on the wall in the room. Great Grandpa Jim read the scripture about Jesus calling the children to him. He read a Shawnee Indian poem. He told a story about a little boy whose mother had died, how the night of the funeral the boy and his father slept in the same bed, how in the dark the boy made sure his father was facing him because everything would be okay then. I don't always feel—or I'm not aware of—God facing me. Perhaps He does, and it is me who has turned away. Today, however, with your great grandpa struggling so to get through his words, I felt God's face—and yours.

When I sign in to our website, I use the password grandpa1. I didn't choose it; it was picked when the site was opened originally. Each time I log in, I think two things. I am, and will always be, your grandpa, the title I take most seriously. I am also reminded, though, of how poor I was at keeping my granddaughter safe. I'm certainly not #1, not the best.

I am proud of what we have accomplished, proud of this latest achievement even if it is only in a corner of a women's shelter. Maybe it will bring comfort to a child. That is important. But each goal we reach is because of my failures as a protector. Each good thing is because of so much bad. We perpetuate your memory but you are still *gone. Your portrait hangs on the wall and with it our cowardice.*

Oh, Reagan, please face me. Help me to know you are truly there. Give me the strength and patience to last until I can know peace.

2/3/08

Nearly forty years ago, on the night that Dr. Martin Luther King was assassinated, Robert Kennedy gave an impromptu speech to a group of supporters in Indianapolis, telling them of King's death and asking for compassion and love. During that speech on April 4, 1968, he quoted a writer who lived thousands of years earlier.

My favorite poet was Aeschylus. He once wrote: "Even in our sleep, pain which cannot forget falls drop by drop upon the heart, until, in our own despair, against our will, comes wisdom through the awful grace of God."

From a voice thousands of years old to a voice silenced forty years ago to a newspaper article to my eyes and, perhaps one day, to my despairing soul. I've read about God's grace. I've written about it. I've prayed for it, especially when you were still alive. I asked God to keep you safe. He didn't. I guess I have to wait until I die to discover why God's grace has to be so awful.

2/14/08

Some people ask, "Haven't you wanted to kill him?" I've said "Yes." I've explained that I could easily drive over him in my car or how I wished for some kind-hearted vigilante to kill him for me...for us...for our Reagan. I tell people how I feel I've let you down by not becoming violent. Then I add: "But I have people who depend on me. I have Bailey. I can't ruin more lives by seeking vengeance." I don't really know anymore whether I'm acting clearheaded or cowardly. Probably both. It was that lethal combination that didn't save you.

I found this recently printed on a Starbucks cup.

The Way I See It #279

Beware of turning into the enemy you most fear. All it takes is to lash out violently at someone who has done you some grievous harm, proclaiming that only your pain matters in this world. More than against that person's

*body, you will then, at that moment, be committing a crime
against your own imagination.*

--Ariel Dorfman

Novelist, playwright and essayist

*Maybe coincidence. Maybe a sign. Maybe a direction or a
warning.*

*I go to Starbucks for coffee and solace. They know my
name. They know my order before I speak. Now they've
given me something even more important.*

3/2/08

*I measure the passing of time by trips to the cemetery,
by Reagan's Rescue achievements, by legal decisions, and,
especially, by my bedtime ritual of saying goodnight to you.
All the rest seems blurry.*

*The winter grave blankets will soon be gone up at
Sunset. My visits will be more frequent as the weather
warms up.*

*I appeared on WDAN the other morning talking about
SBS. Next week, I'm giving a workshop on SBS at DACC
for "Teach the Future Well," an early childhood education
conference. In three weeks the DHS Track team will host*

the Second Annual Reagan Williams Memorial Invitational. We plan on using some of the proceeds for a senior scholarship at the high school.

We have another new judge and another starting date for the trial—July 7, two years since I last saw you, the day of the funeral. More waiting. More frustration. More wounds that will not heal.

Each night, in the darkness, after I've taken my Tylenol PM to help me sleep, I say goodnight to you: "Goodnight, Reagan Emery. Goodnight, Papa's girl. I love you."

Each night, I marvel for a moment at how fast the day has come and gone. Each night, I count down one day closer to seeing you. I briefly hope for a hero's end— maybe at school—cut down by a bullet while trying to stop a shooting. I could die bravely—and sooner, not waiting for a natural death after a lifetime of mourning.

Sleep comes quickly—that's the painkiller—but I awake with a headache and another day of stressful waiting.

Like that, time passes.

3/24/08

And time passes.

Saturday was the 2nd Annual Reagan Williams Memorial Invitational. In the Field House again, selling items at a table in the hallway, WICD there to film for a news broadcast. Bill Pickett from the radio station doing a quick interview. Your mom and dad there, both sets of grandparents, an uncle, some aunts.

2nd Annual means a year has passed. 2nd Annual means another year without you. Or were you there?

You see, my darling granddaughter, I don't know how it all works. Are you in Heaven? If so, how do you spend the day? Or is there day and night, is there a schedule, are there things to do? Though it has been nearly two years, has it been but a second to you? Are you alone like The Littlest Angel or are you surrounded by family? When I get an image of you, I see you on Uncle Frank's lap. I don't know why, exactly, except he would have been tickled by you.

Do you visit us? Did you tap your daddy on the shoulder on the drive to Tennessee? I've waited for that tap, that touch, myself, but it hasn't come. Am I putting my hope in the wrong place? Must I trust in your presence even though I can't feel you? Is that how God works?

I'm writing from our cabin in Tennessee. It's the day after Easter. I didn't go to church—haven't been for several months. I didn't think I could rejoice that He had risen. I didn't want to show up just because it was Easter Sunday. I didn't want to feel anymore a disappointment of faith than I already do. I couldn't get your Easter dress from two years ago out of my head or my heart. So Da and I visited you in the cemetery and placed flowers at your grave and wept aloud.

I am as angry and lost and confused as I ever have been. Nothing gets easier. I'm losing touch with you. You've faded slowly. I'm not old enough to count the days I have left—as far as I know, anyway. I can count the days since I lost you, and I'm moving farther away from that moment when I heard "She's gone." Farther and farther away.

Moses in <u>The Ten Commandments</u> looks at the distant mountain and wants God to explain why the Hebrews have remained in bondage. He wants to walk on that mountain. He wants to see God. He wants a showdown.

I do, too. I want God to explain to me why, despite our prayers, He took you from us. Why didn't He intervene? And why do the courts keep ruling against us—and against your memory?

This is the first week of spring yet winter lingers. That same gray, cold, numb, lifeless winter lingers in my heart. Why won't God come and warm things up? Why won't He show Himself?

3/26/08

There is a local landmark just outside of Gatlinburg, Tennessee, called Alewine Pottery. It's a favorite stop for tourists—no surprise since several local television stations promoting the area run long commercials for the store.

Besides pottery designed and created right on the spot, customers are treated to free snacks, including apple cider, popcorn, cookies, coffee, and marshmallows roasted over an outdoor fire, all accompanied by the music of Lost Mill, a bluegrass group comprised of a husband and wife, Jerry and Joan Paul, who have become friends of ours, and a few additional backup musicians.

Last spring, during our annual Halls-Williams trip to the Smokies, Alewine Pottery was the most pleasant, peaceful, and relaxing couple of hours we spent, so we anticipated a return visit this week. The store is a family business. Everyone who works there is friendly and gracious. The ads on TV really stress the family. Robert Alewine, owner and obvious proud grandfather, features his two precious granddaughters prominently. They are a closeknit family; his granddaughters are, undoubtedly, his pride and joy.

I got to thinking about what ideas we represent in life. The Alewines promote the pottery business, the craft, the skill, but they also embody the importance of family. If one analyzes the commercials, almost half of the message is strength of family.

Maybe the Williamses were meant to represent gracious grieving. The feedback we receive tends to compliment how we have handled our loss so bravely and so positively. Maybe people can look at us and be inspired by our "courage" and "determination."

Of course, I can't look at the Alewine Pottery commercials—especially at the little girls—and not be

envious of what that family has. I pray they are not
touched by tragedy like we have been. Those little girls
remind me of what we lost in you, Reagan, and what I'd
like to have in Aubrey and Ainsley.

Yesterday, during our visit, I requested Jerry and Joan
sing a favorite of mine—"There Is a Time." I came to
know the tune when the Darlings sang it on The Andy
Griffith Show. Now the words resonate deeply—and bring
me some perspective.

There is a time for love and laughter
The days will pass like summer storms
The winter wind will follow after
But there is love and love is warm

There is a time for us to wander
When time is young and so are we
The woods are greener over yonder
The path is new the world is free

There is a time when leaves are fallin'
The woods are gray the paths are old
The snow will come when geese are callin'
You need a fire against the cold

So do your roaming in the springtime
And you'll find your love in the summer sun
The frost will come and bring the harvest
And you can sleep when day is done

The way I feel now I'm not all that aware of spring or summer. On July 2, 2006, the frost came and killed a budding plant. Now I can look forward to sleep when life is done.

And yet a small part of me wonders if I should be enjoying the springtime of your cousins, Aubrey and Ainsley. I don't see them but through you. I'm probably missing so much that way. I just can't give up grieving.

3/27/08

Today, while shopping in a nearby strip mall in Sevierville, we discovered a store with a Boyd's Nursery, and right in the middle of the bears were several Reagan Emerys. It was a surreal moment. Your Da and I spoke with one of the clerks about you. Soon another clerk joined in. Da began to cry, and the older woman gave her a hug and offered a tissue. I promised I'd return tomorrow with one of our Reagan's Rescue business cards. Maybe we can start a ripple here in our second home.

3/28/08

When we think of Sevierville, Pigeon Forge, and Gatlinburg, we remember our June 2006 trip to this area. Shopping for you and Aubrey at the Boyd's Factory, selecting two similar bears (we had to treat you equally in those days)—black for Aubrey and honey-colored for you. Two years later we are still feeling the ripples. Moments then have led to events now. Connections—some coincidences, some signs.

We returned to the gift shop and gave two new clerks and the owner some Reagan's Rescue cards like I said I'd do. I felt awkward and uncomfortable with these new folks. I need to work on my delivery so that I don't ramble. Your daddy, Kristin, Dal, and her boyfriend, JJ, were all standing near me, adding to my discomfort. I had introduced myself as your grandfather; I had talked about losing our granddaughter. I didn't feel like turning to the others and explaining their relationship to me or to you. I guess I have to get over looking at this so personally like it *was my personal loss. I know in my head that it wasn't; my heart, however, views events differently.*

Da and I drove on to Ink Dimensions in Pigeon Forge. Da got a memorial tattoo on her leg—a fairy with wings and wearing a pink dress while clutching a yellow rose. The artist was JR, the same JR who gave me the Dora tattoo a year ago though at a different shop. He remembered your story, remembered me and my Dora. He was as sympathetic with your grandma, even giving her a discount. The tattoo hurt, but she is so proud of it because you are visible on her body. Each person who asks will hear the story.

Later, while shopping around the corner near the Old Mill, we quickly ran into a store with an angel theme, drawn there, like we are so often pulled into Christian stores, because of you. The music playing softly over the speakers was the end of "In the Garden," then a gospel rendition of "It Is Well with My Soul" began playing— amazingly, one of the four songs played at your funeral. I thought back to the gift shop in Nebraska last July when "You Are My Sunshine" began to play.

Coincidence? A sign? We wanted to believe we were compelled to enter that store at that precise moment to hear that particular song so to know that you were present, hovering there with us, not just in tattoo form.

In the afternoon, we visited the Christmas Place, a huge store devoted to all things Christmas. Your Da has had trouble going in there before, but, this time, she suggested it.

We were really just browsing, not interested in anything in particular until I bent down to look at a shelf of Fontini manger figures and discovered a small, blond-haired Shepherd Angel with a beautiful story card inside about a little angel sent to guard a Judean lamb. Eventually successful in intervening in the lamb's life, the now thriving sheep is confronted by the Shepherd Angel who says "The Lord is my shepherd. The Lord is your shepherd, too." For a brief but powerful moment I heard you whisper this in my heart. You knew what I have so recently struggled with. And you became the guardian angel to my lost lamb.

My interest in signs was reaffirmed last night when Da and I happened to turn on HSN to find John Edward selling a DVD set on meditation. He comforted a grief-stricken caller—and us—by saying that the loved one who has passed has not been lost but is with us in a different form. Your grandma and I needed to hear those words, I think, in order to be receptive to you today.

Thank you, Reagan, for sending us signs. I feel, at least for now on this cool Tennessee evening, strangely blessed.

4/1/08

More signs. More connections.

When we returned home I sent an e-mail to our friends, Jerry and Joan, thanking them for their musical and spiritual gifts and telling them about you, my beloved granddaughter.

The next day, March 31st, Jerry wrote back that he'd seen the Reagan's Rescue website, that our efforts could save countless others, that we needed to place our trust in Creator (as he put it). He suggested that you might be our personal Guardian Angel—the thought of it made my heart leap. They also volunteered to send some copies of a new CD when it is finished for us to use in fundraising. We are so blessed to know these folks.

Tonight, Aubrey and Ainsley came with Blythe to say goodbye to Mallory who's leaving for Colorado tomorrow. We brought the dollhouse up from the basement for Aubrey to play with—and both Da and I remembered the last time we brought it up—when you stayed with is in May of 2006. Oh, how I cherish the memories of that day.

Later, Da told me that, as she drove to the high school to pick up Din, she saw a car pass by with the license plate RAE, her name for you. Amazingly, on the way back home, she saw that same car once more. She knew it was no coincidence but a message from you.

Please keep sending them our way.

4/17/08

Yesterday, your Aunt Bailey was cast in the title role of <u>Annie</u> for the Lincoln Park Theatre Company summer production. Its Board of Directors last week chose Reagan's Rescue as the recipient of its fundraising efforts.

Today, I took Bailey to auditions for the adults so she could read with those trying out, and Ann, the director, said that they still didn't have a Daddy Warbucks and wondered if I would be interested in the part. I've been clear up to this point that I couldn't do the role because the trial is supposed to start on July 7, the week before tech rehearsals and opening night. I really didn't know how I could handle the emotional strain of the trial and the time commitment needed for a large musical, especially if the venue was changed and we had to travel to a courtroom in another part of the state. That was my practical resistance.

The rest is probably impractical and nonsensical. I haven't wanted to share what talent I have with this community because this is where you died. I thought—and how embarrassed I am by it—that my becoming a tragic figure as a result of losing you would be the better story than being in another production. Your daddy could find solace in acting; I wasn't ready to get back to business as usual. I wanted all the clocks to stop. I wanted to be Miss Haversham.

I think, Baby Girl, you wouldn't want your Papa to be that way. You so enjoyed my many faces, my reading to you and singing to you. Why shouldn't I share, especially in a musical about a man who saves the life of a little girl and becomes her daddy? We are about the rescue of children in Reagan's Rescue. What better vehicle for getting that message across than Annie?

I get to share the stage with Bailey. We get to spread more SBS awareness. I have to sacrifice my plan for a tragic life and do this in memory of you.

I hope you understand. I hope that this clarity is the message I asked you for.

5/8/08

*Thoughts of you come at such unforeseen times.
Tonight, while sitting in the front row of the Danville High
auditorium judging the Senior Show, the sight and sound of
a girls' tap routine brought tears to my eyes. I thought,
first, of the talent and joy on display. Then I remembered
that you wouldn't be performing in a Senior Show,
wouldn't have the month of May in your 18th year to
anticipate all of the high school rituals which lead up to
graduation. Finally, I thought of your cousin Aubrey's first
dance recital this weekend and how you loved to dance.
How amazing you might have been. How proud your Papa
would have been—your #1 fan, I've no doubt.*

*While I sat in the high school parking lot, the keys in my
hand, I thought of how unfair this all has been: that you
were robbed of life's benchmarks; that you were separated
from us—or we from you; that we continue to wait for
justice. Then a voice in my head responded that there is no
fair or unfair, there are no guarantees, that life simply is.*

*I know I've had these thoughts before. I've probably
written them to you in this journal. Like some awful
carousel, these emotions come round and round again—
sadness, regret, futility, numbness, and maybe for a brief
moment clarity and peace. Then another rotation and*

[276]

another, never getting anywhere but still exhausted. Some may find this odd, unhealthy, but I am not ready to get off the ride. The return of each emotion—like the appearance of a new season or a sunrise—means I am still living and feeling and missing you. That proves the connection is still here. Maybe, then, I should rejoice in those surprising bittersweet memories.

---

27 What I tell you now in the darkness, shout abroad when daybreak comes. What I whisper in your ear, shout from the housetops for all to hear!-- Matthew 10: 27 (NLT)

5/10/08

It is 1:50 in the morning. Sometime within the last thirty minutes I woke up from an amazing dream. So real that tears were pouring from my eyes and my nose was so stuffed up I couldn't breathe without a great deal of sniffing.

The first part of the dream had me following Sen. Barack Obama around Illinois on a series of fundraisers for his Presidential campaign. The final scene with Barack was at some fair with lots of balloons. Instead of being the healthy candidate, he was old, wrinkled, and partially gray. He said that we had a dinner date, but it would be some years in the future when I was old.

Then Da and I got on an old-fashioned airplane from the 30s or 40s—something out of the movie <u>Casablanca</u>. Inside it was filled with passengers, enough to fill a department store. As the plane took off, suddenly a voice began to whisper that this was the plane that would crash because of landing gear falling off. Somehow we were resigned to our fate as I held Da's hand. The plane lurched forward and up into darkness, a crashing sound, a bit of a jarring sensation, and my own inner voice saying, "So this is how it feels. This is not so bad."

The last part of the dream faded in like a movie, sunlight coming up quickly like it was stage lights.

I was in a chair, fully reclined, and covered in a blanket. I suddenly realized that I was old and in the middle of a living room. The door opened and adults I seemed to know ushered in many children one by one to greet me.

*"And who are you?" I would ask and they would
answer and hug me. I somehow knew they were
descendants—grandchildren, great grandchildren. As the
last one greeted me and began to leave, I felt regret
because the one I wanted to visit me hadn't come—my
Reagan. But a voiced thought assured me to be patient.
Then you appeared or a teenage version of you anyway.
You had dark hair, almost black, as if you had dyed it. You
had glasses, too. Your head was cocked to one side a little,
and you had a grin on your face. You came to me, hugged
me so tightly, and told me that soon we'd be together, but I
was aware that we couldn't stay like this. I held you so
close and wailed.*

*Then I was in the back of a bus, looking out the rear
window. You were standing on the side of the highway. It
was dark, except for a light on me and one on you outside,
as I left you behind on the pavement. Then I awoke, deeply
sad and peaceful, somehow sure you sent this dream. Oh,
thank you, thank you.*

Why 1:50? Why 5/10? Is it because of 1/5?

Volume Three

Memorial Day weekend. It meant a three-day break from the pressures of the end of the school year, a little more time to relax, a cookout with the family, a visit to the cemetery, the Indianapolis 500, and thoughts of you. It is a holiday I only really thought of as the unofficial beginning of summer vacation. Now, amidst the flags which line Vermilion St. and patriotic concerts and reminders of war, I can only clearly focus on one grave.

Today, we discovered a lost treasure. It filled my heart with such joy and such sadness. Your daddy and Kristin came over. Blythe and Shane brought Aubrey and Ainsley. After dinner, Shane and your daddy tried to get his old white car started. It has been parked for nearly two years behind the garage. The tires are flat. It's killed the grass beneath it. Vines have begun to overtake it. We even kept the swimming pool on top of it during the winter. It was an eyesore, but today it was a gift.

Shane hooked up battery cables from his truck, parked in the alley on the opposite side of the fence, to the car, long enough for your daddy to start up the engine and pop the trunk open. Besides his saxophone, long thought lost, and a box of kitchen appliances, we found a grocery bag

with some of your books and clothes and a dancing Elmo,
which we have video of you opening on your last
Christmas. Someone turned it on, and, surprisingly, it had
just enough juice left in the batteries to provide about five
seconds of singing and dancing before it stopped. When
had Elmo last danced and sung? Was it when you were
still with us? Did someone turn it on one last time after
you died before placing it in that trunk?

I grabbed the bag and walked clumsily to the patio, sat
down, and purposefully went through the contents. Kristin
carefully folded the clothes—some of them worn, some of
them still with tags—and I stacked them on my lap, thinking
of you in them, trying to remember when you wore them,
even smelling them to see if they reminded me of one of
your visits. I didn't want to cry in front of anyone else. I
looked for tears in your daddy's eyes, in Aunt Blythe's, in
Da's. I don't know whether I saw any. I felt them in mine
and gave myself away to your cousin Aubrey who asked,
"What's the matter, Grandpa?" I put her on my lap and
read one of the books to her, hoping that you would forgive
this betrayal.

None of us expected to find your possessions. I thought
we had surely discovered the last of them some time ago,
but I thank God that we came upon them.

It is appropriate that it is now Monday and Memorial Day itself for I remember you. Although remembering you brings pain, I hope that it also brings honor to who you were. I embrace the pain because I can then embrace you. That's why people will be bringing flowers to gravesites in cemeteries all over the country. Remembering those who have gone on means there are still connections. Flowers and flags and solar lamps provide tangible proof of that connection, like wearing a Reagan bracelet.

I caught part of the Memorial Day Concert on PBS this evening when Charles Durning recounted the horrors of World War II. This beloved actor and American hero is living history. With tears welling up in his eyes and a weak voiced choked with emotion, he described D-Day, the Battle of the Bulge, and the liberation of a concentration camp. More than a half a century later, he bears witness to the sacrifices made in that war. He concluded by saying how terrible it is to recall, but that he owes it to the millions who perished, some of them his buddies, the places where they breathed their last, holy ground.

There is a house in Tilton, an ambulance, an emergency room, and a patch of ground in Sunset that I consider sacred. Now I have a paper bag of relics to cherish as well.

I remember you, Reagan. And I love you. Like the front of one of the shirts we found says, "You are a star." Like the stars at night seem to disappear when the sun shines in the sky, the pain will go away briefly when I am distracted by present matters. When the sun sets, the stars once more appear, having never really left. This bag was here all along. I passed it numerous times every week. It didn't go away. I just couldn't see it until it was revealed on Memorial Day weekend.

I remember you, Reagan.

6/15/08

Today is Father's Day. It is hard to believe that only two years ago I had a beloved granddaughter named Reagan in whom the sun rose and set. I don't feel like celebrating anything today. I'd be fine with no family visits. Father's Day is just a reminder of what preciousness I lost and what a miserable failure I was...and am...as a provider and protector.

I've written before of my feelings toward your daddy. The arrival of Father's Day makes me resentful of his shortcomings as a provider and protector, but it also fills me with such pity and regret. How awful this day must be for him. I suppose celebrating a birthday for someone who is deceased is acceptable within reason, but can you celebrate Father's Day if your only child is not here anymore?

I stood in the greeting card section of K Mart the other day looking for a card for your Great Grandpa Jim when I spied the face of Dora the Explorer looking up at me from the display. The card was meant to be given by a child to her Daddy. I began to tear up, fighting the urge to cry because I didn't want Da to see me sad. That was the perfect card for you to give your dad, and, for a brief moment, I considered buying it and filling it out on your behalf. I didn't know whether that would be cruel or not. I didn't get the card, but now I wish I had.

This past week has been difficult on many of us. Da ended up working a couple of days with the Polyclinic nurse we saw when we took you in to have your bruises checked out. Da was filled once again with guilt and regret over not carrying through on the phone call to the abuse hotline. What if we had called? Maybe we would have lost contact with you, but perhaps you would have been alive.

Your Aunt Blythe ended up standing in line at K Mart right next to Ryan Allhands. She had both Aubrey and Ainsley with her, and they were fussy, so she was at a real physical and emotional disadvantage. When she got to the car she realized that she was parked right next to him. It took her twenty minutes to calm down enough to drive away. I couldn't say very much to her to make her feel better. Some father, huh? Some protector.

I attended a workshop in Bloomington on domestic violence and the role of the paramour. I realize again just how a textbook case this all is. The next day, on Thursday evening, we got word that the defense attorney has filed a motion for a change of venue. We have to wait a week before the judge makes a decision.

Good things have happened, too. We got a $100 donation to the Lincoln Park Theatre Company Save a Child Fundraiser from Sunset Funeral Home employee Tammy Hopper on behalf of her church, the New Life Christian Center. That was a blessing. I was able to write a letter of recommendation for Tawnya Morgan as the YFRC undergoes staffing changes.

The folks at Sunset keep looking out for us. Groundskeepers began their frequent summer mowing rotation recently and cleared off all grave decorations, setting most of them under nearby trees. When Da and I went up to retrieve those moved items we didn't find any left. Mike Puhr actually boxed them up for safe keeping, and I was able to pick them up earlier in the week. They do still treat us like family, and I am grateful. Having you taken from us was enough. Having your grave robbed of its decorations would have been a symbolic replay of that violation.

A few weeks ago, I finished a book that Great Grandma Sharon gave me entitled <u>Life After the Death of My Son</u> by a pastor named Dennis Apple. The chapter headings alone intrigued me because they sounded so familiar:

> Will It Always Hurt This Much?
>
> Will Our Marriage Survive This?
>
> Am I Losing My Mind?
>
> Where is God?
>
> I Don't Want Him to Be Forgotten
>
> His Birthday Is Coming
>
> I Love My Church—but Sometimes It Hurts to Be
>> There

The last three chapters suggest places where we might end up, truths we might come to accept eventually:

> I Didn't Cry This Morning
>
> I'm Beginning to Live Again
>
> A Wounded Healer?

Rev. Apple suggests that "Sorrow shared is sorrow halved." We cling to each other, therefore, as a family to get through. We share our grief and our fumbling to pick up the shattered pieces with others who may yet benefit. We continue to find comfort in the words and acts of others. We dread the coming days of trial and injustice. We anticipate the joy we can spread through _Annie_. I savor the time spent with Bailey.

I look forward to the close of this day.

6/24/08

Some days conclude with me carrying the CD player out to the brick patio, turning on the four songs that were played at your funeral, and looking up at the stars as they pour down their light, wondering which star is you. The tears normally flow between the lines "Please, don't take my sunshine away" and "Tell me why the stars do shine." Some days I cry earlier—morning, afternoon, evening—but I've begun to look forward to this quiet and lonely ritual, a moment with you.

The last few days have been so much about you. We sold bracelets at Arts in the Park in preparation for the fundraiser that the Lincoln Park Theatre Company will hold which will benefit Reagan's Rescue.

Yesterday, a status hearing was held, resulting in a continuance until October 20, another hearing for September 15, but no change of venue. Your daddy said that it was time something went our way. Da was very upset that we would have to wait once again for the trial to start, afraid that justice would not be served, afraid that she will lose it if the verdict is not what we hope for. I'm so worried about her. She misses so much; she hurts so deeply, darkly.

I received an invitation to speak to another Kiwanis Club about Reagan's Rescue and SBS. And our loyal friend and reporter, Barb, wants to set up an interview for an article about Annie.

Those invitations are the small lights in the vast darkness like your star against the night sky. That light keeps me living however dead I sometimes feel.

6/30/08

I've had a sick feeling all day—a headache, a pain in my chest. I think I'm dreading the next few days because we begin to replay all those events from two summers ago. Two summers. Hasn't it been more like ten years?

I'm sitting at your grave. I brought flowers although I'll probably bring more on Wednesday. It is such a beautiful, cool evening, I didn't want to let it slip by without coming to see you.

Your marker looks so bare without some mementos left behind. It's kind of like how my spirit feels without you— empty, bare, lacking in life and love.

I don't know if you'd recognize me the way I look now with no beard or mustache or hair of any kind. I'm completely bald, ready to play Oliver Warbucks in Annie *with your daddy and Aunt Bailey.*

More importantly, I don't think you'd recognize the lifeless man I've become. I just don't have much passion anymore.

Would you know my name if I saw you in Heaven?

Sunshine, I'm in need of a visit, an unmistakable sign. I want me back—the Papa you'd be proud of. I know I can't have you, for now anyway, but maybe you can have me.

7/2/08

I'm thinking a lot about sunshine today. Your aunt Bailey sings about the sun coming out tomorrow in Annie. *She plays a character who believes that everything will*

[290]

work out for the best eventually. The thought of tomorrow can clear away sorrow.

Today in the newspaper our friend Barbara wrote an article about how we are doing on this second anniversary of your death. Above a photograph of Bailey, your daddy, and me is the word "Tomorrow." The article deals with the support of the community, the upcoming production, and the fundraiser for Reagan's Rescue. It also talks about closure. Your daddy has found some, and I'm proud of him for being so strong and for being able to share that strength. I'm not that strong, I guess. My closure will come when I die—oblivion or a reunion with you.

Today, Griefshare talked about the good in grief, yet another example of the messages we get, the support we receive, through God's grace. It happens too often to be just coincidence, and I shared as much with Barbara during our newspaper interview yesterday.

Good grief is accepting the fact that you died, accepting the sorrow, but believing there is more to come. The illustration in the devotion includes the promise that the sun will shine again and that a brand new life awaits the survivors.

The Book of Ruth declares: "He will renew your life and sustain you in your old age" (Ruth 4:15).

[291]

We didn't want this life, but we can't go back. We must focus on the good we can do in your memory.

I asked for a sign. I think I got it.

Thank you, Sunshine, for the joy you brought me and for the cherished memories I hold dear.

7/13/08

Tonight, I had a terrible dream. It wasn't about you, but the tears I shed were like the tears I had when you appeared in the dream about our reunion. These tears oozed out like oil, and my cries were silent. This dream was about your Aunt Bailey.

We were living in a kind of Nazi Germany, and we were like Jews. Our freedoms and possessions were taken away, and we existed in what seemed to be a large institutional building—part school, part warehouse, part antique or general store full of our former material wealth but now on sale for anyone.

Occasionally, groups of young people would attempt to escape, and, as Bailey's father, I would worry for her safety. I would never see her caught or killed, but I witnessed this happening to others. I also remember standing in the center of a small, multi-tiered arena, with people of various ages and ethnicities all sitting in little compartments waiting for their numbers to be called. I bravely conversed with several of them, promising to relay messages and mementos to their loved ones once they were gone. I seemed to be carrying out some kind of heroic mission.

Then I was in a school cafeteria setting with a loudspeaker blaring something about "Working, keep working." Bailey, in a pumpkin-colored outfit was carrying dishes. I couldn't say much to her for fear that she would be punished.

Suddenly, two Nazi-like officers came up to her—my baby—and both of them knocked her in the head with their skulls, laughing as she fell out of sight.

What was different about this dream was my almost immediate ability to do the same to them, bloodying them with repeated blows of my forehead or my sledgehammer-like fist. Then I went on a rampage, striking and bloodying scores of Nazis like the leader of a rebellion or revolt. Other "Jews" followed my lead, and mayhem ensued.

I woke up with one last thought of Bailey and words echoing from the play The Diary of Anne Frank: *"She puts me to shame."*

[293]

I don't know what it all means, but I have some guesses. Through this experience in Annie, I've gotten closer to Bailey. My character nearly loses her in the play, and I've struggled with conveying the proper emotions in some scenes because Annie in jeopardy is Bailey in jeopardy and you in danger, too. I didn't react effectively when you were being abused; maybe I now can when my own Bailey is victimized. I am sure there is more to it, more interpretations, but I'm weary. It is 4 a.m., and I've been up for nearly an hour.

I know the dream did not have you in it, but I woke with fear for one little girl and regret for another and maybe proof of a courage I sometimes fear is lacking in me. I wish I had the resources of Oliver Warbucks. Then I could create my own safe world and have armies at my disposal.

7/22/08

Our production of Annie has come to an end. Despite some challenges—the set, the heat, the oppressive humidity—being involved in the show was a positive experience, not only for us as a family but for Reagan's Rescue.

We sold wristbands to the cast and the audience. Each night, a 50/50 drawing was held. One of the winners, our good friend Carol Cunningham, gave back $60 to us. Cotton candy was sold, more people participated in the Save a Child campaign, and all of the Custard Cup proceeds are being donated to Reagan's Rescue. It was difficult not being touched by the efforts of so many caring, generous people.

Off to the side of the stage was a big wooden display with signatures of donors and handprints in pink and purple. After the final performance, when the adrenalin had gone away, I stood before that board and marveled at the goodness of people.

I was also profoundly touched by how many cast members wore Reagan bracelets during the run—even on stage. You were certainly there with us.

Another example of this goodness happened on Sunday morning without my knowledge. The cash box from Custard Cup was accidentally left behind in Lincoln Park on Saturday night. Early on Sunday, a jogger found the box, figured out to whom it belonged, and returned it without any expectation of a reward. There are good people in the world, Reagan, even though I don't always believe it.

We sang "The sun will come out tomorrow" numerous times. It may not come out during my lifetime, but, one day, in Heaven, when I see your face, when I see your light, when I see "my Sunshine" again, then life will be bright and sorrow will be gone. Until then, like Aunt Bailey sang, I'll have to hang on come what may.

7/31/08

A short trip to Tennessee means thoughts of you so close in my heart and so very far away. We're staying in Echo Bay, the same cabin we were in in January of 2007 when our friends, George and Erin, Da, and I came down to sign the papers to purchase a place at Hideaway Hills. I'm sitting in the same rocker I've sat in before, on the same deck overlooking the same valley—although now there is lush green obscuring the view and a symphony of bugs and birds and the oppressive humidity and heat of summer. Still, I half expect George to come out on the deck, a cup of coffee in one hand and a Bible in the other.

This is still a relaxing place of meditation for me, so thoughts of you easily come.

Yesterday, we went to Dolly's Splash Country, the first time we had been back since June of 2006. As I stood in lines waiting for my turn to slide or climb into a tube, suddenly you were on my mind with thoughts of "The last time I stood here, my little Reagan was alive." I figured I had experienced the last of those moments, but, evidently, I haven't.

At the Christmas Place two evenings ago, as I looked at the cutest Snow Babies, I spotted one that made me think of you—a child wearing a wizard cloak and holding a wand in one hand and stars in another. It reminded me so much of you fixing stars in the night sky.

Of course, at the water park yesterday and with my shirt off and arm exposed, many people noticed my Dora tattoo. Children especially. No one asked about it with words, but there were many curious glances and even stares. I was ready to share your story with anyone who would listen.

I found Reagan Emery Bears in two stores, one in Gatlinburg and the other in Sevierville. The latter even had a small card with a copy of the story that was found on the Boyd's website. I wanted to shout out "That's my granddaughter" to all the customers, but I celebrated silently instead.

Our last blessing was at Alewine Pottery. Jerry and Joan gave us about 10 of their new kids' CD plus about 10 of some of their earlier works with the promise that, if we can schedule it, they'd be willing to do a benefit concert for us. They are beautiful, generous, and compassionate folks. We are lucky to count them as friends. The Lost Mill has helped me find my soul.

8/4/08

I played for a wedding on Saturday. Your Aunt Mallory sang "When God Made You," and, though the song was about people falling in love, I found myself unexpectedly thinking about you.

It's always been a mystery to me
How two hearts can come together,
And love can last forever.
But now that I have found you,
I believe that a miracle has come
When God sends the perfect one.
Now, gone are all my questions about why.
And I've never been so sure of anything in my life.
Oh, I wonder what God was thinkin'
When He created you.
I wonder if He knew everything I would need
Because He made all my dreams come true.

When God made you
He must have been thinkin' about me.

I sat there in the pew thinking about how you'd never get to walk down the aisle. I could only cry and whisper "Unfair." Like the song's lyrics, I wonder why God made you, why He presented me with my most precious gift only to allow it to be taken away. Why did He make all my dreams come true then dash them into bits? Why did we lose our miracle?

I rejoiced with the families through the service and the reception, but I was jealous and suffering inside.

8/7/08

Tonight, I watched the Steven Curtis Chapman family on Larry King Live *talk about the aftermath of the tragic accident that took the life of their 5-year old adopted daughter, Maria.*

I heard one of the boys say his initial shouts of "Why...Why...Why?" proved his belief in God. A daughter said that the Bible promises God is nearer the brokenhearted. Steven, himself, said that he believes God was there in that driveway and wept.

The whole family showed small memorial tattoos they had done. They agreed that they are sharing their story to give hope because they have the hope of Heaven. They have been angry; they've considered not touring anymore (although, ultimately, Steven Curtis Chapman did give concerts again).

The Chapmans' overwhelming prayer has been "God Give Us Strength." They will honor Maria by honoring the One who gave her life.

They related a story about a sign they are sure was left by Maria. On the morning of the day she died she drew a butterfly and wrote the word SEE even though she had only written her name before. She also drew a picture of a flower, only one of its six petals colored in. The Chapmans have six children; only one is whole in Jesus.

Thank you, God, for letting me see this program. Thank you for providing me with the answers I sought, and give me strength—give us strength—as we continue down this path.

13 Sing for joy, O heavens! Rejoice, O earth!

Burst into song, O mountains!

For the Lord has comforted his people

and will have compassion on them in their

suffering.

14 Yet Jerusalem says, "The Lord has

deserted us;

the Lord has forgotten us."

15 "Never! Can a mother forget her nursing

child?

Can she feel no love for the child she has

borne?

But even if that were possible,

I would not forget you!

16 See, I have written your name on the

palms of my hands.

Always in my mind is a picture of Jerusalem's

walls in ruins.--

Isaiah 49: 13-16 (NLT)

9/4/08

Before writing this entry, I reread what I penned the last time and noticed that I spoke to God, thanking Him for answers and asking for strength. It bothered me because, evidently, for a moment I forgot that this is your journal, Reagan. I write these thoughts for you. Am I so confused and unfocused that I would forget that? Oh, I hope not.

I know I am supposed to let you go, supposed to celebrate the time we had, supposed to bless God who gives and takes, but I just can't. Yet I'm afraid that my heart and my spirit are not in a right place. If I am not saved—or saved enough—will that mean I am kept from you for eternity?

I am stuck between the solid rock and the hard place of my heart.

Perhaps I am making progress. I went back to Central Christian last Sunday. I even sang most of the praise songs although I cried during "Blessed Be Your Name." The lyrics were so personal. I am in a desert place. I walk through the wilderness. The darkness has closed in all around me, and I want to be able to say "Blessed be the name of the Lord" and mean it, but I can't.

The song went on to talk about blessing God, "when the world's all it should be" and "the sun's shining down" and suddenly I saw your face—smiling and happy—shining on me. That's when the tears came, and I was walking down the road "marked with suffering." How can I turn back to praise the God who gave then took away?

So many times in these last two years I have had doubts and questions. Somehow answers always seemed to present themselves. Maybe I've found them because I've sought them. After all, I did write "Hide and seek. Seek and find. Knock and the door will open."

Maybe God sent the answers. Maybe, Reagan Emery, you sent them.

Here are what came my way:

—A poem written by Canon Henry Scott-Holland (1874-1918) of St. Paul's Cathedral.

Have you gone into the next room?
Can I speak to you in the easy way I always used?
Are you waiting for me?
Will we really laugh at this trouble of parting when we meet again?

—Next were words from Mother Angelica.

No matter what suffering you have: physical, mental, spiritual—it will all pass, as everything passes.

When you are suffering you have the capability of achieving great things. You can:

1. Create great holiness and become a powerful witness to those around you.

2. By accepting your pain you are doing God's will in an awesome way.

3. By offering your pain to God you can save souls.

God is trusting you with pain. He is trusting you to accept it with love. Don't miss the possibilities.

Lastly, I looked at your myspace. Your heroes were anyone you ever met. And so I am among those lucky people. I was your hero. I only hope that I can be worthy of your love, my Sunshine. Worthy of the brightness of your grave marker, of your smile, of your eyes, of your trust, of your joy and innocence.

Maybe if I can be worthy of you, my precious granddaughter, I can be worthy of Him who made you.

9/7/08

Today, your family attended a special Grandparents'
Day Service at Great Grandpa Jim's church. Four
generations of Williamses sat together, including your
Great Grandpa, Da and me, Aunt Blythe, and your cousins,
Aubrey and Ainsley. Your daddy was there. And you were,
too, for we were reminded of the suffering of the Hebrew
slaves, the first Passover, the exodus from Egypt, and,
many years later, the Lamb of God's sacrifice, His blood
the ransom paid for our souls to enjoy eternal life in
Heaven.

You were there, Reagan, because your family was
gathered together for a celebration. But there was more to
it. Pastor Divan explained that God knew of the Hebrews
and the length and depth of their suffering. God is, after
all, a God of transcendence, reigning from above, but He is
also a God of imminence, aware of what's in our hearts,
aware, it seems, of the number of hairs on our head. Once
again, your Papa was being told of the immeasurable
enormity of God's plan, so big we cannot fathom, but that
God was there with our little Reagan when you were scared
or injured or even when you died.

Humans don't like waiting for an answer to prayer.
Sometimes they don't like or understand or agree with the

answers God sends when He does respond. I'm sure the Hebrews were confused by the things Moses told them. In that confusion and anger I can relate even though thousands of years separate us.

You were there, Reagan, because your Papa pondered the words of the service and felt like they were meant for him. I was given a glimpse of that door to you—a doorpost smeared with Christ's blood which allows me to cheat death and live forever.

Although I should be happy, I was also reminded in this gathering that a space beside me on the pew was empty—at least from my limited mortal knowledge. Maybe you were there beside me after all, my angel, and it was imperfect human me unable to see you.

Forgive me for missing you every day. Forgive my tears. Forgive my very human weaknesses. Please be near me each day and guide me in what is right.

9/17/08

Lessons continue to come my way. Sometimes the message is just enough to keep me going and headed in the right direction—like a few breaths from an oxygen tank while drowning in the sea.

I went back to church this past Sunday and played keyboard in the Praise band. Some of it was empty playing—all the right notes but none of the passion.

One of our new pastors spoke about God's U-turns, citing Saul's conversion on the road to Damascus and his name change to Paul.

I know about U-turns. Mine happened on July 2, 2006. And what God has made out of this change in direction we are still finding out. If losing you was, indeed, God's will, then we hope to one day discover why our journey was disrupted. The message Sunday spoke to my heart even if only partially. I did feel that I was meant to hear the pastor's words. I experienced momentary peace, like the sun peeking out behind a cloud.

This week at school, I read an essay from one of my students about the loss of a loved one. How did she conclude? Decades of waiting are nothing compared to eternity.

How miraculous when a student can become a teacher!

Lastly, we received a box from your Great Aunt Laurie. In it were framed pictures of you, a hummingbird feeder for our front porch, and homemade scarves made out of pink and purple yearn. Todd and Laurie also sent a $100 check for Reagan's Rescue.

I wrote to thank them, and Laurie wrote back with words so gentle and loving and understanding (like Laurie herself). She said: "Sometimes I try to relate to God from a human father (or mother) point of view. After all we are His children. Think of when our kids get mad and angry with us. We understand, we want to comfort them, but we also understand that they just need their space. We just wait and hope for the least little softening towards us. The love we feel for them overwhelms us and slowly they come around and write things like 'I love you, Dad' on our myspace."

I want to say "I love you, Father God," but my anger and pride keep me from uttering the words.

Reagan, you're closer to God than I am. What should I do?

Baby, your Papa needs you.

10/5/08

I'm far away from home today, the farthest point in my trip to share the accomplishments of Reagan's Rescue and to tell people about Papa's girl.

Da was supposed to come with me, but she got injured at school, and she also thought it was important to be there

for your Aunt Flyn at yesterday's marching band
competition and in tomorrow's Homecoming Assembly.

I had to come—to meet people I've become acquainted
with over the Internet, people who have provided answers
when we needed them and hope when we were down. I had
to come for your sake, Baby Girl, because I promised you
would not be just a victim but a cause. Still, I miss Da and
your aunts. I am very lonely.

Here in this remarkably beautiful city of Vancouver,
autumn has arrived with its cooler temperatures and the
reds, oranges, purples, and golds of changing leaves. The
air smells of the sea and evergreen trees and big city bus
fumes. When I open the sliding door of my sixth floor
room, I hear seagulls squawking, the engines of seaplanes
as they land, and the conversation and laughter of people
in the courtyard below. The dark gray water of Coal
Harbour shimmers beneath a cloudy, pale blue sky.
Everything is so clear and peaceful and alive. People jog
or rollerblade or bike or walk along the seawall. They are
French, Asian, Australian, British, American—Canadian. I
haven't seen anyone smoke. Life seems so clearly defined.

I wonder if Heaven is like this place.

I came to Vancouver to present a workshop entitled
"One Small Candle: Creating an SBS Advocacy Group."

I told my audience about my Sunshine. Some cried. Some occasionally nodded and smiled at me. When I was finished a few came up to congratulate or thank me.

I met Debbie Dycus and Pamela Rowse-Schmidt from the National Shaken Baby Coalition, just two of the many experts touched by SBS personally who have helped us. When I watched Debbie care for her great niece, Taylor, a wheelchair-bound survivor, I wondered again whether we were somehow the lucky ones. Debbie's mother has wondered the same thing.

This evening family members gathered for a brief candlelight vigil. We watched a DVD that Debbie put together of children who were shaken—both survivors and non-survivors. There were four pictures of you, Reagan. The one of you lying on your back in the leaves. The one of you covered with icing on your first birthday. The picture we later used for your grave marker. Finally, my favorite, with you in your daddy's lap. The tears really flowed and with no effort.

I know I've written this many times before, but oh how I miss you.

How poor my life has been since losing you. How poor it will always be.

10/8/08

I'm on the final leg of my trip, at Denver International Airport waiting for my flight to Indianapolis and then a late drive home. Although I am closer to Danville than I have been since early Saturday morning, the waiting makes me feel like I'll never get back.

What a miraculous couple of days! Since leaving Vancouver yesterday morning, I have felt somehow blessed—undeservedly so, however.

I sometimes wallow in self-pity, usually when I am alone. I lost my Sunshine, and no one else can feel just the way I do. My grief is something I own, something I cling to. I find myself slipping more and more, calling you my daughter before I recognize the error and correct myself. The amount of grief I found at the SBS Conference was every bit as real as mine, and some of those family members in attendance had lost their loved ones years before you left us. I don't deserve any special awards. What I need to do is work even harder in your memory. Like Darryl Gibbs from Yonkers, New York, founder of the Cynthia Gibbs Foundation. At the gathering for family members this past Sunday night, Darryl got a chance to hold another couple's baby, sharing that eight years had gone by without his holding a baby. You see, Reagan, I don't have you anymore—and it breaks my heart—but I've held your cousins, Aubrey and Ainsley. I can find something to be thankful for.

And then there's more...

I got through US Customs so quickly, made my way to Fall City, Washington, to meet Karolyn Grimes, the real Zuzu from It's a Wonderful Life. She sent a signed poster from the film several years ago and, around Christmas 2006, our first without you, she sent an autographed Christmas ornament from the movie The Bishop's Wife, which she signed "In Memory of Reagan." I wrote to her and asked if I could visit her in her home and see her museum, and she graciously agreed.

I told her about your Aunt Bailey being named for the family in It's a Wonderful Life. I reminded her about you and the conference I attended. She shared with me her difficult life after Hollywood as an orphan and of the community which rallied around her. She told me about losing family members. Then she said that people need to get on with their lives, not dwell in the past but hope for a brighter future. I know she was sincere, certainly experienced enough with grief, loss, and "Hell on Earth," as she called it, to be able to give that advice. It was a remarkable hour. We have angels in common, that's for sure.

When I flew out on Saturday, I was nervous and lonely. In the seat next to mine, a woman named Ruth and I began talking, and we found we had much in common. She was from Effingham, Illinois, the town where I was born. She had family up and down central Illinois. I told her about our family, the conferences I was going to, and, of course, you. I really felt God placed here there to ease my mind. She had lived in Seattle and was returning for a visit, so she even helped me get through the airport.

Today felt the same way. I left your cousin Jessica's house, drove downtown to see the Space Needle. I got in the wrong lanes of the Interstate but turned off at the right exit. I discovered a McDonald's near the base of the Space Needle, so I didn't have to pay for parking. Then I drove to Pike Place Market and found a parking place right in front of Starbucks, just as another car was pulling out.

When I arrived at the Seattle Airport, there was a computer glitch with my reservation. In talking to the ticket agent, I found out that I could get on Standby and leave Seattle earlier. When they began to board the plane, however, I was told there was no room and would have to leave later during my originally scheduled flight. The plane was delayed; the lengthy cleaning time put the flight behind even more. As the boarding was almost concluded, I went up to the desk to ask if there was any seat left and there was. The attendant suggested I leave early because my original flight would be running late and I might not make my connection to Indianapolis. I boarded the early flight then and there.

During that flight, I read my horoscope in the newspaper. It said: "If anyone gives you a warning, be thankful. Don't take a chance by not following through to correct an error."

In the seats in front of me sat a mother and her baby daughter. We smiled and waved at each other. She really perked up when I played peekaboo.

I thought of you and cried. I miss you, Reagan.

Later on the plane...

I have been reading a book called The Gift of Grief *by Matthew Gewirtz, a rabbi, who writes very clearly, profoundly, and practically.*

He says: "...every time we engage our pain and become stripped down because of being present in our pain, we are in touch with our deepest sense of insight and purpose. When we come out of that state, we may even feel our pain more deeply. However, we also bring back new insights into ourselves, and the more we engage in the process, the more we are able to see our inner truth. The pain won't magically dissipate, and we won't get back the life we once had. But we can start to rebuild our lives using the insights we have gained by facing our suffering head-on."

That's a lot to consider, and I'm only halfway through the book. I can see, though, the genesis of Reagan's Rescue in that quote. Only through facing and fully experiencing our grief can we reach the core of our souls— the flame. Only through that flame can we gain enough insight to help—to rescue—others. We can rebuild our lives and the lives of others; one small candle can light a thousand.

And lastly…

No sooner had I finished my visit on Tuesday with Karolyn Grimes and started to pull out of her driveway than Ian called—I mean your daddy called—to say that Ryan was taken back to jail. I don't want to get too hopeful or too filled with glee because our lives have been jolted before, but I am glad things turned out that way. There is another continuance, February this time. At least we can get through the holidays.

At least there is some justice again. Your Great Grandpa Jim always taught me patience. Things will work out though maybe not on our terms or on our timetable. I have probably written this to you before, but it applies here. When your daddy called with the news, I reminded him of the lesson in patience. Then I told my boy that I loved him.

11/2/08

It has been a weekend of rituals and a time for missing you.

Friday night was Halloween. The neighborhood held its Halloween parade. Aubrey and Ainsley in matching dresses were here to participate. My thoughts, though, ran to you. As children walked by and our front yard filled with family and friends, I whispered my hope that you were with us.

Saturday, Da and I curled up on the sofa to watch <u>Meet Me in St. Louis</u>. Once again, I cried as Judy Garland sang "Have Yourself a Merry Little Christmas," clinging to my faith that we all will be together one day.

This morning, Central held its All Saints Sunday service as we lit candles for those who passed away this year and then for any family members we still mourn. Mallory came to church this morning, the first time in more than half a year. We walked together to the table of candles, tears dropping off our cheeks, where I lit a votive for you.

This morning's message dealt with Hebrews 11 as the writer lists those heroes of the Old Testament whose faith sustained them—"Now faith is being sure of what we hope for and certain of what we do not see. This is what the ancients were commended for." (Hebrews 11: 1-2)

Noah, Abraham, Enoch, Moses, and all the others were called by God to go to a distant place—sometimes a literal destination, sometimes a mental and/or spiritual destination—and these heroes went even though they did not know where they were going or what conditions would be like.

Something in the message spoke to me because we were called on July 2, 2006, to journey to a place we knew nothing about, called to wear armor of a warrior.

Hebrews 12 continues the challenge:

"Therefore, since we are surrounded by such a great cloud of witnesses,

Let us throw off everything that hinders us and the sin that so easily entangles,

And let us run with perseverance the race marked out for us." (Hebrews 12: 11)

As I lit that candle, I thought of you and your perfect and innocent example. I thought of my grandparents and great-grandparents standing beside you. Such a great cloud of witnesses, I am determined to throw off every hindrance in an effort to persevere this race marked out for us, my eyes fixed on Jesus and on the promise of Heaven.

These rituals bring me great sadness. They renew my grief, but I feel closer to you and to understanding than I did just three days ago.

11/9/08

I continue my individual journey toward healing or, at least, to being more healed as I will never fully recover from grief. In recent weeks, I have decided that my only hope in a reunion with you, Reagan, is through renewal of my faith. And, whether they know it or not, people in my life are helping me toward that end.

I took Da to Indianapolis yesterday to a Gift and Hobby Show at the Indiana State Fairgrounds. I kept our destination and purpose a surprise until the last possible moment. Karolyn Grimes was there selling movie memorabilia and signing autographs along with her companion, Chris. I wanted Da to meet her.

We bought Chris's book about Karolyn's life and career, and I was reminded of just what hardships she endured—her mother's death from Alzheimer's; her father's death in an automobile accident, which left her an orphan; her first husband's death in a hunting accident; her second husband's death from cancer; the suicide of her teenage son. Despite these losses, she has been capable of surviving and healing and now touches the lives of others through her films, travels, and personal appearances. Others including me. Karolyn survived and so she teaches me that I can survive as well.

When the people of Israel were trapped at the edge of the Red Sea, Pharoah's army approaching them from behind, they cried out to Moses who comforted them: "Don't be afraid. Just stand where you are and watch the Lord rescue you." (Exodus 14: 13)

Psalms 46 says we should "be still" and know that He is God.

In the song "Trust His Heart," Babbie Mason writes:

> *God is too wise to be mistaken*
> *God is too good to be unkind*
> *So when you don't understand*

When you don't see His plan

When you can't trace His hand

Trust His heart

And Ecclesiastes 3: 11 reminds us that "He has made everything beautiful in its time. He has also set eternity in the hearts of men."

I know that Heaven is in my heart. No more sadness. No more goodbyes. No more loneliness. I don't understand fully why this happened, why God needed it to happen, but I know we can help others who are hurting and grieving. And one day, we'll see you again.

11/27/08

Today is Thanksgiving. I have found it difficult to be thankful for much these last two years, but I want you to know that I am thankful for you—for the time we had with you and for how you've continued to inspire and challenge me from Heaven. I have a precious little girl who is with me constantly. I have important work to do on behalf of children everywhere. And I have wonderful memories that make me sad sometimes but mostly make me feel happy and loved.

Recently, someone sent me a poem that was read at Princess Diana's funeral. This person sent it to give us some peace.

> *If I should die and leave you here awhile,*
> *Be not like others, sore undone, who keep*
> *Long vigils by the silent dust, and weep*
> *For my sake—turn again to life and smile,*
> *Nerving thy heart and trembling hand to do*
> *Something to comfort other hearts than thine.*
> *Complete those dear unfinished tasks of mine*
> *And I, perchance, may therein comfort you.*

12/21/08

Tonight, we all attended the Christmas candlelight service at Great Grandpa Jim's church. Mothers and children from the Women's Shelter at Your Family Resource Connection were there. The evening began with a dinner, followed by the service, and then dessert and presents for the YFRC families—a blanket and bag of toys for the kids and a scarf and bag of grooming and toiletry supplies for the mothers.

Reagan's Rescue donated Disney DVDs and books for the playroom.

[321]

*Your Aunts Mallory, Flyn, and Bailey sang a song
entitled "One Candle" about the spreading of the light and
a wish for God's peace.*

*When all of our candles were lit, the entire congregation
joined in on "Silent Night." That's when our tears began
to flow. Your daddy, Mallory, Da, and I all began to cry.
Maybe it was the simplicity of the moment, maybe the
longing for "calm" and "heavenly peace" we find so
elusive. I listened to the words I was singing as if I'd never
considered them before, especially "love's pure light,"
"radiant beams," and the hardest to get out, "Wondrous
star, lend thy light" and "With the angels let us sing." I
sensed you with us hovering somewhere nearby. A silent
prayer went up from my numb heart—"Reagan, our
wondrous star, lend us your light."*

*It doesn't get any easier, but three Christmases have
come without you. The years get shorter. I am that much
closer to seeing you again. I can make it. I can survive
with the love and support of my family and friends and with
your heavenly light as a guide.*

12/24/08

I sit next to your Christmas tree filled with Doras and butterflies and stars. I look at the lights on the tree so soft and warm and glowing, and I feel a peace radiating from it.

Like I've done for three Christmases now, I read Dora's Christmas Adventure aloud, lifting each flap to discover the surprise beneath. I have faith that you sat with me although I felt no weight from your body. One day I hope to discover you again and hope, too, that people can hug in Heaven.

Sunshine, I will visit the cemetery tonight and spend a few moments with you on this holiest of evenings. I've had so many Christmas rituals to cling to over the years. I never thought visiting my granddaughter's grave would be included with Christmas crackers and eggnog and watching A Christmas Carol. I guess I never realized a lot of things.

The other night at Great Grandpa Jim's church, two different people said how "blessed" I was to have such a beautiful family. My first reaction was to remind them of our loss. How could I be blessed without my Reagan? But I do have a beautiful family on earth and in Heaven. They are talented and sensitive and honorable. We share so many wonderful memories. We've been through so much, growing closer through it all. We have much to draw on as we face an uncertain future.

Yes, despite so much, I am blessed.

Merry Christmas, Reagan Emery. Papa loves you. The love you had for me is your continuing gift.

12/25/08

Last night, I visited your grave. That's a word I don't like to use because it reminds me of death. Cemetery seems more neutral to me. The outcome is the same no matter what word I use, but I like to envision you as living on, existing with us. Grave is too finite.

It was bitterly cold and very dark—no moon although the stars were out. Most businesses were closed except for gas stations. Streets were mostly empty. Last minute shoppers filled Kmart's lot.

I felt terribly isolated. I guess what gave me comfort was knowing that some churches were holding services somewhere in town.

Your marker was hard to see. I did make out some frozen leaves on its surface and made plans to stop on

Saturday when the temperature was warmer so I could give the marker a good cleaning.

I sang "Tell Me Why" and "You Are My Sunshine," told you how much we loved you and how much we missed you.

As I prepared to return to my car, I looked up and caught a glimpse of a male deer taking a few strides before disappearing into the distant woods. Because I only caught a few seconds of his movement, I questioned for a moment whether or not it was a vision or my imagination. I'm convinced, however, that what I saw was real. Another gift from you?

I had been crying. Now I began a mix of laughing and sobbing. I must have looked crazy.

Thank you, Sunshine, for another Christmas Eve miracle.

1/3/09

Because the tree was beginning to droop and dry out, we decided to take Christmas ornaments down and pack them away until next November.

I took a few extra moments to hold those decorations associated with you—the little Shepherd Angel we got for *our nativity set, the photo of you in the Christmas tree frame, and the Always Remembered ornament that your Great Aunt Elaine sent to us two years ago. I can't remember whether I ever read the back of the box or not, but today, this is what I found written there:*

I know I am still with you in your prayers, your thoughts, your heart.
And though you cannot see me, I will always be a part
Of life's sweet celebrations in those times when you reflect
On how, though times are different, through our love we still connect.
We'll see each other someday when our spirits are free,
Until then, I am with you because you remember me.

I guess I need to ask, do we still connect through our love? I remember you, certainly, and so you're with us, especially when we gather as family. Yes, you are in our hearts and memories, but is your spirit there? Are you free to visit? Until I know that answer for certain, there will always be the lingering and damaging sadness of grief.

I put away your Snow Babies Joy ornament, once again aware that Joy is the one emotion I have never regained.

With the new year comes the realization that we've dealt with your loss for parts of four different years. How we hope that 2009 brings us some peace.

1/5/09

Your 5th birthday. Though you are frozen in time, always 2 ½, I can't help but wonder what you would have looked like at 5 or 10 or 15 or 20. Still, you'll always be my baby girl.

Late this afternoon, we picked up your daddy, stopped at the garden center for balloons—5 white, 5 pink—then drove to the cemetery. How beautiful the day was. The sky was pale blue. The wispy clouds looked like tulle or white caps on the ocean. There was very little wind to speak of.

We let off the balloons and watched them for ten minutes as they rose up and up until they were tiny black specks.

A few minutes after the balloons launched, a flock of geese in a near perfect V pattern flew over our heads, honking and honking.

Great Grandpa Jim said, "A flyover" as it reminded him of an Air Force spectacle. Suddenly, one of them broke off from the group, heading east as the others

*continued north. I thought of Memorial Day observances
when one jet breaks off from the rest.*

*It was a beautiful part of the day and a memory I will
always cherish.*

1/20/09

Blessings and opportunities keep coming our way.

*Our friend Stefanie brought me a surprise birthday
present last week, a money order from a friend of hers as a
donation for Reagan's Rescue. Da and I were touched by
the gesture from both our friend and a stranger who,
nevertheless, believed in our cause.*

*I received an email from Gary Perry of Wichita, Kansas,
whose 3½ year old granddaughter was killed in November,
a victim of domestic violence. Someone from the National
Center on Shaken Baby Syndrome suggested he contact us
about our fundraising and advocacy efforts.*

*The similarities between our losses are astounding.
Like your Papa Gary, this Gary was the maternal
grandfather. Natalie, with red hair, was his first
grandchild as were you. Natalie's father and mother were
no longer together. Her mother was living with a
boyfriend. They, too, shared a younger child together. The*

boyfriend, entrusted to care for Natalie, took her life. The investigation and judicial system have taken a long time to act. He is heartbroken, clinging to a faith, looking for answers, seeking a purpose.

We spoke on the phone for about thirty minutes the other night, sharing emotions, asking questions, commiserating in grief and shock.

He is planning a fundraiser in April and has asked us to attend if possible. Da and I would like to go if we are able. I am glad that we can provide Gary and his family some help. We are farther down the road than they are. Maybe in comforting them we can find additional purpose for our own journey.

I have the chance to speak to a high school group in Indiana later this month and to a group of nurses and childcare providers at a Child Development Seminar at DACC.

These opportunities reassure us that we are doing what we need to do. In reassuring us, they bless us, too.

1/26/09

In recent days I've received e-mails from Joni Markel whose niece was a victim of SBS and from Erin, a former student who just wanted to know how we were doing and how our advocacy efforts were progressing.

Then today I received an e-mail from Debbie Dycus, co-founder of the Shaken Baby Coalition. She wrote simply: "It is with a very heavy, broken heart and empty arms that I let you know that Taylor Nicole received her angel wings on Saturday, January 24, 2009 at 1:45 p.m."

I quickly responded: "I am so very sorry, yet I am comforted that she is finally free and ready to soar. Maybe Taylor and Reagan will meet up and play together." I told Debbie to call if she needed anything and sent condolences to her mother as well.

A few hours later she wrote back:

"As I was holding her and she was slipping away I named off all the friends she would have to play with and Reagan was one of them."

Sunshine, I met Debbie and her niece face-to-face in Vancouver. Debbie was so helpful and encouraging to me. And as I looked at Taylor I wondered about how we could have coped had you lived and been in her condition.

Papa wants you to look for Taylor. I'm sure she'll be up and out of her wheelchair and whole again. You two play together. Show her around Heaven. And make preparations for that day when we'll all be together once more.

2/3/09

Great Grandma Edwards died last Friday. Her funeral was held yesterday down in Paris.

You never met her here on Earth for she had been in poor health in the nursing home for many years. You came close to her when we took you to see my Grandma Williams and we had a five generation picture taken. Great Grandma Edwards was in the same facility, but her memory was poor, and I don't think she would have understood who you were.

She would have been your Great Great Great Grandma, and how she would have loved you. How she would have delighted in watching you play.

She was born in 1906, which made her 102 years old. The pastor who spoke at the funeral reminded is that between 1906 and 2009 was the dash, her extraordinary long life. He then asked us to think about our dash. I thought of mine, but soon my thoughts turned to yours.

2004-2006. Your dash didn't last long, but you made an impact on all of our lives, and you continue to touch lives.

In my last entry, I asked you to look for Taylor Nicole. Today, I ask you to look for Grandma. She'll be rocking away in a favorite chair. You'll hear her chuckle. She may be surrounded by loved ones who have passed away, some of whom you've already met. You push your way through. You get in there and introduce yourself.

I know she'll delight in you.

3/19/09

I haven't written in over a month and a half. It isn't that I haven't had anything to say. My heart has been full. But Da and I have been busy, especially with show choir competitions on weekends, and it seems that I could never find a stretch of uninterrupted time to spend with you, Sunshine. Besides, I was afraid that what I had to say would not be said well or not important enough to write about.

The truth is I have felt a great deal like the season. The month of February and the first half of March have been dreary, gray, lifeless. Those words pretty much describe my soul. The gray was not the color of storm clouds or fog or mountains in the distance—all sights I love and why gray is usually my favorite color—but, rather, the gray of dirty snow and muddy gravel and pavement. Lifeless. Cold. Nondescript. And like this last month and a half, the gray lingered. I didn't see the fog roll in. No little cat feet. No peaceful, enveloping approach. I woke up one morning to find myself in the fog with no sense of direction, with no movement or force. All of my life seemed...well, like Hamlet put it, stale and flat.

We had to drive over to Indiana on a couple of weekends, each time battling sleet and extremely icy roads. Vehicles up and down the interstate were in ditches, some even upside down. Instead of driving the speed limit or faster, we had to slow down to 25 miles an hour, even getting off the interstate one night to drive back to Danville on a two-lane highway. I think it was the most treacherous driving conditions I've ever encountered, at least in recent memory. I wanted so much to reach our destination safely and quickly. Instead, our trip would seem to last an eternity.

Those drives seemed to mirror the lingering winter and the winter in my soul.

Despite my spirit's stagnation, we did know some blessings. As has always been the case, God provided us with glimpses of goodness and opportunities to minister to and teach others.

A grandfather grieving over the loss of his granddaughter is how I've been perceived and defined for two and a half years now but a grandparent—one of many—who has become an advocate of Shaken Baby Syndrome awareness.

We were able to raise over $1000 from the sale of coupon booklets for Elder-Beerman's Community Day event.

I presented a workshop for the Early Childhood Conference at Danville Area Community College.

You were cited once again as a non-survivor of SBS and Reagan's Rescue was mentioned as an organization in Senate Resolution 49 designating April 20-26, 2009, as Shaken Baby Awareness Week during Child Abuse Awareness month.

I've received two invitations from ladies' clubs in the area to speak about what we're doing.

Debbie Dycus sent along information about another grieving grandfather whom I may be able to help.

I received an e-mail from a former Schlarman student who is now a nurse at Carle Hospital in Champaign. The simple offer of her help, her willingness to put me in touch with other child advocates in the area, brought a momentary ray of sunshine and a warm breeze to the chill of winter.

Next week, the high school athletic department will hold the third annual Reagan Williams Memorial Invitational.

All of this has happened while we have continued to wait for a day in court, let alone justice. The trial has now been continued to July 20. I remember last April wrestling with the decision about whether or not to commit to playing Daddy Warbucks in Annie, afraid that the trial would coincide with production week. Now we're looking at a year later, and even that date may not work if a jury can't be seated.

I know that the delays have contributed to the gray lifelessness of this winter.

I need spring.

3/23/09

I probably attach too much sentimental value to things, but when those items belonged to you or are associated with you, I can't really help it.

Today, we are trading in my little Ford Aspire for another vehicle. I've had this car for fifteen years. I still vividly remember the day I drove it home and how excited the kids were. I washed it every week. We went through a lot together—torrential rain storms in South Carolina, snow in Colorado, trips around the country. What memories we share.

But I find that the most difficult part of giving up this vehicle is not having the backseat where you used to sit. You were always so happy when your daddy and I would pull up to your daycare to pick you up. I could reach back and hold your hand, that's how small the car was.

After you died, I remember how loudly I wailed as I drove to teach a night class in Hoopeston, how I'd rest my hand, palm up and open, hoping you'd grasp it. How I shall miss this car.

3/26/09

At the last minute, I got the idea to donate the Aspire to Kars 4 Kids, so I had a few extra days to spend with it. I even took a couple of pictures.

When the guy came and loaded the car onto the truck, I got emotional again. Da did, too. I will have memories from the car but I won't have that backseat where you sat. In some big or small way perhaps you are, once again, able to help out other children. Were it not for your connection

[336]

to the car, I probably would have traded it in without a second thought. I think donating it was a better choice.

We had another amazing day for Reagan's Rescue. *The News-Gazette* had an article about this Saturday's track meet.

I received an e-mail from Chip, the grieving grandfather from Shelbyville. It's too hard for him to speak right now, but he said that he would eventually call.

We received a check for $1500 from the A. L. Webster Foundation. That's $1000 more than we asked for. $500 was supposed to be for the poster campaign using the photo and message from the billboard design. The foundation gave us an additional $1000 for the website.

In the same batch of mail, we received a catalogue from Realityworks which includes an SBS simulator, a doll with a clear plastic skull and a visible brain inside. The cost is $689.00. With this extra funding from the Webster Foundation we can swing this purchase.

Your Papa needs a kick to the seat of the pants every so often to stay on track and to not give up. All of these certainly were that kick.

4/11/09

The Saturday before Easter. Da and I took small pink roses to your grave, held each other, and cried like we'd just lost you.

We talked about holidays. Christmas is difficult to get through but there are traditions and rituals we cherish which provide a framework for December and January. And Christmas is appreciated mostly inside where a warm fire keeps the chill away. Easter is about the changing of seasons and outdoors and longer days of light. I look through the front door or windows and see the yard where you sat, so pretty in your pale yellow dress. I also see an empty yard and no granddaughter. Perhaps it would help if Blythe and Shane came to visit with Aubrey and Ainsley but they're gone to Kankakee for three days to be with Great Grandpa Dave and Great Grandma Cookie.

I colored eggs tonight while Da worked on Easter dinner. We missed you, Reagan, so very, very much.

5/1/09

Across from the entrance to Walmart there's an abandoned lot where a farmhouse used to sit. The family who once occupied the house moved out; the house was torn down. Now the lot is overgrown with weeds. A gravel-covered lane leads up to where the house used to be. Over the last few years the driveway has begun to fade under a layer of brush, nature's way of reclaiming its own. There once was a home at that site; now the clues to its past are few.

As I drove from Walmart to the cemetery the other day and saw that neglected property, I realized how similar our lives have been without you, my darling granddaughter. We've all felt abandoned, lost, demolished. As for me, what once was a heart filled with love and hope and purpose is now empty. I suppose some part of me still exists, some glimpses into who I was, but I am fading. And there are days when I fear that you are fading away, too. Oh, I still have pictures to look at and videos to watch and memories written down in these pages, but I don't—can't— carry them in my memory very well. The road which leads to July 1, 2006, and beyond is getting harder to discern. My memories are fuzzier, so I have to rely on photographs to recall who you were and what we had.

It scares me. I never want to accept losing you. I never want to become too complacent. Only when I feel pain, only when I'm overcome with grief, do I feel closest to you.

Today in my darkened classroom I stared at your picture—the one in which you're lying on your daddy. I talked to you, apologized yet again for not saving you, and then I looked a few inches to the right at the framed cross stitch that Da did for me so many years ago. It read: "When God closes a door, somewhere He opens a window."

I guess I never made the connection—or don't remember it, anyway. That line from <u>The Sound of Music</u> always inspired me, especially when we endured some setback or move.

When you were taken from us, God closed a door (a door like so many other doors we've encountered these three years). Although Reagan's Rescue came out of our grief and guilt, I don't always know whether that is the window which opened. I'm frankly still waiting for Him to tell me in an undeniable way.

Maybe in my brief moment of despair this afternoon, He sent me the assurance of that framed message. Maybe the whole moment was random. I wish…I wish I knew.

My fuzziness (or lack of focus or doubt or numbness) is one reason why I haven't written much in this last month. There's so much I want to say but nothing I can write with any clarity. It's like when I'm driving all alone in the car,

wanting to talk to you but able only to whisper "Oh,
Reagan..." I feel like such a bother, such a disappointment.
I should have volumes to share with you, but all I can get
out is your name.

In April, we planted silver and dark pinwheels for
prevention of child abuse around the sign in the front lawn
of Central Christian. The marquee noted that April was
Child Abuse Prevention month. How those pinwheels
shone in the sun!

In April, we lost our beloved Aunt Gin. She's with
Uncle Frank now and, I trust, with you. Get to know her,
Reagan. We adored her so. She'll get a kick out of your
antics.

In April, we found out that the Reagan's Rescue PSA
was submitted by WDNL to the Illinois Broadcasters'
Association for consideration in its annual awards
presentation—and the radio spot is actually a finalist in the
small market division.

In April, we met the new Assistant State's Attorney who
will be handling the case from now on. Our hopes are,
once again, renewed.

Please know, Sunshine, that what I can't always say
aloud I feel very strongly in my heart. You are always
there.

5/3/09

I don't usually go back and read what I've previously written so I can't be sure about never repeating myself. I guess I write about what I'm feeling at the time.

Sometimes when I walk in Springhill Cemetery I listen to the CD of The Secret Garden. *Inevitably, I cry several times during the score.*

Recently, Danville Light Opera's board chose The Secret Garden *as its spring production for 2010. I'll be directing. I'm doing the show in your memory as the story and the lyrics resonate so deeply with me right now. The musical is about loss and redemption, healing and hope. It speaks to me very profoundly, and I trust it will speak to the audience.*

I used to cry during the song "How Could I Ever Know," sung by the departed Lily to those she left behind. I heard your small voice in the lyrics, you see.

Now I cry at other moments. "Lily's Eyes" reminds me of Reagan's eyes. "The Girl I Mean to Be" makes me think, with sadness and regret, of the girl you'll never grow to become. "Hold On" encourages me to weather the storm, to endure, although sometimes I find the thought unbearable. I guess I can say that the tears I shed are the result of a good cry, a healthy release of my emotions, the small doses our therapist spoke of.

Though the play is scheduled for a year from now, I'm already planning. Nothing is too good for my Sunshine.

5/20/09

Tonight, I took a walk through our part of town—our regular two mile trip up Franklin to Winter, over to Oak, down Oak to Voorhees, over to Walnut, and home. I listened to <u>The Secret Garden</u> on my portable CD player, listened to lyrics about dying and grief, winter and spring, illness and health, cruelty and love, holding on and giving in. The neighborhood in the full bloom of spring, the smells of flowers and newly-cut lawns, the animals that froze when I neared them then scampered off or trustingly resumed their business (robins and squirrels and so many rabbits), the clear blue sky and the beautiful, evocative music I was listening to gave me a brief peace I have not felt in a while. I believe I was meant to take it all in.

I reached the house before the CD was over so I took a seat on the brick patio and let the songs play out, their words and melodies as much gifts from you as from the composer and lyricist. Lily begs Archie to think of another way to hold her in his heart. Right then I glanced at the latest solar light to be on your grave, wondering why it hadn't come on yet when the others had. Not five seconds later, it blinked on. I've always thought of that light as a sign that you're here with us. Like a No Vacancy sign in a motel window or an Open sign in a storefront.

After my walk through our neighborhood, I felt like you were home.

7/2/09

Another July 2nd. Another sad trip to the cemetery to be with you. Another cleaning of your marker. Another bunch of flowers tied in a pink ribbon.

It's a mild day for early July. Temperatures are in the 70s. Some sun but the sky is mostly overcast with gray clouds. No rain though. Maybe the sky reflects my physical, emotional, and mental states. Crying is harder though I still cry every day. I know there's blue in the sky somewhere. The gray still lingers.

Another 12:25 p.m.

Another reading of your favorite books while your Papa straddles his wooden, wobbly camp stool. And always you look up from the ground and smile at me, surrounded by butterflies.

I never made the connection—or have forgotten—that in the book Touch and Feel Home *there's a photograph of a clothesline and the question "What's behind the rough towel?" And when I lifted up the piece of terrycloth, I found four butterflies. And on the last page a mirror, gloriously smudged, most likely from you.*

I feel old today—all week really. It's not just this date. We're holding a candlelight vigil at Central Christian tonight. Planning has been necessary but also strenuous. The trial is supposed to begin in three weeks, so I am filled with dread. It doesn't help that a couple of celebrities in their early 50s died this past week from heart attacks and that I'm turning 50 in January. All this while trying to prepare for a weeklong trip to Tennessee starting Sunday. And I've had a tightness in my chest—like a gas bubble— that won't go away. I don't want to die; there's so much left to accomplish. But then I'd be reunited with you.

Another year. More waiting. More wrestling with who I am and what I believe.

More you.

7/7/09

Today marked three years since I saw you last, since I touched you last, since I nodded to the undertakers that I was done looking at your tiny body and that they could seal up your casket for the short drive across Vermilion to the place you would rest.

In the three years that have passed not a day has gone by that I haven't cried for you. Though I would like to believe that I am healing, I still return each day to a place so low, so dark, that I doubt I've healed at all. The possibility of healing was a theme of the vigil last Thursday night. I believe I was convincing to those who gathered at the church. They admired my strength, incapable of understanding how I could keep this fight against child abuse going. I don't convince myself.

I've included a copy of what I said. Convincing or not, what I put together was done out of love for you, Reagan. And that love remains the purest emotion I've ever had.

Today, we went to Dollywood, taking your cousin Aubrey with us. While watching her fearlessly get on ride after ride, I was struck early in the day with a sense of regret (if that's the right word) that you weren't on vacation with us. I also remembered that the last time we were at Dollywood was a month before you died.

[346]

Later, in the afternoon while playing in a children's water park area, Aubrey came across a butterfly. Da picked it up, the butterfly resting on her finger until she placed it safely in a tree. Its wings opened and closed slowly, deliberately, as if waving to us. Just prior to this happening, I was standing off to the side telling you how much I missed you. Maybe the butterfly appearing at that moment was a coincidence, but I believe it was something more. Da is convinced that you've come to us numerous times in the form of a butterfly—the yellow butterfly that landed on Flyn during marching band practice, the butterfly today, an occasional butterfly that drifts past us while we're sitting on the front porch. And the symbol for Dollywood is, appropriately, a butterfly.

The logo for Reagan's Rescue includes a butterfly. And your Aunt Flyn has an appointment on this Friday evening to get a tattoo of a butterfly, its design from a photo she took of your grave marker.

Maybe all of these encounters simply indicate how much we still remember and honor you. Maybe they merely reflect our obsession with trying to find signs. What I hope they mean is that you are still a presence in this world, still reaching out to us in love.

Three years later, four states away, you are still a part of who we are.

Sometimes the various thoughts I have about you, Reagan, come at me like a heavy snowstorm. The flakes are beautiful but their iciness stings. In this past month little memories and connections have come and gone. Sometimes they hurt to think about.

While listening to <u>The Secret Garden</u> CD, another line jumped out at me. I've heard it before, but I don't think I've ever considered how appropriate it is to our lives these past three years. In the song "How Could I Ever Know," Lily tells Archibald, "And find some new way to love me/Now that we're apart." We love you through our memories, through every tear shed, every regret felt, but we know those things don't accomplish much. In Reagan's Rescue, however, and in the production of <u>The Secret Garden</u> I am preparing for, I hope we are able to love you, too.

While on the drive back from Tennessee two weeks ago, I heard a song by Martina McBride on the radio. It's called "Anyway."

[348]

You can spend your whole life building
Something from nothin'
One storm can come and blow it all away
Build it anyway

You can chase a dream that seems so out of reach
And you know it might not ever come your way
Dream it anyway

God is great, but sometimes life ain't good
When I pray it doesn't always turn out like I think it should
But I do it anyway
I do it anyway

This world's gone crazy and it's hard to believe
That tomorrow will be better than today
Believe it anyway

You can love someone with all your heart
For all the right reasons
In a moment they can choose to walk away
Love 'em anyway

You can pour your soul out singing a song you believe
in
That tomorrow they'll forget you ever sang
Sing it anyway
Yeah, sing it anyway

I sing, I dream
I love
Anyway

I don't know if I ever heard the song before but I listened to it as a grandpa who knows the loss of my prized angel. I was struck by the reference to the storm because that symbol has appeared numerous times in these last years— even weeks before you died, in special music I asked our friend, George, to perform at church, "I'll Praise You in the Storm."

On July 2, 2006, a sudden storm did wreck our lives, but we've had to rebuild to keep from losing so much more.

I pray to God to allow me to see you again, and, though that dreams seems so far away, I dream it anyway. Though the world seems crazy, I dream and hope and build and love anyway.

[350]

God is, indeed, great. I've said it as grace. I've sung it in that old Methodist hymn "How Great Thou Art." I've repeated it in the reading of the Psalms. I believe it more now after The Shack. *I've certainly sensed it on a mountaintop.*

But life is not good. Prayers aren't always answered the way I need them to be answered—even prayers that are a matter of life and death.

Last Sunday, I asked for prayers for the Green and Williams families as we faced a court hearing (and another continuance, as it turned out). Deann said something in her prayer that spoke to me, the gist being that we don't always understand God's plans, but we know that He is. We know that He was and will be.

It's a beautiful evening. The weather is cool and dry. Crickets serenade the backyard. I sit at our patio table, writing by candlelight. There's a bright crescent moon out. The air smells a little smoky. Sometimes I get whiffs of the chlorine in the pool. Rosie's just inside the backdoor meowing for me. I'm waiting for Da and Aunt Bailey to get home from the DLO play at DACC.

I miss you, Reagan. What I wouldn't give right now for a "Papa? Papa?" and a face peeking around the corner.

8/19/09

There have been strange occurrences at 1508 N. Walnut. We originally chalked them up to active cats, Charlie and Rosie, or some unseen critter like a mouse or a bat, but we wonder if the cause is more spiritual. We hope the cause is you.

On the mantle in the living room a candle was tipped over though several vases and angels were left undisturbed. On another day but on that same mantle a picture of Blythe and Bailey was face down with, again, nothing else disturbed. And in a large vase at the other end of the mantle branches of eucalyptus were rearranged. These recent unexplained events had us thinking about other eerie moment when JJ, your Aunt Mallory's boyfriend, heard a child's voice in the basement say "Hey" or when toys in the basement would turn on with no one around them or in our many encounters with lightning bugs or butterflies or hummingbirds.

I have prayed for a sign, have hoped for irrefutable proof of your lingering spirit. Part of me doubts all of these events as nothing more than coincidence but more of me clings to a connection that defies the grave. Oh, how I want to believe, how I want to know. I am so tired of being

adrift and aimless. What little faith I have is not guiding
me toward Heaven's shore.

You know, ships lost in thick fog needed a lighthouse
and foghorn to bring them safely to port. I need my
Sunshine. I need to hear a "Hey" too.

9/3/09

This evening, while walking through Springhill
Cemetery, I was listening to Girlyman's <u>little star</u> CD when
I heard the lines: "as for Jesus, you never felt much, but
you prayed/ 'cause you needed to believe that you could be
saved." The song has military allusions in it, but I heard
the lines as one who has dealt with a three year long battle
within my soul. In just a matter of seconds I thought of how
numb I often feel, how so far away Jesus seems to be...or
is. I thought of my prayers. Not traditional praying, I'm
sure, but a reaching out, a calling out, a hope in salvation
which brings me to you, Reagan. All of these thoughts in a
few seconds.

Then, as I passed the mausoleum, I glanced over to the
left (I usually look and veer right at this point), and there,
on the other side of the fence, three deer emerged from the
woods and stopped to stare at me. I paused and looked at

them. I even gently waved to them—I think to thank them. Just yesterday, I was telling my seventh graders about my Christmas Eve encounters with deer. I can hardly believe that, a day later, I am in another cemetery facing more deer.

Later, after walking my mile-long loop around the old section of the cemetery, I cut again through the new part and saw in a far corner of the grounds a young man walking hand-in-hand with his little girl, a blonde probably around two.

I don't know if they were for me or if the deer were sent as a sign, but I came away feeling strongly that that was the point.

As the evenings have gotten cooler and my walks more leisurely and reflective, I've used the time to think about you, Sunshine. Much of the music I play seems to serve as a soundtrack for our story. Lyrics that I never paid much attention to suddenly seem to speak so clearly to our time together and our time apart.

"Stardust" for instance—the Nat King Cole recording. It's a song about being parted, about a love lost and clinging to memories as elusive as the dust from stars. The melody and the orchestration may be as beautiful a song as was ever recorded.

I walk our neighborhood streets and see the full moon and the ghost-like clouds and the twinkling stars. I feel the gentle breeze of approaching autumn. I hear my footsteps on the pavement beyond the music in my ears. I hear these lyrics:

> *High up in the sky the little stars climb*
> *Always reminding me that we're apart*
> *You wander down the lane and far away*
> *Leaving me a song that will not die*
> *Love is now the stardust of yesterday*
> *The music of the years gone by*
> *Beside a garden wall*
> *When stars are bright*
> *You are in my arms*

And so on...

I stare at these words now and connections like lasers go out in different directions: The Secret Garden and "a garden wall," the little star CD and "the little stars climb," "Our bright, shining star Reagan" and "the stardust of yesterday."

This is the only time I'll say it, Reagan, but we both know that, though I hope you read over my shoulder, these journals will one day be read by others.

So, for this one time, to all those who pick up this book—my children and grandchildren and great-grandchildren and beyond—if you want to know who I was following Reagan's death, listen to the music with which I filled my head. Pick a cool evening, lit by the moon and the stars, walk through your neighborhood, and listen to Nat King Cole sing "Stardust." Feel the regret and sadness in it. You'll hear what's left of my spirit in its haunting refrain.

9/7/09 2:27 a.m.

Two mornings ago, while walking through Spring Hill where I encountered the three deer, I listened to the <u>Joyful Sign</u> CD from Girlyman. The last track included these lyrics:

> *I will be right here. I will be right here.*
> *Right behind the door where I left my love before*
> *I will be right here. I will be right here.*
> *I know about rapture, the feeling that you've*
captured what you'll never own.
and these:

> *Right inside the room where I always wait for you*
> *I will be right here. I will be right here.*

and:

I want to call you

Cause everybody knows the truth of letting go is that you never do.

I will be right here.

An hour ago, we woke up to a crash. Your Aunt Bailey dropped a fan in the hallway which caused Bronte to get scared, and, somehow, our family portrait fell to the floor, the glass in the frame shattering. The photo is okay, and the frame can be used again, but the loss is greater. This glass had your fingerprints on it from when you used to point to family members. I guess the loss wasn't complete because I was able to save a section of glass which had been right over the images of Da and me. I found a gift box in the basement, lined it with paper towels, and carefully placed the shard inside.

The lid, ironically, had a cartoon image of an angel on it. I didn't tell Aunt Bailey about the treasure found on the glass.

I feel like I've lost you again.

9/8/09

Yesterday afternoon, Labor Day, I walked my three miles to and through and from Spring Hill. Same cemetery but yet another CD, this time from Alison Krauss.

When I walk I pick out an album on my I-pod that suits the weather, the time of day, and my mood. Sometimes, it's music with a strong beat so that I'll pick up the pace; other times, it's quieter tunes when I want to think.

I have never chosen an album so that a song will come on at a certain place. My last few trips around Spring Hill are examples. The fact, however, that certain songs have played with words so relevant to my grief and to you, my angel, can't be just a coincidence.

Alison's Krauss's "Jacob's Dream" tells the story of two young brothers who get lost in the mountains after wandering away from their cabin. After a daylong search by one thousand men, the boys are found cold and still. The first two choruses have the boys crying out for their parents, promising that they'll never wander away from their cabin door. The last chorus, after the boys have died, has altered words:

> *Oh mommy and daddy, look past the tears you cry*
> *We're both up in Heaven now, God is by our side*

As you lay us down to rest in the presence of the
Lord

Know that we will meet you here at Heaven's door
You can imagine, Reagan, how sad Papa got. We've talked
about Heaven's door, haven't we? I've asked you to stay
there and wait for me. It's all I really have to look forward
to.

Right after that song, Alison Krauss sings "Away Down
the River." Once again, the words had special meaning:

Baby dry your eyes
There's no need to cry
Cause I'll see you again
It might be a while
Before you understand

I'm just away down the river
A hundred miles or more
Crossing over Jordan
To the other shore
I'll be standing waiting
With all who've gone before
I'm just away down the river
A hundred miles or more

Now the pictures on the wall

Will help you to recall

They're not there

To make you sad

But to remember

All the good times we had

When it's time to leave

You're gonna feel the mountain breeze

And the snow will fill the stream

And carry you to me

I guess I'm mostly touched by these two songs because they could be your words to me. And, maybe, though sung by Alison Krauss, they were sent from Heaven.

10/27/09

It has been a stressful month and a half. Da and I, your daddy and mommy, and Papa and Da Green have met with both the Assistant State's Attorney, Kavita, and the State's Attorney, Randy, a couple of times to talk about a plea agreement in this terrible case. Originally, we wanted to try the case before a jury, but, as the November 2 trial date neared, we began to weigh the options and consider how much we could all lose if a jury rendered a not guilty verdict. Shaken Baby Syndrome as a form of child abuse and a cause of death would be questioned. Your mommy would have to deal with shifting blame. Ryan (I don't even like writing or saying the name) might be able to walk out of jail to hurt and abuse other girlfriends and children. We all decided that we wanted him to get something instead of risk him getting nothing.

Later today, he is supposed to plead guilty to manslaughter. His sentence, determined by the judge at a later date, will end up being drastically reduced from what he might've received if convicted of first degree murder.

It is some justice, but it is no victory.

Last month, I was asked to consider running as a Democrat for State Representative in the 2010 general election. That request began a month of information gathering and soul-searching. Running for office would have been physically and emotionally draining. It would have meant giving up many evenings and weekends to travel around the district and talking to voters. Part of me was flattered to be asked. Part of me was filled with pride at being able to represent the people of Vermilion and Champaign County. I told so many people—from friends to local Democratic leaders to state Democratic workers—

that I was no politician, but I so admire John Adams and Harry Truman that I really wanted to give it a shot. Selfishly, I thought of the setbacks I've endured in the school district, seeing a run and a win as a chance to show up some administrators. I think when that thought entered my mind, I began to doubt the whole idea. Financially, I would have had to risk my job, my tenure, and my salary; at fifty plus, I didn't want to have to start looking for a new career (if I didn't win re-election or opted not to run again). I also didn't have money of my own to sink into a campaign.

Faced with a dilemma and waffling daily, I began to look for signs, even praying for guidance.

Actually, several weeks before I was approached to run, I sent up a prayer to God while walking through Springhill Cemetery. "What's next, Lord?" I asked aloud. About a week later, I heard the news that Rep. Bill Black was planning to retire at the end of his term and that he had already named a successor. I remember standing in front of the radio, listening to the announcement, and wondering if I could handle political office. A week or so later, Dan and Nancy Brown pulled up in the driveway and posed the question. I met with State Senator Michael Frerichs and the chairperson of the Vermilion County Democratic Party to gather insight into the election process. I called Lori DeYoung, the former Democratic contender. I also sought the advice of Barbara Greenberg, Carol Cunningham, Dr. Kathy Houpt, Kelli Simpkins, and Stefanie LaReau as well as your Great Grandpa Jim. They were all supportive of a possible bid.

And the signs? They came from both sides. I had a dream about my Great Grandpa Edwards—I think the only one I've ever had. It was in a classroom filled with children. He walked by me, almost floating like he was on a conveyor belt, and both smiled at me and nodded his head affirmatively. He used to be a teacher in a one-room schoolhouse. I interpreted that as a vote for staying in the classroom. A few weeks ago, I attended Great Grandpa Jim's church and heard him deliver a special benediction that spoke to my heart:

> May the Lord disturb you and trouble you,
> May the Lord set an impossible task before you,
> And dare you to meet it.
> May the Lord give you strength to do your best
> And then—but only then—
> May you be granted the Lord's Peace.

That very evening, I received an e-mail from a former student now studying to be an English teacher and crediting me with her decision to go into education.

Back to square one.

Throughout all of this indecision, I continued to ask what you would want me to do. I thought I could do good for causes related to families- and children-at-risk. I thought of the legislation I could enact on a statewide level, not just here in Vermilion County. I just didn't want my Sunshine to be disappointed in me because I have disappointed so many times before. And, if I made the wrong decision, I'm sorry, Reagan.

Eventually, I had to say "No." The stress headaches subsided somewhat, and the indecision, consuming so much of my thoughts, finally ended. What change I can help create will have to come from Reagan's Rescue.

Da and I attended a domestic violence program at the YFRC on Oct. 1. I spoke briefly about the Frost poem "The Road Not Taken" and the choices we can make in our lives and, sometimes, choices that are made for us—like losing you.

*Da and I also attended the Infant Loss and
Remembrance Ceremony at Sunset on October 15. We
were able to share our grief with the grief of so many other
families who have laid their children to rest in Sunset's
Garden of Innocence.*

*I also submitted a workshop proposal for the next SBS
conference to be held in Atlanta next year.*

*And the Future Problem Solvers club at North Ridge is
taking on SBS as a project for the year. Bailey is a part of
that group, and I am so proud of her.*

*We have several hours to go before the hearing. I feel
very queasy today—very weak. I know I must be strong for
my family. For you.*

*I'm sure I'll write more about what happens in court
today later on. Please be with us, Sunshine. We need your
strength.*

---

*Before a judge and a courtroom filled with people, Ryan
admitted to causing your death. Now we wait until
December 21 for the sentencing.*

*Despite the events of the day, I still wish that you could
get a deal, too, Sunshine.*

I love you, Reagan, and I miss you as much as I did over three years ago.

11/1/09

    Christmas music plays in the background on one of our Music Choice cable channels. Though it's a little early, I need some Christmas spirit. This past week has been stressful, but the days have been crisp and orange and gold, and they've brought reflection and an openness to making a connection to you.

    Have you tried to get through? In the last weeks, we've discovered three unexplained puddles of water in the house—one in front of the entertainment center, one in the sewing room in the basement, and one in the living room again, this time in front of the fireplace. We originally thought Bronte or one of the cats might have had an accident, but the spots did not smell. There were also no drips, spots on the ceilings, or leaky pipes to explain what we've come to describe without fear as paranormal activity. I looked for information on the Internet and discovered numerous references to spots like these around the globe, often attributed to a poltergeist. We are not afraid of these strange occurrences because we cling to the hope that it's your spirit coming through, and that brings us incredible peace.

Aunt Flyn told us that, while alone the other day, she encountered a ghost. After heating some food in the microwave, and unable to close the microwave door because her hands were full, she sat down in the living room to eat, only to hear the microwave door slam shut. The most she could utter was an uneasy "Thanks."

Oh, Reagan, are these your spirit reaching out to us? Are they like the deer I encounter in Springhill Cemetery— never when I look for one but always there when I need your assurance?

We move into that holy and blessed time when thoughts of you come so strongly and unawares, the tears flowing so easily. I miss you during the holiday months, especially, and there are times I wish I could die so to be with you.

You are always in my heart, always so very close even as you are far away. Please keep reaching out, please keep coming through.

Just one other thing...this afternoon, one of the cats, we think, knocked over the ceramic angel that sat in the center of the mantel above the fireplace. This figure had been a part of the flower arrangement that Papa and Da had made up for you for your funeral. It's probably not all that

important, but it broke my heart, like losing a piece of you
again. I kept a fragment of wing that I'll put with the glass
with your fingerprints on it. Another shattered piece.
Another fragment. More brokenness.

---

1 Don't worry about the wicked

or envy those who do wrong.

2 For like grass, they soon fade away.

Like spring flowers, they soon wither.

3 Trust in the Lord and do good.

Then you will live safely in the land and

prosper...

5 Commit everything you do to the Lord.

Trust him, and he will help you.

6 He will make your innocence radiate like

the dawn,

and the justice of your cause will shine like

the noonday sun.

7 Be still in the presence of the Lord,

and wait patiently for him to act.

Don't worry about evil people who prosper

or fret about their wicked schemes.--

Psalm 37: 1-3; 5-7 (NLT)

12/31/09

The general consensus about 2009 is that it has been a terrible year. The hope is that 2010 turns out to be better. I guess the same can be said for our family. 2009 was a year of cautious highs and surprising lows. The court case was continued several times. Then came word that a plea agreement had been reached. We hoped that Judge Clary would give Ryan the maximum sentence of fourteen years, a vastly reduced penalty from life in prison. On December 21, the sentence was handed down—seven years in the Department of Corrections. With time served and good behavior, seven really means a little over two years, not much more than the length of your time with us. We were in shock, the same kind of numb we felt on July 2, 2006, when we received the frantic phone call. It was a shock like the moment I met Da in the hallway of the emergency room and she told me you were gone. Once again, we were left wondering if we failed you. What didn't we say? What could we have done? What did we overlook?

Judge Clary said some things from the Bench that I disagree with—that Ryan didn't mean to kill you, that our emotions should not matter in sentencing. I believe that Ryan meant to harm you and did so on numerous occasions. The judge also never asked about the financial impact statement that we filled out. Nothing. Silence.

One of my resolutions for 2010 is to oppose him when I can. Of course, I don't know whether or not this is the action I should take from your point of view. Perhaps you are safe and secure in Heaven looking with pity at your family trying feebly to come to terms with reality and to face the future in a more positive way. We are, after all, imperfect unlike you, glorious Angel. We can always use a sign.

Since the sentencing came just days before Christmas, it cast a shadow over much of what we did. A lot of these past two weeks has been a blur.

And we've run into so many people out and about who, out of habit, have asked: "Have you had a good Christmas break?" or "How have your holidays been?" We don't want to bore people with specifics. Maybe those who ask are not aware of the events of December 21. Maybe they've forgotten already. Maybe they don't consider how difficult that question is to answer. Maybe we should answer with an automatic "Great" or "Relaxing" or some other vague statement.

Da and I were in line to see a movie the other day. We stood behind some acquaintances of ours who were with their grandchildren. When the man asked how many grandchildren we had, I faltered for a bit, looked at your Da for help, and finally stated "Three" with no other explanation. It bothered me that I wasn't prepared with an answer. I will be prepared from now on. "Three" I will say and think to myself, Two on Earth and one in Heaven.

I made the fourth trip to your grave on Christmas Eve. It was raining buckets as I shivered, wet and cold, under an umbrella and read the Dora Christmas book aloud, fumbling between the pages, the flaps, and the umbrella handle. Later, at night, after all the festivities were done and food eaten, I returned for our quiet night together. I sang "Tell Me Why" and "You Are My Sunshine" like I have now each Christmas Eve since 2006. I couldn't help but think about how quickly the year went by. I can't help but hope that the remaining years of my life go by as quickly until I am reunited with you.

I've included the words I spoke on the stand as part of my Victim Impact Statement on December 21, 2009. I've also included words of a friend, Charlie Hester, a survivor of domestic abuse who credits you, Little Girl, with saving her. [NOTE: See the sections entitled Victim Impact Statement on pg. 531 and Operation Shrink Charlie's Big Butt: How Reagan Rescued Me on pg. 535]

People have written letters to local papers about their displeasure with the sentence. [NOTE: See the section entitled The Sentencing on pg. 543 for the comments which appeared as a result of the judge's decision] *You continue to be a cause, Sunshine. You will continue to be a cause as long as I have breath.*

1/5/10

It would have been your 6th birthday today, and that number makes me realize that you would have been less a baby—less a child—and more a girl. This early part of January is a time of changes. Out with the old and in with the new. Like the two-faced god Janus for which January is named, it is a time for looking to the past and looking ahead to the future. Because 2010 was the end of the decade, people looked back at the past ten years and anticipated a better year and a more promising decade to come.

Some Christmas decorations are still up. Lights still shine in windows and on trees indoors and bushes outdoors. Other folks have already thrown their bare trees out into the front yard for the city to pick up.

We began to pack away Christmas decorations since today is the 12th and last day of Christmas, but Da and I were too tired to put everything away. We'll stretch it out over this week.

I say this because we are at that point of change, of transition. We need to move on in our grief even though there's so much left to take care of. We need to make plans for the future even though we don't want to let you go. We look behind us all the while keeping tabs on what lies within us.

This afternoon, as I left North Ridge, I saw a deer grazing on one of the snow-covered baseball fields. I couldn't help but think it was a gift from you.

Mallory, JJ, Da, your daddy, and I released ten pink balloons from the cemetery, some of them with messages for you. We were afraid that they would get stuck in nearby trees, but their tangled lines all pulled apart, and each balloon cleared the tops of the trees and, minutes later, disappeared in the bleak, frigid evening air.

You never knew JJ, Sunshine, but you would have loved him, just like your cousins, Aubrey and Ainsley, do. He would have delighted in you.

Your Great Aunt Elaine sent me a message on facebook, a quote by Jeffrey Glassberg: "Beautiful and graceful,

*varied and enchanting, small but approachable, butterflies
lead you to the sunny side of life. And everyone deserves a
little sunshine."*

*Like a butterfly (and how you loved them), you, too,
were all those things—beautiful, graceful, certainly varied,
enchanting enough to capture my heart, small and always
approachable. You led us to a sunny, joyful place. I don't
know whether we deserved you but I hope we can be
deserving of you.*

*Happy birthday, my Angel. I'll try to smile for you.
Forgive me the tears I still shed. They reflect my love for
you.*

2/13/10

*Your Papa is in a musical this weekend. It's called The
Spitfire Grill. Aunt Mallory plays the leading role of
Percy, recently released from prison, who comes to a small
town called Gilead to start her life over again. I play a war
deserter named Eli, an emotional cripple who doesn't
speak except with his expressive eyes. Since I don't have
any lines, I've had a lot of time to listen to what the other
characters say and sing.*

Throughout this run you have been with me in a very powerful way. I've carried the card from your funeral in my pocket. It has the picture of you kneeling next to our dining room table, the same photo we used for your marker. On the back is your 2 year old picture and part of the description from your obituary. In between scenes, I clutch it in my hand and rub your image, then it goes back in my pocket.

The plot of <u>The Spitfire Grill</u> deals with topics that are very personal—loss, violence, family, loneliness, guilt, depression, hope, redemption. The story is not ours, but the emotions are. The song lyrics and the score capture so perfectly what I feel. Although I am not in the play very much, I am present for many of the most emotional moments in the show. I feel those emotions very strongly— as Eli and as your Papa.

Aunt Mallory sings a song called "Shine." I kneel beside her and cry because I long for this kind of peace:

> *There's a darkness in me*
> *As deep as this valley*
> *And things that I done*
> *I can never repay.*

The days I regret
Are too many for countin'
There's sins river water
Will not wash away.

But if you can turn this whole valley to golden,
And burn till the colors of paradise shine,
Then maybe your bright mornin' light can discover
A diamond of hope in this dark heart of mine.

Later, Hannah, played by our neighbor down the street,
Alice Cowan, sings a song called "Way Back Home."

It is late in the day,
It is late in the day.
Would you please find your way back home?

There's a lamp in the night,
There's a lamp in the night.
You can follow its light back home.

I will wait for you here until morning.
And on to the end of the day.
I will wait for you here until morning.

[376]

I promise I won't turn away.

When Alice sings these words about missing her son, I think of those evenings I've gone out to the backyard, looked up at the stars, and waited for you to come back to us.

I guess I can confess that whatever strength my performance has is because of you being in my pocket and in my heart.

And in Aunt Mallory's heart. When her Percy says to Hannah, "I know what it is to lose a child, Hannah! I do. And mine can never come back," I can hear the personal anguish in her voice and see the tears in her eyes. I would say that seeing my daughter upset like that breaks my heart, but my heart has been broken for some time now. Again, in that moment on stage, you are very much with us.

3/31/10

I am writing once again from Tennessee, a place we have come to for peace and the rejuvenation one gets from nature. We never forget you, but in the Smoky Mountains, and with all the activity with which we fill our day, we can go longer stretches without being so sad.

We vacationed here a month before you died. Papa and Da returned three months after we lost you to look into buying a cabin. We have come back numerous times since. Papa has always drawn strength from the mountains. In these last few years, I have needed a lot of strengthening.

Since I last wrote in these pages, so many things have happened—some exciting, some very sad. I have wanted to sit down before this to catalog it all, but I have found precious little peace and alone time to gather my thoughts. After a while, I was overwhelmed by the amount to record. I'll try my best, though, to summarize the events of late February and all of March.

The most important occurrence, I guess, is the day I realized that I hadn't cried for you. I went for more than three and a half years crying every single day. You know how I was afraid to stop crying, afraid that you would not love me anymore or that I would, with my lack of tears, dishonor you. Well, now that pressure is off, and I will have to learn how to honor you in more positive ways. I am sorry, Sunshine. Even as I write this, through tears, I know that your life and your loss are still the single most important parts of my life's story. They always will be.

Not that it matters all that much, but I believe the change occurred as I began rehearsals for The Secret

Garden. *Though it is an emotional show, and I am surrounded by many friends and family members (including your daddy), I have found the very act of directing this musical and bringing this story to Danville audiences to be cathartic and uplifting even. The story is about loss and grief and the reclamation of not only a garden but also the hurting characters who inhabit it. The story is about me and you and your daddy and Aunt Mallory and Aunt Bailey. This piece of beauty we create is our way of healing others while healing ourselves. And the healing seems to be working.*

My faith, however, is as numb as it ever has been. I have stopped attending services although I want to return. I just don't feel any impulse, any breath of life, any spirit. What rejuvenation I have experienced has been because of spring. Temperatures are warmer. Trees and flowers are beginning to burst with color. I am walking once again through our neighborhood or the cemetery.

Maybe my soul is like the garden. Maybe it is wick. Maybe there is magic just under the surface "waiting for the right time to be seen," like Dickon sings in The Secret Garden. *Maybe souls have seasons, too. "The Circle of Life" is how Elton John coined it. And that leads me to February 20.*

I received a call from my former student and friend, Julia Sullivan. She said she had bad news. I thought she was going to tell me that she couldn't be in The Secret Garden. Instead, she told me that her mother, Barbara Greenberg, had died earlier that day. Barbara had become a valued and trusted friend, an advocate for abused women and children, and, as a Commercial-News reporter, a champion for Reagan's Rescue and, although she never met you, for you, too. She spoke at Ryan's sentencing. She counseled me, encouraged me, thought of us so often. I miss her terribly. I hope that she's gotten to know you. She was a woman of great strength, courage, and conviction. She will live on in her two amazing daughters, Julia and Kate.

And the other events? Because of the light sentence that Ryan received and the public outcry, State Representative Bill Black introduced House Bill 6213 which called for longer sentences for those convicted of killing children through abuse. Bill was outraged by the miscarriage of justice in our case. I only wish the bill could be named for you.

Great Grandpa Jim and Great Grandma Roberta went to Springfield to testify in front of a committee. Just last week the bill passed 112-3 in the House and now goes to the Illinois Senate.

The Future Problem Solvers at North Ridge, of which Aunt Bailey is a member, won the state competition for their "I Can Prevent It" campaign to raise awareness of Shaken Baby Syndrome. The project was inspired by your life.

Tomorrow, April 1, Great Grandpa Jim and Great Grandma Roberta return to Springfield to pick up an award from Prevent Child Abuse Illinois at the Governor's Mansion. Reagan's Rescue won the central region Program Excellence award. Since we are in Tennessee, they are going in our place. And I am pleased for them because they have been so deeply touched by your loss and so involved in our advocacy efforts that they should be acknowledged.

And last Saturday, March 27, was the 4th Annual Reagan Williams Memorial Track Meet at Danville High School.

What this all means is that my Sunshine lives on and on. We can't hug you or kiss your cheek or forehead, but we can share you with the rest of the world.

Gee, I almost forgot. We have been invited by the National Center on Shaken Baby Syndrome to present a workshop in Atlanta this coming fall at its international convention. We'll take what I prepared for the Vancouver conference and update. And what amazing updates there will be.

We do now share you with the world. Your light continues to shine.

5/23/10

Da was cleaning out her closet this evening and trying to organize the bedroom. She found a picture taken at Great Grandpa Jim's house of me holding you. You have a baby carrot in your right hand and a flowered purse hanging on your right arm. You look relaxed; I look happy and proud.

I just gained a couple more seconds with you.

7/2/10

Like your birthday and Christmas Eve, July 2 is marked by ritual. For the fourth time now, I've come to Sunset's Garden of Innocence around noon to be with you at that minute you passed into Heaven.

This day is always emotional, like reliving the events of that July Sunday in 2006. I write in your journal for a few moments then glance at the time so that I don't miss 12:25. Each time I've come here, with camp stool in tow, I've been at a very different place emotionally. I wrote to you before about Papa's numbness, that I reached a point several months ago when I realized that I hadn't cried for a few days. That might be a sign of healing, but those tears were proof of emotion, proof of feeling. Nothing has replaced those tears, and so I feel very little. No peace or goodness has filled the hole. No anger or bitterness has darkened it. So I live without a core. That's why I cling to ritual.

Here it is—12:25 p.m. I've been sitting under the nearest shade tree for, though the humidity is low and the temperature on the high end of comfortable, the sun, in a blue and cloudless sky, is fierce at this time of day. The breeze is fragrant and gentle. Around your marker are a bunch of white, pink, and purple flowers I brought; a Reagan wristband; a Dora doll; and a balloon and flower pot from Julia. A slip of paper attached reads "With love from my family to yours—Julia."

We couldn't have ordered a more perfect day.

These last couple of months have been full of activity. A man who heads a social agency in Springfield contacted us about partnering with his organization. Da and I sent out posters to churches in the area in the spring. Now we are ready to send posters to local taverns and pubs. I just ordered large magnets for cars and vans to advertise Reagan's Rescue along with postcards. Da and I are starting to make plans for the SBS conference in Atlanta this coming September. Today we ran an advertisement in the <u>Commercial-News</u> *to publicize our website and mission and to memorialize you.*

I guess the biggest development has to do with the North Ridge Future Problem Solvers competing in the FPS International Conference in La Crosse, Wisconsin, from June 9-13. We are so proud of all the kids did to spread awareness of Shaken Baby Syndrome—especially your Aunt Bailey because the project was difficult for her sometimes. Though they came in fourth, and were understandably disappointed in the outcome, they met both kids and adults from around the world—England, New Zealand, Singapore—and around the nation, and they did, indeed, spread SBS awareness and your story. Reagan's Rescue also benefitted by gathering attention and picking up some marketing materials like magnets for the refrigerator and a 3-D cutout of our logo—a little girl reading her hand out to a butterfly. We'll take her along to Atlanta.

I need to go home now, Sunshine. I need to spend the day with Da and, hopefully, with your daddy, too. Your troubled Papa also needs to reclaim his spirit—somehow. As always, I could use a visit from you, in a form that I can recognize.

I love you, Reagan Emery. I just hope that you've been standing by my side while I've been writing this.

I never forget you, my bright angel.

Later...

I checked messages on facebook and found two quotes left by Julia.

"Life is eternal and love is immortal; And death is only a horizon, And a horizon is nothing save the limit of our sight."—Rossiter Raymond

"There is a sacredness in tears. They are not the mark of weakness, but of power. They speak more eloquently than ten thousand tongues. They are messengers of *overwhelming grief…and unspeakable love."—Washington Irving*

7/15/10

    Today is Thursday. I am waiting for your Aunt Bailey to get done with her voice lesson. While I'm sitting here in the van, I'm thinking about the events of this past Monday and the ironic timing of it all. You see, Monday was one of those days of firsts I've written about before. One was planned; the other was not.

    I've had a cyst on the back of my head for a couple of weeks, and, since my own home remedies and treatments were not working, I decided to go to Urgent Care at the Polyclinic and have it checked out. I approached the trip with some dread because I had not been in that room since the day Da and I took you to be checked out by the nurse. It was the day we found bruises on your body. It was the day we faced a sign telling us that the Urgent Care staff would no longer treat children your age. It was the day a compassionate nurse allowed us to bring you back anyway. It was the day Da and I tried to make a report to the Abuse Hotline but were denied because we did not feel comfortable giving our names. That was also the day we will regret to our dying hour.

That return to Urgent Care was enough of a milestone for me, but fate had more in store.

Around 11 p.m., we received a call that your daddy had hurt himself while playing tag in Lincoln Park with some of his friends. He ripped open his scalp pretty badly and, bleeding profusely, was taken to the Emergency Room at Provena.

I got dressed and drove to the hospital. Da could not because it was in the Emergency Room on July 2, 2006, that we found out you were gone.

I approached the entrance with an even greater dread. What if my boy had not survived? What if something went horribly wrong while he was being treated? That anxiety— coupled with reliving memories of that terrible Sunday afternoon—nauseated me.

There was the spot where I saw Da crying, clutching a tissue, and telling me that you were gone. There was the chair I sat in as I waited for detectives to question me and your daddy. There was the room Sister Joann took us into so that we could cry and ask "How did this happen?" There was the place where I called my sisters in Colorado and where I heard them wail. That was the place my life changed forever.

Once inside one of the examination rooms, I sat at the foot of your daddy's bed and watched as the nurse and the doctor sopped up blood and stitched his head back together. I was angry at his carelessness, yet I marveled at his resilience and his fun-loving nature, made the more impressive by your loss. I also felt helpless. That's an emotion I associate with the ER as well.

7/28/10

Last week, we had to make the difficult decision to put Bronte down. She was our faithful, loving, and gentle dog—our old lady—since your Aunt Bailey was a little girl. We rescued Bronte from the county animal shelter the day before she was to be euthanized. We saved her again shortly after that when we had her treated for heartworms. This time, however, old age had taken its toll. It was time to let her go.

It was an agonizing decision. We even backed out of it once already. We certainly felt—and still feel— responsible. And our house lacks something now.

[388]

Your daddy and Aunt Flyn took her to the vet. Your daddy was with her when the drug was administered. Da wrote a note for your daddy to read, encouraging Bronte to find you in Heaven. If pets do live on in Eternity—and we've read confirmation of that possibility from both a medium and a Christian writer—then we find peace that Bronte is your new companion.

I miss you so. Take care of each other until we join you.

---

1 God is our refuge and strength,

always ready to help in times of trouble.

2 So we will not fear when

earthquakes come

and the mountains crumble into the sea.

3 Let the oceans roar and foam.

Let the mountains tremble as the waters

surge--Psalm 46: 1-3 (NLT)

9/12/10

Last week, in my 7th grade Language Arts class, I talked to my students about how life offers us no guarantees, no promises—of happiness, of time. I taught them this idea because I believe it is an important one, even for twelve and thirteen year olds. As Friday approached and I anticipated leaving for the International Conference on Shaken Baby Syndrome in Atlanta, I felt a certain dread. Wouldn't it be ironic if something unexpected happened to us on the trip? Then I could really drive the point home. Well, the unexpected did occur.

We left Danville around 4:40 p.m., en route to Effingham for a candlelight vigil sponsored by the GFWC Illinois Federation of Women's Clubs. Da and I were in our new van; Mallory, Flyn, Bailey, and JJ were in the big white van. I had been asked to speak as one who lost a loved one to domestic violence. Mal, Flyn, and Bailey were going to sing "One Candle" during the lighting ceremony.

An hour into the trip, as we were pulling off Interstate 57 to eat dinner in Tuscola, the white van quit running. Mallory pulled onto the shoulder on the exit ramp. The plan had been to attend the vigil in Effingham, an hour away, and then for Da and I to continue on to Mt. Vernon where we had a motel reservation. Mallory would drive everyone else home.

With time running out to make the vigil at all, we had to decide what to do. Tow the van and, if so, where? Pile into our new van, attend the vigil, then drive all the way

[390]

back to Danville? Not go to Effingham at all? Aunt Bailey didn't feel well, so she didn't want to sing. Da and I didn't want to leave everyone either, and we had borrowed a large keyboard from the school that we couldn't abandon.

Eventually, your uncle Shane drove two hours from Indiana to pick up Mal, JJ, Flyn, and Bailey who waited at a restaurant. The white van was towed to a nearby town to be fixed. Da and I drove on to Effingham, making the vigil in time.

I had time to think about the injustice of it all. We were all volunteering to participate in an SBS candlelight vigil. I wrote a short speech; the girls practiced a song. Why weren't we allowed to get to the location and share what we had come to share?

Maybe there is no great Plan, I thought as I drove along the interstate. Maybe there is no will of God. Maybe everything is, indeed, random.

Now, a couple of days have passed, and I will admit to being a little less skeptical. The van did break down on an exit ramp at the edge of a town within walking distance of gas stations and restaurants. No one was hurt. It was just plans which had to be changed. And my own children assured me that everything would be okay. They returned home safe and sound. My son-in-law reminded me about the nature of family. Da and I got to the vigil. We still touched lives, and we made some connections which may be useful in the future.

And I'll certainly have a good story to tell my students when I get back to school next week.

9/13/10

I've often thought, dear Granddaughter, that one day I would have nothing more to write, that our advocacy work would come to an end, our projects all tapped out. This evening, as I sit in our room at the Intercontinental Buckhead Atlanta, I realize this work on behalf of children will never be finished. New ideas will be formed. New challenges will present themselves. New contacts will be made.

Da and I arrived here in Atlanta on Saturday evening. I met with the tech guy to download my PowerPoint presentation into the system, and we settled into our 16th floor room. On Sunday morning, we attended several workshops, met some very knowledgeable, helpful, and generous people, and got inspired to take our awareness campaign to the next level. We also reconnected with people I met in Vancouver—Debbie Dycus from the Shaken

Baby Coalition, Danielle Vazquez and Ryan Steinbeigle from the National Center on Shaken Baby Syndrome, and several other advocates and family members from 2008.

On Sunday afternoon, we drove into the city and visited the Martin Luther King Jr. National Historic Site, the world of Coca Cola, and Centennial Olympic Park.

On Sunday evening, we attended a very emotional Family Reception. Da felt uncomfortable, hurting that most of those who were there were family members of survivors. Everyone in the room introduced themselves. I said that we lost you in 2006, that we mostly remembered reading to you and singing to you, and that you kept us alive and keep us alive even now.

This morning we presented our workshop entitled "One Small Candle: Creating an SBS Advocacy Group," an update to the presentation I made in Vancouver two years ago. Da didn't want to talk much because it is still hard for her to control her emotions. The room we were in (Hope1) was full. The presentation went off without a hitch. I think we informed a lot of people and touched many, too.

We will come away from this conference with a renewed sense of purpose and with some exciting new plans. We are so fortunate to be a part of this SBS awareness network.

We are lucky, too, to have you as our granddaughter, our light, our cause, and our inspiration.

12/12/10

   I am actually upset and shocked to discover that I haven't written to you for three months. I didn't realize I had been so neglectful. All I can do is apologize, Reagan, and hope you can forgive me.

   Each month since our trip to Atlanta, Reagan's Rescue has been asked to participate in an awareness event.

   Da and I helped present an SBS workshop at the annual Prevent Child Abuse Illinois convention in Springfield in October. Lucky for us that our school district went on strike in September while we were in Atlanta because Da and I got our personal days back to use for the state convention.

   In November, I returned to Springfield to speak in front of a statewide Family Violence Coordinating Council meeting made up of representatives from all of the judicial circuits in Illinois.

   Tonight, Da, your daddy, Mallory (and her boyfriend JJ), Flyn, Bailey, Grandma Roberta, and Grandpa Jim all attended a Christmas dinner and service at the YFRC. I ended up reading a Christmas story (wearing Da's glasses because I didn't bring mine) since Grandpa's voice was going.

Though Mallory, Bailey, and Flyn sang three beautiful and moving songs ("Where Are you Christmas?" "Christmas Lullaby," and "Believe") I managed to keep it together emotionally. Then we sang "Silent Night" with all the mothers, their children, and members of Grandpa's church, and I came to verse 4 and the words "With the angels let us sing." Tears clouded my eyes. Maybe they were tears of sadness or regret; maybe they were brought on by pride for my granddaughter is an angel singing and dancing in Heaven. I imagine you with your great great grandparents and with Uncle Frank and Aunt Gin— everyone, all the host praising God and singing in one mighty chorus. You there, my Littlest Angel, running from one knee to another, from one embrace to another. When I miss you the most, this image brings me comfort.

I will not neglect my writing to you again. I'm sorry it has been so very long.

12/25/10

My hat from my Christmas cracker on Christmas Eve.
Pink—for you. [I placed my hat in the journal, one of many
such mementos.]

12/31/10

Oprah re-ran an interview with author J. K. Rowling,
who shared that, were it not for the illness and death of her
mother as well as the writer's own battle with depression,
she would not have penned the <u>Harry Potter</u> series. Her
great fame and fortune were born of loss.

As I look forward to the new year and beginning a book
about you, Reagan, I'll take this interview as a sign. It can
be done.

1/2/11

We're going to be taking the Christmas tree down in a
few days, and I will be filled with melancholy to see it go.
This particular tree has been active this year. We've had
several ornaments fall off, which has never happened.
None of them has broken, thank God.

What is strange is which ones fell. First, the It's a
Wonderful Life ornament with the bell ringing. Next, Da's
rooster. Finally, last night, an angel ornament that your
Aunt Elaine gave us, one we keep next to your picture
ornament and the Snow Baby ornament we have for you.
Are you sending us messages, little one?

1/5/11

Another January 5. Another trip to Berry's Garden
Center for balloons—five pink and five white. Another
somber trip to the cemetery. Balloons are passed out (with
warnings for Aubrey and Ainsley to hold on tight), a circle
is formed around your grave, we count to 3, and then we let
them go. On this particular birthday, they flew toward the
north. One year it was to the east, another to the west.
Sometimes the temperature has been mild, other times
bone-chilling like today.

One year the balloons disappeared almost immediately
into the low, dense clouds. Other times, they took many
minutes to turn to specks and then rise out of sight entirely.

As I flip through these pages, I cannot believe that five
years have gone by. Maybe it is indeed a blessing that my
life seems to be accelerating and that my memory is not of

individual days gone by but seasons and years. I don't dwell so much on how I am moving farther away from you but instead on how closer I am getting.

Great Grandpa Jim told me that, with time, I would heal. There will always be scar tissue and a numbness. I will always miss you, Reagan. I will always love you and consider myself so fortunate that you loved me.

5/1/11

Once again, as I turn through these pages, I am surprised—shocked even—to find that I haven't written to you in almost four months. I have thought about you every day. I have missed you every day. Maybe this is what healing is like. Maybe I didn't have anything profound to say.

These last few months have included some of the regular rituals—the track meet at the high school; another SBS workshop, this one in Kankakee with Great Grandma Cookie, Great Grandpa Dave, and Great Grandma Sharon in attendance; another pinwheel display and Reading Rock-a-thon at North Ridge; and holiday gatherings filled with activities and noise and overcrowding, all colored a little by regret. Aubrey and Ainsley are growing up so fast, but I still can't look at them without thinking of you. I don't suppose I'll ever get over that comparison.

The new activity this spring was Monical's Pizza Community Day for Reagan's Rescue on April 11. We raised a little over $500, which means the three Danville restaurants brought in over $2500 worth of business on that day. We have a second event planned for July 5 in Kankakee and Bradley.

As I write this I am sitting in the second seat of the white van, occasionally on the verge of tears, thinking about all that we've done in this vehicle. I'm especially thinking about that Father's Day afternoon in 2006, when I took you home, not knowing that I would lose you two weeks later. I'm thinking about opening side doors, hugging you tightly, then hugging you again.

I told Da about my reluctance to sell the van, and she understood. I know that I am emotional about things. I know that I have some very strong attachments to things, but they are things which serve as direct, tangible connections to people and events in my life. This second seat on the right hand side was where your carseat was attached. It is a space that you occupied at a critical moment, a moment I then inexplicably considered driving away with you to someplace safe. Oh, why didn't I act on that impulse? Maybe one irrational decision might have altered a chain of events which would have meant your living and not dying. Maybe. Maybe not.

I've begun to doubt so much this spring. I've begun to feel that there is no plan, just random events, circumstances. I've begun wondering whether death is simply a long sleep, a lack of consciousness, "Death's second self" that Shakespeare wrote about.

But for now, for these next few minutes, I have the interior of this van. Gray interior, rough, rainbow-colored upholstery, an echo of "You Are My Sunshine" or "Tell Me Why," and two hugs for goodbye.

A fourth journal is ready to be written on, Sunshine.

Volume Four

5/21/11

Last evening, your daddy received his Associate's Degree from Danville Area Community College. For much of the ceremony, I was focusing on the length of the program, the stifling heat in the gym, and the rudeness of the audience. Then I realized that the moment was not about me but about my son and your daddy and how he managed to get his life back on track after it was derailed in July of 2006. I know you would have been proud of him. Perhaps, from where you are, you are proud and looking down, walking beside him and resting your head on his shoulder when he needs comfort.

6/10/11

Yesterday began in a surreal way. I listened to a BBC World Service radio documentary on Shaken Baby Syndrome in which both your daddy and I were interviewed. This broadcast went around the world. Listeners heard me sing "Tell Me Why" and heard me relate the details of July. They heard your daddy talk about visiting your grave and about reacting to the sentencing. I hope that we were able to touch people who tuned in.

Later in the afternoon I received a phone call from an aide to State Senator Michael Frerichs about the status of HB 6213. The news was disappointing; the bill seems to have died in the Senate when the session ended last year. So we start over again.

I've always dreaded the day we when we would run out of projects for Reagan's Rescue. It looks like there are plenty of goals left to accomplish.

6/11/11

The lightning bugs are out. I sit on the front porch and look at them glow as they fly in our yard and up and down our street. I look at them with my customary awe for they are truly miracles of creation, but each flicker of yellow makes me sad because I am missing a little girl beside me.

I remember a distant Twelfth Night when you came for your birthday. There was a moment when you realized that the Christmas tree was missing from its corner of the dining room. I showed you where it was—lying on its side in the front yard right next to the curb where it would be taken away by the sanitation workers. You were so let down for a moment. That tree had been a part of the holiday magic in the house. Now it was stripped of its lights, its glittering ornaments, its sweet candy canes, its life really. You understood.

So I look at that same spot next to the curb. I see past the fireflies, past the lights. I see beyond the magic you brought me, beyond the life you brought into this house.

I understand.

6/19/11

Father's Day. It has been five years since we last saw you alive.

Once again, Da and I, separately, scan the greeting card aisles for Father's Day cards for our dads. For a moment we think "Don't forget Ian" and then we remember, and the tears come.

It's always a bittersweet day.

7/2/11

Robert Fulghum defined ritual as the repeated pattern of meaning acts. And so here am I for the fifth time taking part in a ritual important to me, crucial to me. I'm sitting on the camp stool under a shade tree on a humid, early

July afternoon writing in this journal and thinking about you, Sunshine.

Da is up in Kankakee preparing for a ritual of her own—attending her 30th high school reunion. I'm driving up to join her later this afternoon. I told her that it was important to me to be here at this time and place. Like Christmas Eve and your birthday, I mark the passage of time by these anniversaries. It is around those dates when I am especially focused and pensive and eager to hear some idea, some philosophy, some wisdom to get me through yet another milestone.

Since your death occurred so close to Independence Day and because Papa has such an interest in and passion for our forefathers—especially John Adams and Thomas Jefferson—I searched for a clip today on the Internet which might say what I wanted to say on this holiday weekend, and I found a letter that Jefferson wrote to Adams, both men in old age, about loss and the passage of time and reunion. What they were feeling 200 years ago I feel today here in the Garden of Innocence. I've included a copy here.

"...trials have taught me that for ills so immeasurable, time and silence are the only medicine. It is some comfort to us both that the term is not very distant at which we are

to deposit our sorrows and suffering bodies and to ascend in essence to an ecstatic meeting with the friends we have loved and lost, and whom we shall still love and never lose again."—Thomas Jefferson

 I look forward to the day when we have "an ecstatic meeting." I have certainly loved you and lost you, but we will love each other and never lose each other again—some distant, unknown day.

There it is—12:25 p.m.

I sat in a restaurant yesterday afternoon in Indianapolis waiting for your Aunt Bailey to be done with her acting classes for the day, and I caught up on issues of <u>Our Daily Bread</u>, dog-earing devotions which spoke to the state of my heart—if numb is a state.

I read about counterfeit bills and the deception of our hearts. I read Jeremiah 17: 5-11 and recognized myself, making flesh my strength, departing from the Lord, inhabiting the parched places in the wilderness. I have no trust in the Lord. My hope does not abide with Him.

I have made no effort to be a shrub in the desert; I have allowed my spiritual desolation to occur.

I also read about defragmenting a computer, pulling together scattered pieces of information into a whole. The various parts of my life are, indeed, fragmented. Demands *from every direction bombard me, overwhelm me. Like the words of the devotion, "my mind won't stop and my body won't start. Soon I begin to feel weary and useless."*

Like David in Psalm 55: 1-8, my heart is severely pained within me. I am restless in my complaint. I cry out—and cried out—to God to hear my supplication, to give ear to my prayer. I feel, like David, betrayed by so much that I should have been able to rely on. And still, years later, I have few answers and even less wisdom. I would have thought that, by now, I would be more at peace, but I am farther adrift than ever.

Reagan, if there were ever a time I needed a sign from you, it would be now, my sweet angel.

I don't much like who I am anymore. I loved myself the most when you loved me. I loved life the most when you were here.

7/30/11

Your Papa Gary called us yesterday to let us know that Ryan had been released from prison. We weren't prepared for the news as we were originally led to believe that it would happen sometime in January of 2012 and then in September of 2011. I don't know how to feel except that

I've come to learn that there is a difference between the law and justice.

Yesterday, as we drove from Gatlinburg back to Pigeon Forge, we were listening to the cast recording of <u>Little Women</u>. Your Aunt Bailey was just cast as Beth, the sister who dies in the story. Much of the show is about carrying on despite hardship and letting go despite loneliness, grief, and pain. The mother sings a song called "Days of Plenty," and when we heard the lyrics, Bailey, Da, and Papa all began to cry. Some of the words were:

> *I never dreamed of this sorrow,*
> *I never thought I'd have reason to lament,*
> *I hoped I'd never know heartbreak,*
> *How I wish I could change the way things went!*
> *I wanted nothing but goodness,*
> *I wanted reason to prevail,*
> *Not this bare emptiness.*
> *I wanted Days of Plenty.*

> *But I refused to feel tragic,*

[407]

I am aching for more than pain and grief.

There has got to be meaning,

Most of all when a life has been so brief.

I have got to learn something,

How can I give her any less?

I want life to go on.

I want Days of Plenty

You have to believe,

There is reason for hope.

You have to believe

That the answers will come.

You can't let this defeat you.

I won't less this defeat you.

You must fight to keep her there,

Within you!

So believe that she matters!

And believe that she always will!

She will always be with you!

She'll be part of the days you've yet to feel!

She will live in your bounty!

She will live as you carry on your life!

So carry on,
Full of hope,
She'll be there,
For all your Days of Plenty.

Funny how unexpectedly you fill a room, a van, our hearts.
Like you never really left us—really.

9/3/11

    I'm tidying up the den and the desktop piles. I once
again came across a note from Ann and Bud Yohnka from
Kankakee which included a donation and a poem by Robert
Browning. The first time I read it last month I cried, for the
first line reassures "If I forget, yet God remembers!"
    I want so much to believe that.

      If I forget, yet God remembers!
      If these hands of mine cease from their clinging,
      yet the hands divine hold me so firmly I cannot fall;

      And if sometimes I am too tired to call for Him to
      help me,
      then He reads the prayer unspoken in my heart

and lifts my care.

I dare not fear
since certainly I know that I am in God's keeping,
shielded so, from all that else would harm,
and in the hour of stern temptation,
strengthened by His power.
I tread no path in life to Him unknown.
I lift no burden, bear no pain alone:

My soul a calm, sure hiding-place has found:
the everlasting arms my life surround.
God, Thou art love! I build my faith on that.
I know Thee who has kept my path,
and made light for me in the darkness, tempering
sorrow
so that it reached me like a solemn joy;

It were too strange that I should doubt Thy love.

10/7/11

For most of the month of September, your Aunt Bailey
was appearing in a musical called <u>Little Women</u> *at Myers*

Dinner Theatre in nearby Hillsboro, Indiana. Your papa became very attached to the company, the score, and the characters. I was also touched very deeply by the story, especially by the loss of Beth.

One day, while in the library at school, I found a copy of the novel by Louisa May Alcott and read the chapter about Beth's death entitled, "The Valley of the Shadow." I don't think I've ever read a more painful and yet peaceful description of what it's like to lose the one person to whom you are closest, "one only gone before."

I've included here the pages that affected me the most.

I usually get sad when a play which I have been in or have directed comes to an end. Seeing Little Women end its month-long run brought similar feelings. I think it was mostly because I could not separate Beth's loss from your own. And though a frail Beth pleads with her older sister Jo to let her go, I still find letting you go difficult, even impossible.

I've also included lyrics from Jo and Beth's song "Some Things Are Meant to Be."

Though I am far from you, I have so many memories to sustain me. Like the two sisters sing as the tide turns endlessly at the seashore, we lived for loving each other.

You were mine and I yours. That bond, unbroken by years or death, remains.

[Jo: (spoken) When you were first born, not an hour old, I told Marmee...

Beth: (spoken) Beth is mine!

Jo: (spoken) Everyone has someone special in the world, and I have you; my sweet Beth. Give me a task to do.

Beth: Let's pretend we're riding on a kite. Let's imagine we're flying through the air!

Jo: We'll ascend until we're out of sight. Light as paper, we'll soar!

Beth: Let's be wild, up high above the sand, feel the wind, the world at our command.

Let's enjoy the view, and never land.

Jo: Floating far from the shore.

Beth: Some things are meant to be, the clouds moving fast and free.

Jo: The sun on a silver sea.

Both: A sky that's bright and blue.

Beth: And some things will never end.

Jo: The thrill of our magic ride.

Beth: The love that I feel inside for you.

Jo: We'll climb high beyond the break of day.

Beth: Sleep on stardust, and dine on bits of moon

Jo: You and I will find the Milky Way.

Both: We'll be mad, and explore.

We'll recline aloft upon the breeze.

Dart about, sail on with windy ease.

Pass the days doing only as we please, that's what living is for.

Beth: Some things are meant to be, the tide turning endlessly,

the way it takes hold of me, no matter what I do,

and some things will never die, the promise of who you are,

the memories when I am far from you.

All my life, I've lived for loving you; let me go now.]

10/23/11

Your Aunt Blythe posted the following on facebook this morning: "I just looked out the backdoor window to check on the girls playing with the dog, and there was a butterfly...a single butterfly around them. It almost looked like it was playing chase too. We'll never forget you R. E. W.

Uncle Shane's sister, Jessica, commented: "I saw a random Monarch butterfly yesterday and I thought of her too."

On an emotional weekend when we're performing Sweeney Todd, and certainly thinking about you because of the story, this was a validation of you and our connection.

You were "Beautiful" and "virtuous" and I was so "naïve."

11/10/11

Last night, I had a dream about you—only the second since losing you.

Somehow I found a way to travel back in time and warn family members about what would happen on July 2, 2006. For some reason, though, I was invisible and could only communicate by whispering to them. Even then, my words were not heard but were merely strong mental suggestions, like Billy Bigelow speaking to Julie and to their daughter in Carousel.

This all happened in the corner of a restaurant or diner as the family gathered around a table. My pleas were so emphatic and persistent that some people got tired of the warnings.

For some inexplicable reason, Ryan was there, and when he smiled at me, I beat his face in, pummeling and pounding. Again and again. I was able to do to him what I could not in real life. As far as I can recall, that was when the dream ended. I don't think you were even in the dream, but it was about you—about a slim chance of changing the course of events so that you'd be with us still.

I think I had to wake myself up because I sensed that Ryan was determined to hurt you despite my attempts to destroy him. I could not face the inevitable.

It's the middle of November now. Thanksgiving is two weeks away. The days are shorter, the nights longer, the darkness lingering, and I pull in, the depression very real, hitting me very suddenly. The ground opens up without warning, I work to catch my breath, and tears fill my eyes.

The inevitable is that it happened. There is no time travel or wormhole or portal. We must wait—season after season, year after year—until we are united once more.

12/24/11

Christmas Eve and the family—along with Julia—is beginning to gather. I made the afternoon pilgrimage to the cemetery, sat on the new bench under the barren tree, and read two Dora books to you, inviting you to sit beside me. This evening, around 10 or so, I'll return—for the sixth Christmas without you.

Your story has continued to touch people's lives, creating new relationships, making new connections and new friends. Most recently it was with some cast members of the Indiana Repertory Theatre's production of <u>A Christmas Carol</u>—specifically, Constance Macy and Ryan Artzberger (both instructors of Bailey's last summer) along with Matthew Brumlow, Minita Gandhi, and Rob and Jennifer Johansen. I saw <u>A Christmas Carol</u> earlier in December and was so touched by the production that I wrote a facebook message to Constance, telling her about you and my Christmas Eve rituals. She wrote back, telling me about how her son was just a few weeks older than you and how my message affected her and the cast. It was, of course, scenes involving the Cratchit family and the death of Tiny Tim that meant the most to me—and brought tears of recognition to my eyes.

I took Bailey back to the production this past Wednesday, and we were able to visit with the cast in the Green Room.

Unexpectedly, I received a simple but important gift from Constance. Rob, as Bob Cratchit, sings a small bit of a song to Tiny Tim. In it, he says the name "Papa," and I couldn't help but take special notice. Rob explained where the song came from, then Constance pulled out a page from her script and gave it to me. I've enclosed it here.

[Hush thee, princeling, little child of heaven,
Papa's lullabye is the only sound.
Night is falling over the sheep and shepherds;
Hush thee darling, love enfolds thee round]

Like the Cratchits, we miss you, the first one to part from us, but the memories we have of you make us "very happy."

Now to another Christmas Eve dinner and numerous glances at your empty wooden rocking chair.

3/27/12

The seasons change. Time goes by so quickly. The last time I wrote to you we were immersed in the Christmas season; now it is nearly Easter.

There have been no major events, just little things that have happened to us in these last months. Kind of like the mild winter we had. No snow storms; hardly any snow for that matter. Record-breaking temperatures made for a perpetual November or March, and March has been like June.

Da, Mallory, Bailey, your daddy, and I were involved in a musical, the last production on my Bucket List, which means that I've been fortunate to realize many dreams and creative visions, but also that my time in the spotlight is coming to an end! Bailey is in two shows right now, one that will be raising funds for Reagan's Rescue. Flyn is also in a show, so the Williams family credits keep adding up.

Your daddy is looking to return to Colorado. He needs to get out of Danville. He needs to find his way.

Da and I went to Indianapolis a few weeks ago to see the medium John Edward. I doubted that we would be able to get a reading as there were hundreds there probably hoping the same. We met up with our friends Jeanne and Sonnia so the experience meant that much more to us. We left the room with a sense of peace, but Da and I were both disappointed, too—to be so close to our loved ones who have left but still not have the validation. Each month we will get to watch a live show on the Internet, hoping and praying for a reading then.

I had a speaking engagement in early March and others coming up this spring and fall. Da and I are going to

Boston for another SBS conference. The 6th annual Reagan
Williams Memorial Track Invitational was held at the high
school this past Saturday. Another Reading Rock-a-thon is
coming up at North Ridge.

That is what I mean by little things, Sunshine. More of
the same, a little less grief perhaps.

Oh, the ducks are from a band we had to wear to get
into the John Edward event. The card is from Julia, our
dear friend, who supplied us with a bag of goodies for the
trip.

[The card said:

Dear Greg & Marsha,

Safe travels today! And just keep breathing. I'd be a
nervous wreck! No road trip with my mom was ever
complete without these essentials. Can't wait to hear all
about your adventure!

Love,
Julia]

4/7/12

 *It is the day before Easter. While I sit on the front
porch, I hear the sounds of Aunt Mal, Aunt Bailey, your
daddy, Aubrey, and Ainsley coloring eggs at the dining
room table. Occasionally, Da will be heard giving
directions from the kitchen as she finished cleaning up from
the best attempt she could make at a holiday meal. Truly,
celebrating Easter resurrection has not been a priority for
many years. We rarely walk into a church. We rarely think
about organized religion let alone faith. We still go
through some of the holiday rituals—I know I've continued
to describe them to you—but some holidays are not and
may never be the same.*

 You should be sitting at the table coloring eggs, too.

If I could only know that your spirit is here beside us, sharing in this Easter tradition, I might be able to bear it, might be able to enjoy the two granddaughters that are dipping eggs and singing pop tunes with their aunts and uncle.

Sometimes the quality of my life comes down to that hard fact, especially on holidays with traditions meant for children. For all children.

7/2/12

As I drove to the cemetery today, I passed restaurants and gas stations and stores and banks all filled with people and activity indicating that life, indeed, goes on for everyone else. But not for me.

I live life. I get through it. I cope. Six years later, however, I haven't gotten on. Maybe I don't want to. Maybe I can't. But I'm stuck at July 2, 2006.

I think I have only felt fully alive when I've performed in a musical or when I've cried for you. With the first, I have inhabited someone else's life, fully focused, fully committed to being that character for the audience and for me. With the second, I've given in fully to the sorrow still welled up inside. The two experiences are extremes, polar opposites.

Everything in between is always muddled to some degree.

As I've worked on transcribing journal entries for the book I hope to complete one day, I have come across a lot of forgotten wisdom...

It's 12:25 p.m. Six years to the day and time. Another year has come and gone.

Yes, a lot of forgotten wisdom. Most importantly is the reminder to talk to our loved one who has left, to celebrate the good memories, and I haven't done enough of that.

So, on this day, when we've organized a supply drive for the YFRC Women's Shelter, and when it is miserably hot and uncomfortable, I'm going to end this entry and ask you, my Sunshine, to climb up on my lap and help me be happy and a little less selfish.

Do you remember...

7/20/12

We are on vacation in the Denver area, and we awoke this morning to a senseless, horrific shooting at a showing of The Dark Knight Rises in an Aurora, Colorado, movie theater.

Da, Aunt Bailey, Aubrey, Great Aunt Heather, and cousin Hollyn, and I visited the Columbine High School Memorial. We read, through tears, written sketches of the thirteen victims, and I found this scripture passage from I John 4: 4—

> *"You, dear children, are from God and have overcome them, because the one who is in you is greater than the one who is in the world."*

I left a Reagan's Rescue business card in a chink in the wall of the memorial. I felt very close to you while on that hill.

7/22/12

My Dora tattoo is on my right upper arm. Yesterday, at Bolder Ink in Boulder, Colorado, I got a second tattoo, this time on my left calf, of the four Marx Brothers, my favorite comedy team.

I arranged this through the Internet and discovered a talented artist named Dave Regan (I was struck by his name which led me to believe that this was meant to be, just like JR in Pigeon Forge).

I explained to Dave that, when we lost you, I lost my joy, and how the Marx Brothers made me laugh—how their sense of anarchy, the verbal puns, the physical humor, their musicianship all appealed to me and brought laughter.

Dave said that he knew pain and loss but nothing so difficult as the loss of a child. He went on to say that the hardships we encounter form who we are, who we become, and that, without them, we could not grow or enjoy the good things to come. It made me think of the places we've traveled and the people we've met while doing advocacy work. It made me think of meeting Karolyn Grimes and the members of Girlyman and JR and, now, Dave.

We can't go back, so we must go forward in hope. I saw yesterday's tattoo adventure as a turning point for me, a positive sign that I need to move on in joy. It won't be easy, but I believe I must continue in this new direction having turned a painful, blessed, and joyful corner.

7/26/12

We left Colorado for home today, leaving your daddy behind at Snow Mountain Ranch where he's been working for the last two months. He is happy, or says that he is, and I am proud of how he is doing. Saying goodbye last night was difficult. He is 27 ("born in the summer of his 27th year," he keeps quoting), but he is still our boy. We are apart, and we miss him.

He related a story that made us cry. Weeks ago when he heard about the suicide of a young man from our neighborhood, he broke down in tears but had no one to talk to until an older staff member saw that he was upset and hugged him close. Da and I both hurt for him and hope that he will find friends who will hold him when he needs comforting.

You never went to Colorado, but you were certainly present during our trip—when your daddy and I climbed Snow Mountain together (huffing and puffing and sweating) to find an important tree I carved years ago for Da; when I shared your story with Chaplain Steve Peterson who understood why I have had such a strained and complicated relationship with God; when Da and I renewed our wedding vows at Columbine Point—your daddy beside us—and celebrated a 30 year marriage that has endured difficulties and known bliss; when we visited a makeshift shrine at a corner in Aurora, Colorado, for victims of a terrible mass murder and violent rampage a week ago at a movie theater in that Denver suburb (I left a business card at the site).

I have followed that last story since waking up to the breaking news last Friday, mostly in <u>The Denver Post.</u>

Today, a survivor of the Columbine High School massacre wrote a guest commentary in the paper encouraging those involved in the Aurora shooting to believe that things will get better one day and not to lose hope. The four pieces of advice she gave were these:

1. *Talk and give others the opportunity to listen.*
2. *Find gratitude.*
3. *Never give up.*
4. *Reach out and love.*

Liz Carlston, an author of the book <u>Surviving Columbine: How Faith Helps Us Heal When Tragedy Strikes</u>, writes what I have come to know, what we have striven to do both personally and, through Reagan's Rescue, professionally, and what I hope your daddy will come to believe, if he still has doubts.

I want some more time with my son. I want to hug him again.

8/13/12

Yesterday, a piece entitled "Perspectives on God Arise in Tragedy's Wake" appeared in <u>The Denver Post</u>. Writer Electra Draper begins:

> *For almost every person who believes God protects you in your darkest hours—even interfering with a bullet's path—there is another who wonders if it's not only delusional but even offensive to think God personally intervenes to spare one innocent but not another.*

This has been my dilemma from the beginning, especially because we prayed for your safety for months before you died. Why didn't God spare you?

Draper says that evil "acts on faith, sometimes stripping it away but more often…deepening what one already believes about God and a divine role in tragedy."

A survivor of the Aurora shooting contends that he perceived the mass murderer as "an evil presence" who stopped shooting when God arrived.

"God jammed his gun, many have since asserted. Yet a skeptic would ask why God arrived late."

So, do those touched directly by the shootings in Aurora and the Wisconsin Sikh temple, and do we in losing you, accept God's will with grace, thankful for the time we all had with our loved ones?

Draper offers four popular views of God:

1. *Authoritative God who can be loving but also judgmental and punishing (perhaps piloting a tornado or hurricane).*

2. *Benevolent God who is always involved by inspiring, directing, or even physically saving his children, and who doesn't cause disasters but allows some to happen while preventing others.*

3. *Distant God who created the world but doesn't get involved with daily minutiae.*

4. *Critical God who judges souls in the afterlife but plays no active part in causing cataclysms.*

And who's to blame for Aurora, Draper wonders. Responses from readers have included: God, Satan, us (free will), no God, the victims, the perpetrator, mental illness, evil, a result of sins, it just happened.

One idea that I came away with is this: "The enemy meant it for evil, but God will make it for good."

10/1/12

The Twelfth International Conference on Shaken Baby Syndrome came to a close today in Boston. For the third time, your story was shared with people from around the world in our workshop entitled "One Small Candle: Creating an SBS Advocacy Group." This presentation was streamlined for 30 minutes even though we were able to run over because of a speaker cancellation right after us. We conducted our workshop on Saturday, September 29. We met people at different places on their post-SBS journey, and your story touched them.

This afternoon, we took advantage of the sunny weather and mild temperatures to walk through downtown Boston. In the beautiful Public Gardens, we came across the Make Way for Ducklings sculpture honoring the classic children's book and author Robert McCloskey. I couldn't help but think about you and your books and childhood innocence and stories of peril which work out okay in the end.

Da and I head home tomorrow to see your daddy. We're ready to get back to a normal routine.

10/7/12

What normal routine? Almost a week later, and I realize how special and surprising these past few days have been.

I was the keynote speaker at a Vermilion County CAPIT conference on Thursday morning. One of Da's former colleagues at North Ridge, Lauren Whittingham, agreed to watch my class for the morning so I could share our story. CAPIT stands for Child Abuse Prevention, Intervention, and Treatment. It is a coalition of social and child welfare agencies and organizations; the first large gathering was Thursday. It has been a dream of mine for two years now (since the day after we returned from the SBS conference in Atlanta) to create such a coalition whose purpose is to share vital information regarding children-at-risk in order to decrease the number of children who might otherwise fall through the cracks. My speech was well-received. Various people told me later that it put a human face—your face—on what they do. You make such a difference.

Yesterday morning, I manned a table at the Village Mall for what was called the first annual Peace in the Home Domestic Violence awareness fair. Again, I got to tell your story. One woman was so moved that she wants to help us with fundraising.

Another, a domestic violence survivor (and a speaker later on Thursday at the CAPIT coalition conference) told me that all during her two and a half hour drive home she could feel your presence. It gave her peace, and it made her smile.

This evening I was looking up some information on Nathaniel Hawthorne, and I found a quote that reminds me again of how to connect with you: "Happiness is a butterfly which, when pursued, is always just beyond your grasp but which, if you sit down quietly, may alight on you."

The happiness that filled the domestic violence survivor's car is the happiness that now fills my heart.

When you take the u out of mourning, it's a brand new day!—John Edward

I posted this on John Edward's facebook page after copying the Hawthorne quote:

My granddaughter loved butterflies. I miss her terribly. But when I am not busy pursuing her spirit, then she manages to visit me, bringing happiness on her wings.

10/21/12

Sunday—

Today is Aunt Bailey's 16th birthday. While the rest of the family (and Julia) gathered at our house for brunch followed by pumpkin carving, I attended Great Grandpa Jim's church, delivering a speech about Reagan's Rescue and our six year journey. I don't like turning down a speaking engagement or a chance to talk about you.

It wasn't a sermon because I am no expert on faith. If anything I am a disappointment in that area. I did find some scripture passages about suffering (2 Corinthians 1: 3-7) and works or deeds (James 2: 14-24). I also suggested a couple of hymns—"Blest Be the Tie That Binds" and "O Master Let Me Walk with Thee." Great Grandpa Jim chose a third song—"Hymn of Promise."

While singing "O Master Let Me Walk with Thee,' I was struck by the fourth and final verse which began:

In hope that sends a shining ray

Far down the future's broadening way…

Many family members called you Ray or Ray Ray. We all thought of you as our Sunshine, our ray of light now gone on ahead of us. You give us so much hope, so much illumination, and you bring hope to others. So powerful a little girl and a cause.

Last night, Bailey was convinced that you made your presence known when her clock radio—normally untouched and forgotten on her shelf—suddenly came on while she and her boyfriend, Ryan, were talking about college plans. And the song, by Bruno Mars, which was heard dealt with going to college. Was that you, or someone else in the family? We're all having a difficult time putting it down to simple coincidence.

I guess we all need guidance, whether it comes from God or a kind spirit of one no longer with us on this earth.

> *Help me the slow of heart to move*
> *By some clear, winning word of love.*

and

> *Help me bear the strain of toil, the fret of care.*

12/1/12

Your daddy and mommy's friend, Cortney, sent this facebook message on November 30:

> *Was able to witness the impact sweet baby Reagan has made on our community. Tonight, I took a former client to dinner and noticed a purple and pink bracelet. When I asked her if she knew what it was, she told me. I*

felt about a million different emotions and told her thank you for wearing it.

12/17/12

Last Friday, December 14, and your Aunt Blythe's 30th birthday, there was a school shooting in Newtown, Connecticut. Twenty children, ages 6 and 7, all first graders were slain, along with six adults from the school (including the principal and the school psychologist). The shooter had killed his mother earlier that morning. He later took his own life.

I watched the news reports most of the weekend and into today. I watched as a teacher concerned with school security. I wondered if, faced with a similar scenario, I would react with composure some of the teachers exhibited. I wondered, too, if I would face the danger with courage like those staff members who lost their lives.

I also watched as a grieving grandfather who lost the light of his life to violence. One story, in particular, brought back the painful memory of that Sunday in July. After all the children were reunited with their anxious parents at a nearby fire station, there came a moment when an official had to face the remaining parents and tell them that no more children were coming out. An eyewitness described the sound of anguished wailing that went up in the room. I remember my sisters making that sound.

How my heart breaks for those Sandy Hook Elementary School families.

More angels lost—

Like every holiday season, I brought out the Christmas album recorded by the Danville High School Choral Department in 1976. One certain song, Natalie Sleeth's "Baby, What You Goin' to Be?" was always a group favorite and remains, to this day, a nostalgic and evocative track. I don't know why the song created such an overwhelming emotional response in me in December of 2012, but, one night, as I listened to it play while waiting in a parking lot for Grandma Marsha to get done shopping, I was overcome with sobbing. The soaring melody and some of the lyrics made me think not of the Babe in Bethlehem but the baby I was missing. "Did you come to light our way?" the composer asks and my high school friends passionately sing. "Will you save the world one day?" had been the whole point behind the "Rescue" in Reagan's Rescue. Many Christmas songs rank very high on my favorites list, this one certainly among them.

Here are the complete lyrics:

Baby, lying in a manger, slumbering so sweetly,
Whatcha gonna be?
Baby all the world is watchin', all the world awaits
to see
What will you be?
Baby, sleeping in a stable, underneath the heavens,
Whatcha gonna say?
Baby, did you bring the Good News?
Did you come to light our way?

Oh, look, see the cattle asleep, see the shepherds
beside,
See the Wise Men, they bow unto you.
Are you the one who was meant to be Master?
To bring in the Kingdom too?
Alleluia Baby, Hope of all the people,
What you come here to do?
What you come to say?
Baby, can you be the Savior?
Come to save the world one day?
Baby, can you be the Savior?
Come to save the world one day?

Baby, lying in a manger,

Will you save the world one day?

12/24/12

I'm sitting on the bench in the Garden of Innocence on a bitterly cold and windy Christmas Eve morning. Another year has come and gone. Da is home preparing dinner. She'll come visit you later. And I will be back tonight to share a few moments of peace with you.

Our lives change, sometimes sadly and sometimes happily. Great Grandpa Earl passed away yesterday morning. We will miss him for he was a good and gentle man. He loved you so, and I hope that he will be spending this Christmas with his son, Ron, who died in September, and with you.

In the spring, we have two new babies on the way, both boys we think. Aunt Mallory and Aunt Blythe are expecting, so you will have two new cousins to watch over.

Your grave blanket is decorated the way you would like it—with pink and purple and with stuffed toys from Papa Gary and Da Becky. There's Dora and Swiper and Boots, Blue and Baby Jaguar.

Merry Christmas, Sunshine.

1/5/13

Today would have been your 9th birthday. It is not a milestone like 13 or 18 or 21 or even 1 or 5, but, because you are not with us, it is a day to celebrate and also a time to shed a tear. Each January 5 will be important.

Da, Flyn, Mal, and I went to Sunset Memorial Park and released 10 balloons—9 for you in pink and 1 white balloon for a week old boy who was shaken on Christmas and who survives but remains hospitalized in Urbana.

Later in the day we found out that your daddy and some of his co-workers at Snow Mountain Ranch released 9 pink balloons, too. How his friends support him—especially a girl named Dani whom we met last summer on a trip to Colorado. So floating up in the sky today were 18 pink balloons—all for our Sunshine.

The well wishes, the prayers, the love that have come our way today suggest that you mattered and that you continue to matter. My friend, Scott Zercher, sent a message to me on facebook that he looks at the Reagan Bear and a photo of you every day to remind him to tell his children how much he loves them. He added, "Reagan used to light up the room at church every Sunday. I miss seeing her too."

Another friend, Patsy Jones, said you were "indeed a little beam of sunshine!"

During these past years I've often wondered whether we matter to God. The psalmist asks, "What is man that You are mindful of him?" This is a question I will probably continue to ask. I know the Bible provides its answers. Isaiah 49 quotes the Lord as promising, "In an acceptable time I have heard you, and in the day of salvation I have helped you; I will preserve you..." And later, "See, I have inscribed you on the palms of My hands; your walls are continually before Me."

Still, and I can't figure this out, why, if you mattered, if we mattered, didn't God save you?

I'm sorry to bring lingering grief into what should be a day of celebration. We cry for what should have been. We cry for ourselves because we miss you. We rejoice in the life you had. It's hard to believe that six and a half years have gone by because you are ever present, always 2 ½, always lighting up a room, always bringing us joy.

10 Beware that you don't look down on any of these little ones. For I tell you that in heaven their angels are always in the presence of my heavenly Father.--Matthew 18: 10 (NLT)

3/17/13

2013 has brought with it a number of opportunities to share your story and to spread SBS awareness. Each time I get a chance to speak, I am more and more convinced that you are very much alive in the work we do and very powerful in your influence. I am so proud to be your grandfather.

Da and I spoke before a mothers' group at the Center for Children's Services, sharing information on SBS and tips on how to handle crying. We are working with the CAPIT coalition on a newspaper insert for April and Child Abuse Prevention Month. I spoke to a group in Monticello about our family's journey through the many systems in our society—medical, law enforcement, legal, social services, politics, and the media. I get to repeat that presentation in early April for a group in Peoria. And the Danville

Firefighters have invited us to be a part of their Poker Run fundraiser. Just when I think we've exhausted all projects, the phone rings with a new opportunity.

On Thursday, March 14, your cousin, Rowan James Bailey, was born. The last time we were up there was on a special night in January of 2004. I asked your daddy if this was difficult for him, and he wisely answered, "Maybe a little. But that was a happy day." And it was. It certainly was.

All these years later, and through all the changes we have endured, you are still a daily part of our lives—for me, sometimes more real than what is before my eyes.

Watch over us, Little Angel. Especially guard your little cousin, Rowan.

3/29/13

I came across a garden stone outside a store in Nashville, Indiana, today. It read:

> *In the quiet stillness of the night, if the hurt gets really bad, close your eyes and know I'm there and I hold your hand.*

—Flavia

The stone was in the shape of a heart and had the image of a beautiful angel on it. For an instant, I heard—no, felt—your voice.

This evening the film Signs was playing on television. Its debate between people who see signs and those who only see coincidences made me once again question my faith—what little faith I have left—like the minister played by Mel Gibson. He says there will be no more prayers. He is so tormented, so torn. I know that man. I am him.

And I know that soon I must make a move. I must embrace some belief system again.

4/7/13

I went back to church today. It was not at the invitation of anyone. It was at the prompting of my heart.

[A piece of paper folded in half was placed next to this entry with a quote from Herman Melville. It read: "There is a wisdom that is woe; but there is a woe that is madness. And there is a Catskill eagle in some souls that can alike dive down into the blackest gorges, and soar out of them again and become invisible in the sunny spaces. And even if he for ever flies within the gorge, that gorge is in the

[442]

mountains; so that even in his lowest swoop the mountain eagle is still higher than other birds upon the plain, even though they soar."]

This passage from <u>Moby Dick</u> contained words that, I am sure, caught my attention at the time—eagle, soar, mountains, wisdom, woe, sunny. We took on a lot when we created Reagan's Rescue, extra responsibilities on top of the burden of grief. I think it is fair to say, though, that, even in our darkest days, even in defeat or disappointment, our commitment enables us to fly higher than those who might just as well have given up and embraced the misery without the ministry.

5/2/13

This evening, while pondering the question, "Are there just coincidences, or do things sometimes work out because of a higher power?", as soon as I fashioned the question in my head, I looked up to see two deer walking through Springhill Cemetery. Was it a coincidence or a connection to other pleas, other deer, and other answers?

In this last month, I've attended the Unitarian Universalist Church of Urbana-Champaign. It has brought me peace. It has given me hope. It has prompted questions of doubt and faith.

If two people have cancer, and prayers go up for both, why are the explanations so feeble if the outcome is different for the two patients? If one is cured, we praise God for answering prayer. If one dies, it must have been God's will or God's plan, but we are not to understand it because He works in mysterious ways, those ways past finding out. That's the line I've always heard and ignorantly believed. I don't know if it is enough anymore.

I believe in a Creator, but I increasingly doubt His direct intervention in human affairs. Really, don't opposing football teams both pray for victory, the winner praising God and giving Him the glory while the loser is unworthy of the win?

I ask questions of this explanation, this system, because my prayers for your safety went unanswered. Calling your loss a "mystery" and being expected to take comfort in that doesn't work for me anymore. Were Ryan's prayers, or those of his family, answered when he got a short prison sentence and served an even shorter length of time? Were we supposed to buy into some grand scheme, and happily at that, while overlooking the bitter disappointment, shock, and humiliation even?

I ask these questions because I don't know. Are the deer, the butterflies, the toys that turn on unexpectedly signs or coincidences?

Today, perhaps coincidentally, the newsletter arrived from the UUCUC and in it this line from a song in the church's hymnal: "Even to question, truly, is an answer."

Rev. Gehrmann goes on to say: "Asking good questions is a powerful tool for anyone seeking to gain greater understanding. On Sunday mornings we gather to grapple with questions of meaning and purpose, of right and wrong. We ponder timeless questions about God and life and death, and timely questions about current events in the week's news."

Is there the Truth (with a capital T) or a perpetual search for new insight and relevant, emerging truths (with a small t)?

5/19/13

Your daddy left early this morning for Colorado—his third trip out west to work at Snow Mountain Ranch. Accompanying him was Dani, his girlfriend, who flew out this past Wednesday to meet the family before returning with him. We have great hopes for her—for them.

[445]

The first time he went, so soon after you died, was, in hindsight, probably a mistake. Last May, "the summer of his twenty-seventh year" as the song says, we thought this would be the beginning of a new chapter, a positive change, purpose. I didn't count on him missing his friends so much or wanting to be around family. He came back in October for a wedding, in December for Great Grandpa Earl's funeral, and finally, in February for—well, I'm not sure what.

The agreement was that he come back with a plan, including a job and a place to live. Neither panned out. He did end up working a couple of places for a few weeks, but he blew through what money he had and eventually regretted coming back, I think. Maybe you can't go home again.

Grandma Marsha and I tried to make him feel welcome, be he also knew that we were disappointed. Still, we love him. He is our boy. He suffered an unthinkable loss when you were taken from him. Knowing how much to forgive and how much to forget and how much to push and encourage—well, that's not easy.

I encouraged him to "lean forward" toward the future. That's how Jack Kerouac put it—"lean forward" toward the next great adventure. Fulfillment. The chance to be happy.

He will always have parents who love him, but he needs to find his own home, that place where his heart resides.

6/16/13

Father's Day, again, and a part of me always wants to send a card to your daddy. I know this is a difficult day for him. Here's what he posted on facebook:

Had my little girl never left this world and me, I wonder what type of father I would be. Would I be generous and giving like my Grandpa Jim? Would my daughter look up to me as if I were the king of the world just like my brother, Shane's kids do him? Would I teach her how to fish and love the outdoors like J. J. Bailey will do with his little boy? Would I be so unconditionally caring and worried to the point of sleep deprivation like my father, Greg Williams, is with all of his kids? I'm surrounded by so many great fathers. If she were still here, I hope I would have become half the father that these men are. Happy Father's Day everyone.

[447]

7/2/13

It seems such a short time ago that I lay down on the cold ground beside your grave on Christmas Eve. Now it is summer (although the cool, welcome temperature belies that), and I sit here on your bench watching the time and waiting for one moment to remember a terrible thing. July always begins that way—with this awful memory—but this year July will mean spreading awareness and hope and even celebrating our accomplishments.

Tonight, I speak at an Altrusa meeting. Next week, we're on the radio and in Bloomington and back in Danville for the Poker Run fundraiser. Finally, we go to Peoria to be honored as heroes for the work we've done, the work we'll continue to do.

June was a crazy month of activity, soliciting donations for the July 13 charity event. A lot of phone calls and running around town. When I've felt like quitting, I've thought of you, and you have kept me going. That's how powerful you are.

I describe you as forever 2 ½, but I wonder what you would have looked like. I imagine you in charge of your four cousins and probably arguing with Aubrey from time to time.

I still wish for a glimpse of you—2 ½, 9 child, angel, light, smile, whatever.

12:25 p.m. Seven years. Seven years.

And gray skies today, too. And, like the song, and despite those seven years, you make me happy.

1/6/14

Yesterday would have been your 10th birthday, and a busy, wonderful, scary, unpredictable day it was, one of those days when, in the morning, you can't predict what the evening will bring.

Our main objective was the same for any January 5th— taking down the Christmas decorations and visiting your grave to let off balloons.

Snow was falling making the streets increasingly hazardous. Your grandma and I drove to County Market to get balloons (which weren't ready). We ran into a co-worker of Aunt Flyn's who said that she was talking to people about suicide and that she had left for lunch but probably wouldn't come back. Although she's been diagnosed as bipolar, she still has never dealt directly with your loss. I think your birthday yesterday was hard on her.

She puts on a positive front, but she's very sensitive and fragile inside.

In near blizzard conditions we released ten pink balloons, some with messages, into the snowy sky. They sailed toward the south and quickly disappeared out of sight. Your daddy, his girlfriend Dani, and Aunt Bailey were with us. No time for tears—they would have frozen— but it was a bittersweet moment. At least we were together.

After braving conditions (and barely distinguishable roads), we drove to Menards for some supplies then came home to start undecorating.

Soon, however, Aunt Mal called saying that Flyn was sitting outside in the snow and was wailing.

We realized that she needed to go to the Emergency Room after hearing her talk about how stupid she was, how difficult it was to live anymore, how she couldn't put up with Mal's messy house or Grandma Marsha's negativity or your daddy's selfishness. She was emotionally out of control.

I drove her to the hospital (Grandma "couldn't" go because it was a Sunday and the ER, and she still deals with that day in July when she lost you).

They took Flyn back to check her out, and I left to come back home. I called the nurse later to say how worried I

[450]

was that Flyn would leave the hospital, go out into the brutally cold night, and die from exposure (I knew an elderly gentleman who chose to do that after his wife died). She said not to worry, that Flyn wasn't going anywhere.

A couple of hours later, though, Flyn called to have me check her out and take her home. I felt a little manipulated by the hospital and by Flyn herself but I complied. By now the temperatures had plummeted.

All of this happened on a day already emotionally charged because of you and your birthday.

So many people commented on pictures I posted yesterday (1st and 2nd birthdays, the last Easter) as well as photos Dani took of the family on Saturday. You were there, my Angel, in our hearts and in the wristbands we wore. You will always be there—in the ornaments, in the rocking chair, in the photos, in the rituals, on every Christmas Eve, and Twelfth Night, in every balloon that rises into the sky, in every tear we shed, in every smile as we remember the good times.

Happy 10th birthday, Sunshine.

1/8/14

*For some time now—a couple of years probably—
Grandma has been encouraging me to go through your toys
and find some use for them. Toys are meant to be played
with by children, and I have left them untouched as a shrine
to you or a time capsule. Yesterday, we pulled out a toy
box and two totes filled with books, clothes, and toys. As
soon as I opened the lid to the toy box, I heard a voice
coming from the bottom of the box, some toy that came on
by itself even though the batteries should have died long
ago.*

*It was extremely difficult going through these
containers. Tears welled up in my eyes at first, and then I
began sobbing. After seven and a half years I would have
thought this task would be easier.*

*Now your toys are in the guest room waiting for your
cousins to enjoy. And so you will be a part of their
playtime and their happiness.*

4/27/14

*The weather is warmer, the porch decorated for spring,
and we find ourselves sitting outside more and more. That
means we think of you more, of painful memories of sitting*

on the porch and seeking answers to our questions. It also means crying comes more easily and without warning.

I sat out there tonight with my palms facing up hoping to feel your tiny hand slip into mine.

6/14/14

I sent this to your daddy today through facebook:

> *Ian, we received the box today. I haven't opened the card yet, but we did unpack the jars (with towels as an added bonus). Having burgers on the grill tonight, so I'll use the dill pickles. I'm assuming you two put them up. Father's Day is always kind of difficult for me because of you. First of all, please know that I am extremely proud of you. You are kind, witty, curious, and resilient. My difficulty is in knowing whether or not to wish you a Happy Father's Day. I realized this weekend that many facebook friends are posting pictures of their fathers who have passed away, some many years ago, but the bonds are still there and the influence and the love. I think it should*

work the other way, too. You were a wonderful daddy, and, though Reagan is gone in a form we can see, the bonds are still very much there. I'd like to hug you right now, but we'll have to wait on that for a little while. Take care. I love you. Dad

This was his reply:

You know, I think about that all the time. I still consider myself a father, and I will until I truly am one again, which I am starting to hope will be sooner rather than later. What I think about more though is the fact that while she was still here, I never had a good father's day. I got arrested on my first Father's Day, the second year I didn't even get to see her on Father's Day, and we spent the third Father's Day together, but that was also the last day I saw her alive. And I have come to terms with the fact that those first two years, it was my fault that they were bad ones. I can't wait to have a second chance to prove to myself as a great father, like you are. I hope you like the pickles. I'm not crazy about pickles, but I would devour these. I wish we were there. Hopefully we will see you soon! Love you!

[454]

7/2/14

Ritual—repeated patterns of meaningful behavior. Rituals usually bring us comfort as most are attached to joyous occasions or celebrations—birthdays, anniversaries, graduations, weddings, retirements, and so on. Some rituals are sad but necessary if those involved are to work through the sadness. Twice during the year I have scheduled visits which, though bittersweet, are tied to happy events—December 24 and January 5. Once a year I schedule a cemetery visit for a sad occasion—July 2, the anniversary of your death.

Some people I care about and who care about me may think today's tearful visit is silly or unnecessary. Not for me, though. I need this visit. I need this moment. I need to remember.

12:25 p.m. Eight years.

I take some comfort in the cool temperature—just 70 today—as the gentle wind and bird songs caress me. The shade under this large tree as I sit on your bench is friendly and protective. I hear a distant lawn mower, sometimes the whirr of traffic on Vermilion. But most of all I sense peace in this place and in this moment.

Getting here required planning. Flyn picked me up early from summer school. I dropped her off at home, grabbed this journal I already had sitting out, and made it here with ten minutes to spare. When I leave I must go back to the school to record grades.

Ritual is sometimes hard to schedule or bring off.

I'm also thinking for just a moment about your daddy, glad he has Dani to get him through this day.

All of this behavior—these thoughts, these tears, these songs sung and plans made—is meaning. When so much of life doesn't seem to have meaning, this visit does. Sometimes it is the only thing that has meaning for me.

I love you, Sunshine.

Later…

I received this facebook message from my friend and former colleague Sarah Durst:

> *My mother-in-law, who lost her mother a year ago today, posted this poem by Henry Van Dyke. I thought of you.*

> *I am standing upon the seashore. A ship, at my side, spreads her white sails to the moving breeze and starts for the blue ocean. She is an object of beauty and strength.*

I stand and watch her until, at length, she hangs like a speck of white cloud just where the sea and sky come to mingle with each other.

Then, someone at my side says, "There, she is gone."

Gone where?

Gone from my sight. That is all. She is just as large in mast, hull and spar as she was when she left my side. And, she is just as able to bear her load of living freight to her destined port.

Her diminished size is in me -- not in her.

And, just at the moment when someone says, "There, she is gone," there are other eyes watching her coming, and other voices ready to take up the glad shout, "Here she comes!"

And that is dying...

Thinking of you often, G!

It was difficult reading the last few paragraphs through the tears.

7/20/14

Two weeks ago, Daisy got her chain wrapped around a garden fairy statue on the patio. This fairy had been a gift from the Zerchers, a couple at Central Christian Church. Scott was the original drummer for the Praise band.

The statue was brought out each spring and stored away every fall, always in its place on the patio.

The damage was great—both wings broke off and the face as well. Luckily, I could glue the face back on for the break was clean. The wings, however, could not be reattached. So the fairy is now just a beautiful girl (with features similar to yours) who currently sits in the pet cemetery behind the garage.

Most traumatic, I guess, was that the statue joins the broken glass from the family photo and the broken angel from our mantel, three items which represented you. The damage, at least temporarily, was like losing our grip on you again.

8/4/14

Today, I caught up to myself, transcribing every journal entry through July of 2014. Now I start working on reflections and commentary for all these many entries, beginning with these words: "The name of this book is <u>Reagan's Rescue: A Grandfather's Journal, A Grandfather's Journey</u>."

Social Media

The opinions expressed by area residents regarding Reagan's death, the subsequent investigation, and the many legal maneuvers could fill up its own volume. Transcribing it all would have taken too long, shifting the focus of the book to an entirely different theme. Suffice it to say that, when a story becomes public, public opinion becomes part of the story. The ideas expressed were, I believe, sincere even if based on sometimes incorrect, highly filtered, and second or third hand sources. The website for the *Commercial-News* hosted an opinion page. Early posts were compassionate, but soon accusations began to fly. The now defunct All Around Danville Forum began in the spirit of civility, due, in part, to the levelheaded moderators who kept a vigilant eye. Soon, the tone turned accusatory and downright ugly.

This is a summary of some of the opinions that were expressed. They have been copied here as written.

On July 27, 2006, Benny from Illinois began a thread: "I feel bad for little Reagans grandparents. It is too bad they weren't given custody of that precious little girl before this happened."

Another poster, Justice for Reagan, wrote: "Now that the Ryan Katcher case is about closed [a missing person case in East Central Illinois which gained national attention], the authorities can concentrate on bringing justice to Reagan Williams the 2 ½ year old who was shaken to death earlier this month. An arrest has yet to be made and its highly unlikely that she shook herself to death."

Several hours later, christie, in all caps, opined: "AS TO WHAT I HEAR, THE MOTHER OF LITTLE REAGAN WILLIAMS IS LIVING BACK WITH THE BOYFRIEND WHO IS BEING LOOKED AT AS A SUSPECT IN THAT CASE, AS FAR AS IM CONCERNED SHE IS JUST AS GUILTY AS MURDERING THAT LITTLE GIRL, TO ME THAT IS LIKE SAYING WHAT HE DID WAS OK11ORCOULD IT BE MAYBE MOM GOT A LITTLE UPSET THAT DAY, THEY WERE THE ONLY 2 THERE...YOU DECIDE" For the record, Tracy had not lived with Ryan since the week of Reagan's death.

Lydia shared: "They both need to pay for what they did to that little angel"

Fred, from Tilton, suggested: "It never ceases to amaze me all the new names that pop up on here with opinions about people, and things that happen. If you're a new poster I say welcome to you. If you are posting an opinion, but don't want people to know who you are, I think you might consider leaving your comments in your own mind, and not posting them. Saying that, I do realize this world is full of sick, twisted, and sneaky individuals who feel they are 'being cool', saying nasty, hurtful, and cruel things to, and about other people. Really me......Fred"

Pammie Hoskins agreed: "Don't you all few we should leave the answers to the Mna upstairs? Making all these assumptions only causes hurt feelings for everyone. I'm sure we will find out what happened to Little Reagon soon."

Citizen wrote: "There is no hope for justice in this town or in this county, for that matter. Reagan's killer will never come to justice,…"

June C. added: "The little girl that was recently murdered deserves justice. Whoever was with her last seems most likely responsible. I think arrests should have been made by now."

L.P posted: "I must agree tho with the little girl from Tilton. What is going on. Just how many people where in the house that day. And her wonderful grandfather and the kind words he had for everyone including her Mother and her other grandparents. Please don't let this go unsolved."

Another writer, tilton resident, stated: "…the deal with reagon someone had said she moved back in and whatnot but yet you also said that he di it to her child , but little you know SHE was the only one on the home with her the day and night before by herself with the little girl…the child was supposably vomiting all night the night before she was pronounced dead…I was at tilton park for a mudd volleyball tourney when someone said the call was for a little girl not responding..people are so quick to think it was the step father , but fail to realize what the mother may have been capable of! Just because it's her child do you not think she was involved?I know the step father very well and he wouldnt do a thing to that little girl..just go back and look at the story on this in the archives and you will read that she has DCFS on her before , okay well that was BEFORE she had gotten with the"stepfather"…Please , don't let accusation make your mind for you , read up on your FACTS .Thanks !" Okay, Tilton reader, a few corrections: DCFS investigated Ryan and Tracy because of an incident that occurred when they were already living together as a couple but Ryan was watching Reagan; Ryan was not the stepfather; mud has one d. Get your facts straight before making accusations, even veiled ones.

Several weeks went by with no new developments.

In August, Sad wrote: "Reagan Williams. I am just trying to keep her name in the news. It has been 6 ½ weeks since she passed and very little movement in the investigation and I am afraid that someone has gotten away with murder. Please don't forget her and keep the Green and Williams families in your prayers."

My sister from Colorado, going by the name Lanie, shared: "Remembering Reagan…Continue to speak out to everyone about SBS death, get involved with the campaign to prevent this happening to other innocent children. Don't forget Reagan."

Heavy Heart added: "…thanks for remembering Reagan Williams, the shaken baby in Tilton. No arrest have been made and they have 2 suspects—the mother and her boyfriend. However, without a confession, they can't prove who did 'it' and no arrests have been made yet. This is very discouraging! I just don't want people to forget her."

Tilton Resident stated: "Just to let everyone know bout the case with Reagen. The news have made it sound so much worse then it really is." A child died. Could it be much worse? "This lil girl was not treated months ago for a skull fracture and black eyes..she fell in to a coffee table when she just started walking.." Reagan did sustain

[465]

injuries from what Ryan blamed on a fall into a coffee table; however, Reagan had been walking for a year before the accident. She had not just started. That fact is from me, her grandfather. We also have photos of Reagan with two black eyes. "also I am friends both sides..i read some of the report that the mother has and it said that the baby had a small cut above her left eye and thats where the brain damage and bleed was..so she could of fell or something......and there was no other brusing or signs of child abuse at the time of death....Honestly if they knew one of these parents did it why aint there charges or why aint they been questioning???? Just curious..Ryan is not a bad person by far like people are saying...I think people point the fingers too soon!!"

Somebody responded to Tilton Resident: "I personally saw Reagan with 2 black eyes last October 2005. My eyes were not lying."

Grieving from Illinois added: "Yes it is as bad as the news says. Reagan age 2 ½ is gone. Her extended family is saddened beyond words. We should all do what we can to prevent child abuse and see that this never happens to any child. She was a bright light in the life of many people. The joy and sunshine has been taken from her family."

On October 16, BOB began a thread: "Maybe I should say something and maybe I should not but what's up with this investigation into the death of this two year old that died in Tilton…I do not undertand what the heck is taking so long to make an arrest here…The little one can't talk for herself…I'd like to see someone at least in jail waiting trial on this…she didn't even get to really start her life and some sick **&&((&%$$%^% killed her…I've called the County and all they can say is they're investigating it…well what's up…since July good grief…I would go on but I'm probably going to get profane and that's not the way to do things at all…it just seems justice has stopped……"

The writer's hesitancy to get upset, to stir things up, or even broach the subject was refreshing given all the ensuing posting that would go on for years. His sentiments, of course, were ours. I was touched by his willingness to seek answers to his questions; people did care about Reagan's death. The response he received from the county would be heard again and again.

Twenty minutes later, BettyP posted: "I agree with you Bob!...article in the CN today that says they will maybe be closer to the investigation by the end of the month?..Guess we will have to wait and see..I hope whoever is to blame for this is found guilty..Sometimes..the court system…well..just..sucks.." Her closing comment reminded me of Mr. Bumble in *Oliver Twist* who declared "If the law supposes that,…the law is a ass — a idiot. If that's the eye of the law, the law is a bachelor; and the worst I wish the law is, that his eye may be opened by experience — by experience."

A few hours later, PapaJoe responded, "Timing is everything. There will be an arrest at the end of the month (October) because it's just days from the election and the States Attorney is running for judge. Make sense? Politics are not just in our decline in gas prices. It's on every issue that will give recognition to a certain party or candidate. Hmm."

Later than night, Dawn posted, "I would rather have them take their time and make a good investigation and a solid charge to send the right person to jail. No one wants them to rush only to have an improper investigation and weak case so no one goes to jail."

In only one day, Reagan's death had prompted discussions on the nature of civics, police procedures, and politics.

The next morning, new people jumped into the discussion.

A writer named elefan asked, "Wasn't there only two people that really could have done it? I can't remember but I thought the paper had said that only the mother and step-father were at home...you know what really irks me? It seems like there wouldn't be ANY real coverage of the story (besides yesterday's article) if the grandparents didn't push for some coverage. Every time there has been something in the paper it seems like it is because they keep the story alive..."

N!cC!71 concurred: "I feel that way too, if it wasn't for the Grandfather being pushy with them, nothing would probably be said about it...I sure hope they rack the right one!!"

These two posters were right in that both sets of grandparents were trying to keep the story in the public eye. The next three contributors-- Team Player, champagne, and nancyo—agreed that the investigators needed to get it right, and that, whatever happened, the ultimate judgement would be God's alone. That sentiment, though heartfelt, does not really cut it when a member of your family, especially an innocent child, has been taken. Still, I appreciated all of these people taking the time to express themselves.

At the end of November, nancyo pointed out that, since State's Attorney Frank Young had lost his bid for judge, he could concentrate on the job he was paid to do. Another writer, fattypax1, suggested that Frank was "looking for one he can win."

By this time, though frustrated with the perceived slowness of the case (little did we know how protracted it would be), we also walked a fine line—wanting to keep the story in the news and, consequently, on the minds of both the public and the State's Attorney's office; avoiding any action that might harm the case; and moving toward some positive action that might ensure Reagan's legacy while protecting other innocent children.

Caregiver posted that she had called my dad, Reagan's great-grandpa: "I asked what I, a Danville resident, could do. Would phone calls to Frank Young do any good? Pastor Williams asked for prayers for the family and mentioned the bracelets that are being sold for five dollars. The money from the bracelet sales will hopefully help save other children. It every one who reads this would buy one in memory of Reagan and wear it, maybe some good will come from this terrible tragedy." Numerous subsequent posts focused on wristband sales in the area.

About the wristbands, Caregiver wrote, "Granted, it is not much to do, but I felt like I wanted to do something for this poor little angel's memory. Only God and the perpetrator really know all she had to endure before she was murdered. Maybe some changes can be made with some laws and/or with how DCFS handles complaints of suspected abuse.

"As a mother of a 2 year old child," ace_61832 added, "I can not even see the monitor I have so many tears running down my face!!!!! I usually read and not write, but this subject is so sensitive. I have heard a lot of stories of the guy being out at the bars drunk and picking fights with his new girlfriend and others! Let us all remember the precious baby and those who loved her!! And pray that justice will soon prevail for her!!"

Now, wristbands, social action, and Ryan's personal life were introduced into the thread. Some came to his defense while shifting suspicion to Tracy, and more uninformed opinions began to emerge, N!cC!71, for instance, incorrectly, pointing out that DCFS charges were "before his time" when, in fact, they stemmed from an incident in which Reagan was injured on and about the head while in his care. She fairly concluded her post by adding, "I have known the father [sic] for many years and I personally don't think he is responsible and if he is then he deserves to get whatever he gets (specially if its life in PRISON)!"

2007 came. "Frank Young—where are you? Do you remember that a little girl was killed 8 months ago and NO ONE has been arrested?" asked Caregiver. "Frank, if this had been your child, would you have let this go on this long?"

A month later, in February, BOB wondered about the hold up. PapaJoe suggested that Mr. Young would not see another term as State's Attorney, which, indeed, turned out to be true when, aware of the writing on the wall, chose not to run for another term. Poster nancyo argued that "the illustrious Commercial News should be doing some investigative reporting with glaring headlines so it is kept in the minds of all the citizens." This bigger city, hardline approach to journalism was really only a possibility when Barbara Greenberg was on the staff.

The frustration with the State's Attorney and his assistant, Larry Mills, was so great that calls for lynching, getting a rope, using a particular parking garage stairwell that had recently collapsed, killing a young man standing beneath it, all surfaced momentarily before being rightfully squelched by moderator Tuck. A more civil tone returned.

On February 19, Caregiver posted: "…when I asked Pastor Williams what the general public could do to help, he said that the family does not want to do anything that might jeopardize the case like the Gray case. So I have respected their wishes." The Gray case had garnered so much publicity, much of it generated by the family, the entire judicial process had been put at risk. "I wonder if they feel the same way now after all this time. I am sure if she had been my child I would have done almost anything to get justice. Just makes me wonder why her mother, father and grandparents aren't doing more." If the State's Attorney was not doing his job, maybe it was time to contact Bill O'Reilly, Caregiver concluded. O'Reilly and another controversial TV personality, Nancy Grace, were both frequently mentioned as possible powerful voices for getting national exposure.

In a later post the same day, Caregiver shared, "I am curious—has anyone heard anything about the family of the boyfriend or ex-boyfriend? The paper has mentioned the mother's parents and the father's parents. Who exactly are the parents and grandparents of the boyfriend and why haven't they come forward and asked for justice? You would think that if the boyfriend is innocent that his family would want to clear his name." We had thought of most angles to all of this, but, in hindsight, we had never posed that question.

The next day, following a summary of the actions of the Gray/Divan family, SisterLucy shared: "…perhaps it's time for some measures (desperate or otherwise) to come into play for Reagan Williams. Perhaps that is the only way that this little lady will have her voice heard from the grave. Am I advocating violence? Absolutely not!! I am advocating though that we start getting LOUDER in our request for closure on this issue. We can sit here and buy bracelets and post on forums, but how does that influence those in a position of power to hold the guilty accountable? There are lots of ways to fan the flames without resorting to violence, and perhaps the community is being too passive for Reagan."

Madisons suggested a candlelight vigil. We would, of course, hold one on the first anniversary of Reagan's death a little over four months later, not at the courthouse or up and down Vermilion Street as some of these posts suggested but in the front yard of our church, the gathering not a protest but a remembrance and a chance to pass along vital information about child abuse.

In early March, another Vermilion County toddler, this time fourteen months old, became the victim of assault, prompting some to wonder whether the area was soft on crime. Perhaps fairly or unfairly, the theory was put forth that, if a perpetrator had a good relationship with someone in the State's Attorney's office, he or she could get a deal. Caregiver concurred, stating that "there is something wrong with the way this whole thing has NOT been handled." Oddly, and in an unrelated way, she also cited the experience of her neighbor who, evidently, was there in the ER on July 2 when Reagan's lifeless body was wheeled in by the paramedics. Her neighbor shared that neither Tracy nor Ryan even cried. She concluded her post with gratitude that Deegan had been taken out of the house and was safe in foster care since both mother and step-father [sic] should be locked up.

Madisons posted: "Baby Reagan needs an obnoxious, overbearing, loudmouth, advocate to get your local judicial system jump started. This has gone on far too long. Someone has to take charge and see that justice is done. It is inconceivable to me that she has been dead for 8 months and no one has been charged!" Bombarding the State's Attorney's office with letters and e-mails was suggested; ironically, finding the correct addresses proved a challenge for several posters who uncovered several incorrect, outdated addresses on the Internet.

Another writer, marigoldhead, offered a strategy for breaking the case wide open: "It can only be one of two people. Do like they do on law and order…Put them in seperate rooms and someone will break!" Another poster, Jeff, countered with, "I'm sure your sorrow for the family is appreciated but your attempts to portray a TV series outcome as a way to resolve the case may be sorely misguided." The verbal volley that then ensued included discussions about an 18-24 hour window in which the shaking could have occurred, references to other television crime dramas and network news talk shows, further lambasting of area law enforcement and legal personnel (as, according to Madisons, "most times the squeaky wheel really does get the grease"), the validity of news reports and statements by authorities, and the continued need for patience even when the wait seemed unnecessarily long. Poster Jeff vowed to stay out of the fray and listen for a while.

JamNJelly49 reminded forum participants that we should be grateful that "we live in a country where we CAN question authorities" before offering this passionate view: "…this is a child's life we're talking about. She couldn't defend herself or get help on her own. Whatever happened that day, her last conscious moments were filled with terror and confusion. No child should have to go through that. And for nearly a year now, her killer has had to answer to no one and has gone about living their life just the same as before. I think we as a community have a right to be outraged by that."

Jeff joined in the discussion again, explaining that his main contention had always been that the public simply did not know whether there was any negligence in the handling of the case, adding, "In fact, I will go so far as to say, again in my opinion, that they are agonizing over this just as much, and probably more, than you, I or the general public at large, Yes, keeping stories like this in the spotlight is good but accusations of incompetence, with no basis of fact, isn't."

These exchanges happened in late March of 2007. Was there incompetence? Hindsight provided an answer, especially in the original arrest charges which omitted required information and which led to Ryan's release. Later, the inadequacies and untrustworthiness of Young and Mills were evident in crucial medical documents that had supposedly been sent to a Chicago doctor but were, in fact, still in a pile in the State's Attorney's office. Throughout this first year, Reagan's family was told time and again to be patient, to let the investigation take its course, that any public airing of dissatisfaction would be detrimental to the case. We towed the line, doing what we were told.

On April 27, as mindthegap, I posted my own thoughts: "I am one of Reagan's grandfathers. I have read with interest and great emotion all of the comments here. First of all, I commend the forum for being so civil, sensitive, and intelligent (unlike a lot of what I read at the Commercial-News guestbook). Secondly, I believe that many in Reagan's family will, indeed, hold a candlelight vigil near the Courthouse if no arrest has been made by July 2, the one year anniversary of her murder. Lastly, I encourage those of you who are interested to continue to press for answers. Please don't let our 'sunshine' die twice. Never shake a baby! GW"

The responses were swift. "God Bless you mindthegap. Our thoughts will always be with Reagen," wrote flowergirl. "Kindest thoughts and prayers are with you, mindthegap, as well as your precious little sunshine," posted JamNJelly49. "Your granddaughter's story has affected many of us profoundly. It is just so sad...I can't begin to imagine what it must be like for you. I hope the community does not rest until justice has been done for Reagan and your family has some sort of closure," added

[478]

Madisons. "I think about reagen all the time and cant beleave no one has been punished for taking her life," offered whrrll66. BettyP shared, "I don't think you will ever have to worry about anyone forgetting what happened to your granddaughter. We are all very concerned as to how long this case has gone on, and we will reamin concerned until we see justice served. Regardless of who is charged. Like so many others, I can't imagine what you and your family are going thru." And marigoldhead surprised me with this touching post: "Just wanted to send my prayers to you and your family. It has to be very hard. I was one of the ambulance personel from tilton that responded. It was a very hard thing for us to handle also. Again you are in my prayers."

The final post on this thread came from kidsspeakearly, who encouraged writing letters to the editor of both area newspapers, contacting a member of Congress, and calling any number of TV talk show hosts. "It's hard not to point fingers when you think you know who actually killed Reagan. I catch myself doing it all the time. Only Ryan, Tracy and God knows what happened. And hopefully the authorities will figure it out. And as slow as the justice system is, Reagan's family holds out hope that the evidence will be there, that it will be solid, and that there will be a conviction. Act constructively on your outrage and perhaps we can accomplish something positive. And as always, educate yourselves and those around you about never shaking a baby! Thanks for your posts!"

A discussion of Reagan was begun on a different thread on the All Around Danville Forum on August 17, 2006. This thread was devoted to unsolved cases in Vermilion County. BettyP wrote: "Not sure if this is where I should post, but here I go...The case of Reagan Williams...The 2 ½ year old from Tilton that died from shaking baby syndrome July 2, 2006...Nothing has been released about the case. We don't hear anything new about it either. I'm sure they are still investigating but one would think they would put somewhat of a rush on this. I hear second hand, from a close source that the mother is living with her parents, had started seeing the boyfriend of the 3 month old baby boy they share together. I was also told that the parents of the mother wanted her home with them so they chose to put the little boy in foster care. The mother is allowed to see her baby only one hour a week, SUPERVISED..(thank goodness) The mother of Reagan returned to work 2 weeks after the funeral while the grandparents were taking the death so hard they were unable to return to work till just recently. I guess my problem with this whole situation is if the mother and father are both being accused, and each are pointing their finger at each other why..oh why would you continue to see each other..and why..would you put the 3 month old is Foster Care, to bring the mother home to stay with her parents. The mother is working, and could find a small apartment, so that her baby could stay with the grandparents thru this tragic time. I understand the parents want to be there to support their daughter, but losing a grandchild from such a uncalled for, tragic way, I would want to keep the other grandchild close to me. The public already knows DCFS has been involved with this couple before. Obviously there were problems before, to stay with a partner (not pointing fingers at one or the other) because of past abuse of a child, why would one decide to stay with that partner. Some say Love conquers all, but…There is no amount of love for a partner or spouse, that could over-rule the love for my child or children. My heart aches for the grandparents of Regean, but I do question letting their grandson going into foster care knowing that their grandson could possibly be taken care of someone else for the next year or longer..Possibly till he is grown. There are many reasons why children aren't always with their parents, and I understand that, I know first hand myself, but for the reason of child abuse that turns to death, I will never understand why a parent would chose to stay in that situation, and then continue the relationship. The reasoning certainly can't be because there is another child sthat needs both parents, since that child is in foster care. Like I said, I am not pointing my finger at one or the other parent of Regean. I do not know them, nor do I know the grandparents. I can't imagine losing a child or a grandchild, and I hope I never do. I have many friends that have, and I can see how their life has changed. I won't say I know how they feel, because I don't. I just can't understand the situation in this case..and to clarify myself, I know neither is guilty till the results are in, if they ever are, but one or the other done this to a innocent child. One or the other need to pay...I hope this doesn't turn into another unsolved murder."

BettyP seemed reticent, unwilling to stir things up but eager for answers. Without any, she had to rely on second hand information. Were Tracy and Ryan still together? Was Deegan placed in foster care so that Tracy could move home? Dis Tracy return to work after only two weeks? Were both the mother of father of Reagan being accused?

Two and a half hours later, nancyo commented: "I agree that it is unbelievable someone would cover for the other when a child is killed. Your bond with your children are the strongest of all. Or at least with most normal people it is."

About seven minutes later, YNotTango explained: "The 2 adults were the mother and her boyfriend. DCFS had been contacted before because last October, little Reagan had 2 black eyes. The thing that makes me sick, other than the fact there have been no arrests, are friends of the couple who stick up for them."

Ten minutes later, mickster responded: "i'm not going to stick up for either one of them. I know the mother's boyfriend, i babysat him when iwas in high school. All i can say is a lot of rumors get started. They are the only ones that knows what truly happened. and in a lot of cases like this a lot of people point the finger at the man, i am in no way what so ever making an accusation towards the mother, but what is the chance of her being the one that did it? post partum depression can be horrible. maybe that is why she is continuing to see him. maybe he didn't do it. i don't know any inside details, it is an absolute horrible situation. he also has another daughter from a previous relationship and he can't see her now either. they are both suffering form the death of a child, now depression has set in and they can't see the other child either. i can't imagine how they feel. if a true crime has occured, yes, there should be justice, but i can't imagine the guilt and horror they are feeling inside if one of them caused this death. i know from being a single parent i've lost my cool with my kids and i could so easily see how a person could not realize their own strength, not an excuse…i'm not trying to make excuses, but i just think this case is just sad and horrible." The post ended with prayers for the parents, grandparents, and the whole family, the death, foster care, and possibility of one or both parents taken away "so sad."

The next morning, Betty P clarified her comments, explaining that she was referring to Ryan as the father not of Reagan but of the baby boy. She also admitted that most of what she knew was hearsay, then concluded by saying "Partners can be replaced..children can't…"

Soon after, mickster got on once again to speculate on how difficult this would be Ryan and Tracy as parents of the 3 month old, regardless of who ended up being culpable. She then shared the "tuff situation" she was in with the father of her twins and involvement with a murder, "another story for another time." She ended by reiterating

[484]

"there are so many lives and emotions invovled in this tragedy."

BettyP, once again, posted, concluding with "Bottom line is a 2 ½ year old child died for no reason..To say she was in the wrong place at the wrong time, isn't even fair..She had no choice given to her..I'm not out to offend or defend anyone..Its Regean who had to pay the price for what ever the resoning was…My opinion, there is no reason for a child dieing.."

Two days later, on August 20, following a story in the *Commercial-News* about child abuse and neglect, BettyP shared how amazed she was" at the loop holes with DCFS" because she had "never dealt with them." She was also disturbed by attorney Nancy Fahey's suggestion that some cases "fall through the cracks (in the system)." P.Bear explained that few liked attributing the death of a child "to a flaw in the DCFS system, but it happens. A LOT. It is a nation wide epidemic and until Children's Services receives the necessary funding they need; it will continue to happen."

Subsequent posts included the suggestion of allowing the grand jury convene to the need for DCFS procedures to be reviewed and changed if necessary to a firsthand account of the effects of a misused abuse hotline.

This particular thread managed to be civil throughout, with participants seemingly doing all within their power to be open-minded. Other threads resembled a free-for-all. The following comments, from Danville's *Commercial-News* forum on its guestbook, were the hardest to read (and the hardest to transcribe). They were contentious. They were accusatory. Those posting seemed to pick sides, defending and blaming accordingly. Reagan's death often took a backseat to who was responsible. Gossip was accepted as truth, secondhand accounts as firsthand knowledge.

Commenting on the Gray case, Imo, on June 20, 2007, suggested that ending domestic violence should "start at home. We need to parent and protect." Later that afternoon, i think we are all tried of it! blamed State's Attorney Frank Young, citing an entire police department in the county which endorsed Young's run for the judge seat, "anything to get him out of the S. A. Office."

Sarah, from Tilton, blamed Ian, Reagan's father and my son. She wrote, "I am absolutely disgusted by the way DCFS and our State's Attorney have handled this whole situation. It's very unfortunate that either the Green family or the Williams family should have to go through such sorrow because of the mistakes they have made. Second, I am a friend of the family so I know first hand how Reagan's natural father was to her. I don't mean to cause any harm by saying this, but he was a good father to her, once a month when he had time to be with her. He apparently had better things to do most of the time though…I just don't buy all these things about him being 'father of the year'. He wasn't a bad father, he was just an absent father." This post, from a self-proclaimed friend, hurt nonetheless, bringing up mistakes we made (as if we needed reminding) and Ian's seeming inability to spend more time with his daughter. Sarah went on to blame Frank Young's procrastination for keeping Deegan away from his mother and grandparents as well as allowing the one suspect in the case, "a sick and cruel individual," to "share our streets with us…"

It is probably important to make this point here after all of the posts that have been shared and before the remaining posts have been revealed. At the time of these active forums, I had no knowledge of the identities of the writers who used nicknames. The most I could usually tell was the educational level of some of them, based on their grammar usage or lack thereof. I often guessed at identities, based on a name, a nickname, a relationship described, or the content of the post. For instance, I did know several Sarahs in Ian's life but could not accurately identify which one had written the previous entry. I did know the next writer.

On July 2, 2007, the first anniversary of Reagan's death, K Crouch posted the following: "To whom it may concern: It sickens me to find people displacing blame for Baby Reagan's death. Here are the facts: 2 people were in the house. Sure, Ian may not have been around as much as he could have. But, that's in the past. His actions did not result in Reagan's death. The system failed, once again. He and his family were trying their best to remove Reagan from a dangerous situation. Please, before you blame innocent parties, read a newspaper. Send your love and sympathy and support to the families, not malicious blaming and bad mouthing."

The next day, Anon wrote: "To those commenting on Reagan Williams and her family- No one knows the whole story. No matter how close you are to either family, you do not know the whole story. The point is we as a community should band together and stand to fight for her justice and keep her memory alive with education. No matter if you friends of either family, the point is both sides (including this community) lost a wonderful baby girl. I know everyone has feelings on this case, trust me. I have more that you would care to know, but we must look past our own bias and remember what we are here to do. Tracy Green needs just as much concern as does Ian Williams. Before you bash and name call, know the truth. Becky Green was never noted as saying Tracy knew different, because Tracy has never said such a thing. If Becky did say this, it was out of anger."

Weeks later some of the more vitriolic posts appeared in rapid succession over the course of that day on the *Commercial-News* Guestbook.

In response to posts by CN Reader and Melissa, My opinion too! Wrote: "CN Reader, I think the mother was just as guilty, she let this go on for how long? How many times did she get turned in for abuse to this baby? I Ilso think DCFS should be at fault too. So yes, the so called mom should be right up there with the boyfriend. I heard that the mom nevered cried once at the funeral. Melissa, maybe you didn't know the mom as well as you thought you did? Why did she stay with him till the baby ended up getting killed if she was such a great mom? That is just my opinion..." To be honest, the question of Tracy's remaining with Ryan despite domestic abuse crossed my mind as well. One might speculate that what happened in that house in Tilton is a textbook example for it had all of the characteristics of the cycle of abuse: the act itself, the regret, the promises, the pleas for another chance, the forgiveness, a short-lived period of peace, and then another act. To this day I do not know about the events which led to Reagan's injuries. I also do not know how many times DCFS was contacted beyond those on record which I read about myself. I have never been aware of more than one visit to the house because of head injuries Reagan received. The writer, however, in asking how many times Tracy was turned in for abuse is able to plant doubts (and probably made up numbers) in the heads of readers seeking an answer to that question. Somewhat ironically, My opinion too! ends with this suggestion: "So enstead of blaming lets keep them in our prayers till this is over and let baby Reagan rest now."

A half hour later, just venting enthusiastically concurs: "She is just as guilty for letting this go on as he his. I hope she gets what he gets!!! RIP Baby Reagan!!"

Imo also agreed that Tracy was "just as guilty as who ever killed her baby daughter:

#1 She should have died trying to save her.

#2 She should have told exactly what happened instead of staying quiet for a year.

#3 She allowed this bum to live with her and her child.

[490]

#4 She put her own wants ahead of the childs needs.

The childs natural father also should have taken more responsibility for the protection of this child when the problems first arose."

Clemmie added: "I read in the newspaper that the mother had taken her to the ER with her head swollen and she said she fell when the attending doctor said there was no way that injury was caused by a fall. This was before the fatal injury. She covered up, she didn't leave him with that baby. It doesn't take a genius to see she didn't protect her baby. If anyone hurt my baby like that, I'd call the police on my way out with my baby as would most mothers. People on a jury have a duty to be objective and listen to the evidence. But we have a right to read things, analyze things and come to a conclusion. If you don't, you might believe OJ is innocent, or leave your baby with Ryan Allhands, or let Michael Vick board your dog. As the song goes, and the verse, Bless the beasts and the children, for in this world they have no voice, they have no choice."

An important detail became a litmus test for guilt. Did Tracy cry at the funeral? If so, did she cry enough? If not, were her lack of tears hiding some secret? I do not remember. Like so much which occurred on that day, let alone that week, many of the details were a blur. I cried.

[491]

Weeping can be heard and seen on the tape of the service. I was not aware that emotion was being judged on July 7, 2006.

CN Reader fired back: "To my opinion too! Nice name..You HEARD? Are you serious? So because you HEARD this it must be true right? Small minded people have absolutely no business.....well nevermind..And because she didn't cry at the funeral is probably the stupidest thing I have ever heard.....Your response deserves no more response from me.."

Minutes later, melissa from Pennsylvania, in a lengthy response to several of the points that had been made in the last forty-five minutes, suggested that we too often blame victims (a woman who is raped may have dress provocatively, a woman who is abused might have said the wrong thing, a woman whose child is abused let it happen) and that, in the eyes of the law, Tracy had done nothing to deserve losing her daughter. The writer went on to suggest that, based on her own grandmother's lack of tears at the funeral of a husband of sixty-five years, not crying could have been an indication of shock and not guilt or a lack of caring.

Former Danville Resident, responding to Clemmie, wrote: "If she lied to the doctor about what happened when she took her to the emergency room…then she's as much a part of the crime as the person that actually shook her. It's called being an accessory!"

Dawn weighed in: "When you have a child it is your responsibility to keep that child safe no matter what is going on with you. She failed. She knew about the abuse since the baby was in the emergency room several times and she stayed and didn't stop it. She definitely has culpability in the crime that was committed no matter what was going on with her. I would NEVER let someone like that abuse my child while I stood by and knew it was going on."

Clemmie warned: "Brace yourselves, you know Allhands' defense is going to be the mother did it and then it will be a he said, she said argument. I just hope that a conviction is possible and they have all their ducks in a row after all this time."

AL shared: "I know Reagan's mother personally and it is upsetting to see so many people coming out against her. The fact of the matter is, he is being charged not her. Does that make her fully innocent? Not necessarily, but she has paid for her mistakes more than anyone can imagine. No one has the right to judge her for the decisions she made in that relationship. If you have not walked in her shoes, then you do not know. So please let the system do its job and try not to render judgement in matters in which the circumstances are not fully known.

Len from Westville, who claimed friendship with both of the parents, addressed Melissa, CN Reader, and My opinion too!, reiterated the need for open-mindedness and sympathy, adding: "And yes, I was there at the funeral I saw the mother and father all of the family members crying and sobing for Reagan you have no right to say that no one shed a tear you weren't there to see it with your own two eyes who cares what you heard. That's what is so bogus when things like this happen people have nothing better to do with their life then make up stories just to entertain themselves. It hurts me so much to know that people get pleasure out of inflicting pain on those who are already grieving. It blows my mind how heartless and inconsiderate people can be. Is there no longer any compassion left in this world?"

CN Reader responded: "I've said many times before that a lot of the people in the forum are wolves carrying shot guns…and with blind folds on as well…"

Another poster, lynn, explained the difficulty she had in extracting herself from an abusive relationship, this after promising that she would never get in one. She closed with: "You cant just walk out it is not that easy. Especially if you have no one to turn to. So let the jury decide. Remember judge not let ye be judged."

K.D.F. of Danville shared: "I think there needs to be some sort of action on reagan's mother because her job in life was to protect Reagan. She had to know that Reagan was in trouble. The last time Reagan was abused was not the first time. There were calls made to DCFS before Reagan was fatally injured. Yes, in some cases abused women do not have places to go. I dont think that is the case here. Granted, I dont know the mother, but her parents live here, Reagans father lives here and Im sure the Williams' would have taken Reagan in temporarily if her mother wasn't able to leave her boyfriend all at once. As a mother, you do what you HAVE to do to protect your children. IF the mother was being abused by her boyfriend then she should have called the police. She should have done SOMETHING!!!! I seriously hope she never regains custody of her son. Here's the word for today. NEGLECT. 9hope I spelled it right..wouldnt want the spelling police to get me!!!).

Sherry Scarlett, a name I with which I was familiar, pleaded: "To all of you who wish to post your 'opinion' regarding the Reagan Williams case...please step back and let the law take care of it. Your opinions are very hurtful to all who are personally involved! Unless you know the families and have been there holding there hand, you don't have the right to lay blame. My son is a close personal friend to Ian and Tracy. He was there the minute Reagan was born. He is still there to this day to support both families. Trust me! I know what is going on. Let our justice system take care of it. Everyone else, please just listen, don't talk."

Danville Native wrote: "Take off your rose colored glasses, people. I don't give a darn if Reagan Williams' mother was being abused herself, she has a moral obligation to protect her children. From what I have read, she did have resources. It seems like at any point she could have taken her child to Reagan's paternal grandparents' home and they would have been glad to have her." This was our intention throughout May and June. We offered to take Reagan temporarily until Tracy could figure out her situation. "I don't give a darn if the mother herself was being abused or is a victim, because that's not was she is-what she is in an accessory to murder because she allowed her child to be with the man. She should be facing the same charges."

Crystal stated: "C'mon if Reagan's Grand parents only got to see Reagan on the weekends and they noticed the abuse and sought help, why wouldn't her main Monday-Friday caregiver, her mother notice anything? Reagen's mother adlegedly had her infant son removed from her and her boyfriends custody by social services, why didn't Regan's mom say hey can you help my baby girl too, or i would like to give Reagan to her dad or grandparents, because my boyfriend is beating her & i, she is not safe." Deegan was taken from the home after Reagan died. This writer, like many, had partial facts with which to work. Still, her argument was well-taken. There were options; unfortunately, a decision was not made until it was too late. Crystal went on to make several points: people were mad at Tracy for what she didn't do for Reagan; this case should be a wake-up call for others in a similar situation; grandparents' rights are often overlooked.

Cortney, Tracy's best friend and a friend to Ian as well, explained the challenges of an abusive relationship: "For those who do NOT know what abuse means, it is not as simple as just packing up and leaving. It takes several tries, usually about 7...and you have no idea how many times the mother of Reagan tried. You have no idea of the circumstances that led up to Reagan's death. I sat next to

Reagan's mother at the funeral, for those of you who think she did not cry, she did. She has everyday since. Do you not think she feels horrible enough? The story is not as cut and dry as you may wish. 'Why didn't she just leave?' Well, because if it was that simple for Reagan's mother and many others, we wouldn't have to worry about things like this. The question SHOULD BE…that we shouldn't be asking why she didn't leave….we should be asking why he did such a thing to a wonderful baby girl. Why he did such things to a wonderful mother. Think all you want, but please educate yourself with facts about abuse and the world around you before you decide to pass judgment."

A Georgetown resident, just my concern, commented: "While I don't know, and don't want to know who killed that pretty little girl….I can't help but think that there is more to this story. One of the main reason's I feel that the mom needs some blame is due to the fact that she, herself was under investigation for bruises appearing on that child. Our lovely DCFS office was in charge of this investigation. I personally think that both of these people should have to pay for this crime."

A new poster, INOU, wrote: "I read with sadness about the arrest of Ryan Allhands. I am sad because the mother was not arrested with him. For the entire time she has hide the fact that Ryan did it. If there were only two people with the little girl and the mother took her to the e.r. that means Ryan did it and she knew it. Why cover for him? I just don't get it. Only time will tell if she is guilty, if not by law…but by GOD!!" Once again, a writer was confusing several facts, blending them together incorrectly.

Another Person in the Mix called for rational thought and silence: "Did you really think that Tracy, through the advise of her lawyers was allowed to speak? Do you not think that maybe for one instance she wanted to scream outloud 'Ryan did it!'? Once again…just listen…don't talk!"

A writer named danville friend attempted to clear up some misinformation. The little boy, Deegan, was taken after Reagan died. Tracy wasn't covering for Ryan; she wasn't allowed to talk about the case while it was under investigation.

Shari Ellis pointed out that nothing would heal the loss of a child then hoped for some closure "for the family of a precious little girl."

The last post of the busy, contentious July 19 went to a child, A from Georgetown: "i am a 12 year old who new ryan since i was born he is a very nice and caring guy i know for a fact he didnt do this he is the nicest person ever i want him to be set free he used to make me laugh when i saw him he is an awesome guy all the people that think he would do this are wrong."

July 20—a new day and a new round of posts.

At 7:57 AM, Danville Reader wrote: "I'm a friends of the Williams family and the Green family and yes I was at the funeral, not that it matters BUT the mother DID NOT CRY at the funeral. She walked around talking and laughing hugging her friends having a gay ole time like it was a party. I never once saw her shed a tear and I was sitting close by behind her! It really don't matter that she cried or not, no big deal to her I guess. But you can bet your sweet cookie if that was my baby girl laying up there in that casket like that they wouldn't be able to hear the service from my crying. If she had anything at all to do with it, it will come out and she will get her dues, if not by the law she will have to answer to GOD at the end. God Bless both sets of Grandparents, we must keep them in our Prayers these next few weeks or months which ever it takes to get this matter solved. Rest in Peace now Baby Reagan." Like so many posts, I had a hard time figuring out the relationship of this person to Reagan's family and the motivation behind the message. Since the writer claimed to be a friend of both families, attendance at the funeral service makes sense, but what kind of friend goes on to bash Tracy for not crying then states that the amount of crying doesn't matter then asks for God's blessing on the grandparents? Phrases like "having a gay ole time like it was a party" and "you can bet your sweet cookie" suggest a malevolent tone or a deeply rooted need for opinions to be recognized to bolster self-esteem.

Cynthia from Danville delivered a strong defense of Ryan and, conversely, doubt regarding Tracy. "I am a good friend of Ryan I am sad to hear about Ryans arrest. The day of Reagans death It was Ryan who picked Reagan up when she was crying,Ryan that didn't think she was acting right Ryan that called for Tracy something was wrong,the 2 of them that knew they needed help,the 2 of them that worked on her until help arrived.Few days later that Tracy and Ryan were holding on to one another,supported one another,there for one another. Yes, those who know Tracy know Ryan wasn't at the funneral. It wasnt because he didnt want to be therehe did,He didnt go because the grandparents were throwing a fit and already blaming him and he wanted it to be easier on Tracy not because he did it or because he didnt care. Ryan was hurting just as much as Tracy.The first thing mentioned was baby shaken nobody wanted to hear anything else.The talk about the abuse Ryan did Is this the truth or has Tracy decided the start talking bad about Ryan because she is scared of being blamed? Has anybody ever thought that when Reagan was only 2 yrs old accidents do happen.For one of them not to be arrested then or within the weeks that followed just maybe they were telling the truth they didnt do anything.I dont really want to point a finger at Tracy but if everybody that knows Tracy is pointing at Ryan why not everybody that knows Ryan point at Tracy. As far as calling him a bum, You need to take a look at what he has done. He had a good job, he was buying his home,he didn't move in with Tracy She moved into his home he was taking care of his children and he was helping support Reagan. The children were not going without anything they needed. To be only 21 yrs old I think he was doing pretty good for himself. So how do you get off calling him a bum? I beleive in Ryan just as his girlfriend and will stand by him 110% also. I wont put the blame on Tracy either because I beleive that Reagan did fall or something to cause her injuries and that neither one is to blame. I feel as though the two of them did everything to protect her, to help her. I think it is all because of the mention of baby shaken that it was classified as a hommicide. That should have been an accidental death. I hope out of the goodness of Tracys heart that she hasnt decided to start telling lies about Ryan so the pressure is off her.Maybe Tracy and Ryan did do everything right and in was a mistake Maybe it really was an Accident I will stand by Ryan no matter what I pray that everything works out for Ryan." Reading this comment the first time and, later, transcribing it were both excruciating and maddening. In the hospital on July 2, Ryan explained that Reagan passed out on the sofa and that he notified Tracy who was taking a shower. There was no talk of picking up a crying Reagan. Did Ryan and Tracy stay together for several days after Reagan's death? Do I remember "throwing a fit" at the thought of Ryan at the funeral? No, though we did decide that his presence ill-advised and neither needed nor appreciated. The fall against the coffee-table resulting in severe head injuries had happened in October while Reagan was in Ryan's care; it had nothing to do with the injuries Reagan sustained on July 2. The coroner's jury ruled her death a homicide rather than a suicide because she was not old enough to self-inflict the injuries that took her life and no accident was reported by either Tracy or Ryan on that July 2. To be honest, the poor grammar and spelling also irritated the English teacher in me (and this was not the only post rife with convention issues). How can one take poorly written crap like this seriously? Yes, I am fully aware that the grammar found on public forums like this does not really matter compared to the seriousness of the death of a child (especially when it is your first grandchild and the light of your life). Had I been in any number of other occupations, I probably wouldn't have noticed, but Reagan's papa just happened to have a degree in English.

TILTON READER leaned over the proverbial small town back fence and shared the following news: "I bet none of you guys knew that Tracys mother (Becky Green) was arrested thursday early morning @ 2am for going to Ryans moms house telling her not to be mad and she still wanted to be friends..and she knows he is INNOCENT!!! Whats up with that!!"

Zorba pondered: "Regarding the recent arrest in the Reagan case, I read in the newspaper this guy has a fiance? My Lord, I know this woman just had a baby by someone else a couple months ago! How do you get a fiance that quickly?Someone better be checking on that baby! Where do these people come from? This is straight out of a Jerry Springer episode!"

A poster from Colorado calling herself Someone that cares shared personal information. I was able to read between the lines here and realized that the writer from

Colorado was my sister, Elaine. She explained: "I am a survivor of extreme mental and physical abuse…No one can understand what happens and how deep it can go until they have walked in a victims shoes. I've been told by Experts in my case it was just as if I'd been brainwashed. So please stop the harsh words against Tracy. Many times even immediate family and Medical experts can't recognize how severe the abuse can affect someone's mind and the ability to make rational decisions. Many times the victim can't even tell the family what's really happening behind closed doors or how she even feels. I urge everyone to get out where ever you live and support victims of Domestic Abuse, help to make a change for them and stop the blame. My love and prayers are with every family members and friend of both families. We love you Reagan!"

Paula from Danville responded directly to Cynthia, but even her impassioned post contained misinformation: "…do you seriously believe that a Doctor cannot tell the difference between a toddlers fall, and "Shaken Baby Syndrome"? This has a name because it has symptoms-severe brain trauma-it has a name because it is caused by severe shaking of a young child. The Doctor goes by all the tests performed on the child-he doesn't just stick his finger up in the air and say, hmmm I think this is child abuse." So far, so good. Shaken Baby Syndrome, also known as Abusive Head Trauma, does have very distinct symptoms which cannot be created any other way. "You and a very few others are trying to associate domestic abuse, and battering with what was going on in that house, and the reason this so called "Mother" of this child remained quiet. This woman is not 40 yrs old-she isn't even 30 years old. She wasn't subjected to anything for years and years, and brainwashing? She must have taken a 'Speed Course' in it then." Now the writer was saying the killing of a child did not fall under the heading of domestic abuse. "Now I see that her own Mother went to the young mans Mother's house to try to make nice. How much more obvious can it be? She doesn't want that family to imcreminate her daughter-so she goes over to make nice with them. Good for them that they weren't buying it." How did Paula know about the details of the conversation between Tracy's mother and Ryan's mother? "I read in the newspaper that the newest fiance of this fellow says it was an accident. It is no accident that this child died. She was murdered." I appreciated her bluntness, but I had to wonder just *what* was an accident? What was Ryan telling his new fiance? Was someone actually admitting that something was done to Reagan that caused her death? "I also read here that on the advice of her attorneys she was advised not to talk. HUH??? If she was so abused, the first time she was interviewed by the police with her legal counsel present, she should have told it all. And then the cause wouldn't have taken over a year to seek justice. But she didn't say anything-no-she knew the truth and that truth would not have set her free. Please do not insult the intelligence of these readers to say this was an accident caused by the toddler." Again, I appreciated the writer standing up for Reagan, but the topic of Tracy's not talking was misinterpreted.

A poster calling herself annonomous reader tried to inject some faith-based sense into the discussion, citing bad things happening to good people, God's will, how we all sin and no one should cast stones. The writer ended by suggesting that we can all learn from this whole terrible nightmare.

The final post of the day was submitted by JLO of Dvegas and meant for an earlier writer: "Paula-you shouldn't believe everything you read here. Tracy told everything to the police, time and time again. EVERYTHING. She left NOTHING out. She has been advised by her attorney not to speak to the newspapers or reporters. That in itself is commons sense, during this year

[507]

long investigation, the impending trial. There will be a time when Tracy will be able to comment on this tragic matter. I hope all of you, who point fingers, state non-truths and don't know the facts will be able to open your mind, and ears to listen."

The posts started in the middle of the night on Saturday, July 21. At 2:09 AM, Concerned poster asked: "Could everyone who posts about the REAGAN WILLIAMS case please at least spell that child's name right? If you have so much to say about it, please give that baby girl the respect she deserves by at least spelling her name right. It's bad enough that you are all criticizing her mother and father so harshly. She is a beautiful angel in heaven, and the believed guilty suspect is in custody. Let this matter lie in the courts hands. Who are we to cast judgement on these people who lost a child anyway? I think that if you're not God yourself, then you have no right cast judgement on these parents. I'm sure they loved that baby more than life itself. Do you not think they don't see these horrible things you post? Let this family grieve in peace. Sometimes it's better to keep your opinions to yourself. I was always taught 'If you have nothing nice to say, then don't say it at all'. Thanks."

The suggestion was ignored. At 6:50 AM, Cynthia wrote: "Paula, I'm not stupid and saying a doctor can't tell the difference between a fall and a severe brain trauma But severe brain trauma doesn't mean they had to be shaken. Something else could have cause it. What everybody fails to hear is closed head trauma "consistant" with Shaken Baby Syndrome It doesn't say it was Shaken Baby Syndrome." What other event could cause the triad of injuries? "Maybe they are telling the truth they didn't shake her. I am not saying there was any kind of abuse at all was going on in their house. I don't beleive for a minute there was any such thing. Tracy was at the PSB for 7 hrs. that day." Which day? "I don't think she kept quiet about anything I think she said all she knew just as Ryan did. That's why there was no arrest. She wasn't being abused and if she is the one saying it now it's just to make Ryan out as the bad guy so she doesn't have to worry about them going after her. I think they only made the arrest because they were being pressured by the grandparents and they pointed the finger at Ryan so that is who they went after. They don't want to beleive her Mother could do such a thing." For the record, we did all we could not to pressure the police or the State's Attorney's office to avoid damaging the case. Personally, I wanted the responsible

[509]

party to be arrested and to pay for Reagan's death regardless of who it was. "I know for a fact that during the 6 hr. time frame they have for Reagan's injuries to have accurred that Ryan wasn't even around home for 2 of those hrs. So if it wasn't an accident then Who's to say what went on when Ryans was gone? Ryan was just the boyfriend not the real parent So why not blame him? I don't care what anybody says I will believe him no matter what." Given that Ryan later confessed to causing injuries that led to Reagan's death, I wonder if Cynthia still feels the same.

Paula responded to another writer: "Then JLO, why did Tracy stay with the guy if she told all when the police first questioned her? She continued to live with him and put their own fears of both being arrested, to cover up the murder of her child. The excuses some of you are making for this woman make me ill. This was not a one time event, this child was being repeatedly assaulted until she died." At least Paula acknowledged the possibility that Reagan's death was not caused by one unfortunate accident but by systematic abuse.

The next evening, July 22, CN Reader shared: "I just wonder if people really want to know why Tracy did this or Tracy did that (pardon if I misspelled her name) maybe they should ask Tracy? I mean everyone seems to think they know what happened that terrible night, and they all seem to have their own opinions as to why she stayed with Ryan but have they asked Tracy herself? Probably not because they don't know her. I don't know her either but I'm not assuming anything about her. I'm not saying I do or don't have sympathy I just think if you want to know why someone did or didn't do something then why not go straight to the 'horses' mouth? If you dare." I am not sure to what "terrible night" she is referring.

On Sunday morning, July 23, Todd L. Schultz of Tilton wrote: "Sure glad someone finally got arrested for the reagan death. I cant believe it took so long. May god be with the family."

JLO from Dvegas posted: "Paula & to anyone else who think Tracy stayed with Ryan. I just really knew all of you knew Tracy like I did. You just really have no idea what she went through, before, after,,,and now. Like I said, someday…you will get her full side of the story. Until that day comes, please stop stating things that aren't true. The fact is, she was moved out of that house 4 days after Reagan died. She did not STAY with Ryan. They have not been a couple for over a year now. What I love about our country is our right to freedom of speech. You're all entitled to it, your opinions…but please, don't judge this entire issue until you know the whole story and ALL THE FACTS. Not rumors, not speculation, not heresay. 'Better to remain silent and be thought a fool than to speak out and remove all doubt.' Abraham Lincoln"

Several hours later, Dawn opined: "Tracy should have moved before Reagan died. Too late after. If there was no history of abuse before that time I might feel differently, but there was."

Rachel, Ryan's fiancée, also stepped into the fray: "To everyone who has been considerate to Ryan's family's feelings, thank you. To the rest, that's okay too because you are entitled to your own opinion. I'm not going to rant and rave about what Ryan's like because I'm engaged to him, it's obvious that I believe him and love him and have all the faith in the world in him. Let me just say that there are multiple victims in this case. Not just one. I mean no offense to either Williams or Green family. But before every one talks about what a monster my fiancee is make sure you actually know Ryan (personally), before you comment and be considerate of everyone's feelings who is involved in this case, not your own. Thank you to all of the continued support that everyone has shown. We both love all of you. Thanks!" Because of her relationship with

Ryan, Rachel was free to post. I am not sure whether she was accusing the Williams and Green families of calling Ryan a monster. The Williams family certainly kept public comments to what had been reported in the media; in fact, typically, any reference to Ryan included in an article was a matter of record and used by journalists to provide background information for readers. Perhaps the reference to the families was to explain how Ryan's family and friends were hurting, too.

Jason H. posted: "It looks as if Mr. Allhands will be going to court to prove his guilt/innocence. I see he is also scheduled for court on July 27 for crashing a vehicle and running since he had been drinking. Would the crashed vehicle happen to be a Cadillac Escalade?"

A writer named just venting shared: "This whole Regan case why is this Tracy Green not oin the PSB as well (don't know either of them) she was there and did nothing plus has had calls to DCFS before?? What are we thinking people. Lets get real for a minute…just my two cents worth."

Lacey explained: "I read all of these horrible things about Ryan Allhands everyday. I went to high school with Ryan, and honestly I didn't see anything in him that would lead me to believe he was capable of this." Remember, anyone can get frustrated enough to shake a baby, even someone who wouldn't seem capable of abuse; however, there were signs of abuse for months—head trauma, bruises, black eyes. "In this country we are supposed to be innocent until proven guilty, not guilty until proven innocent! I really hope that every single stitch of evidence is evaluated in this case. I would hope he doesn't take the fall simply because people are looking for someone to blame. Often times we are so eager to 'close' a case (especially one involving a young child) that we are blinded by emotion and not facts. I feel so sorry for Rachel, everyone critisizes her for standing by Ryan, but the fact of the matter is, no one knows what happened that day. There is nothing wrong with her standing strong and having faith in her decision to believe in him."

Another poster, mother of 2, wrote what I perceived to be as fair a comment on the tragedy as was possible: "It is sad to see everyone bickering back and forth about the Reagan Williams case. The way I feel is I am friends with one of them and I do stand by their side, but in all actuality I don't know who did what, I was not there as were any of you. More than likely we will never fully know exactly what happened and for how long it went on. The only facts we do know are that innocent little girl died and they arrested only one person! I personally am glad I won't be on the jury because it is probably going to get nasty in that court room. I pray for the families of Ryan, Tracy, and Ian because the pain over the last year has been hard enough without the pain they are about to endure when the trial begins. By what I have read on this commercial news message board I hope Ryans lawyer request a change in venue for his trial because it doesn not look as though a fair one may take place with all the publicity this story has recieved. Like I said previously I am friends with one of them but I do not feel down grading the other results in anything. Please leave the families alone, they are dealing with a lot without your negativity. And for the record I did attend the funeral and it was very sad..Tracy looked as though she had done nothing but cried for her little girl. Everyone grieves differently. At my fathers visitation and funeral I was able to walk around and smile and laugh at memories of him. That did not mean my heart was not broke and I did not love him because I did and still do. My prayers will continue for everyone involved in this!"

Conversely, SMM of Tilton relayed a message to Rachel: "You should be glad he got arrested. If not only for the fact that he committed a horrible crime, against an innocent child none the less, you should be glad that you and your family will never have to go through what the families of Reagan Williams have been through. You have a baby daughter, and you still want to stand by his side? That's just sickening that you would put your own child in harms way. Maybe DCFS should do their job and investigate you. It was only a matter of time before he treated you the way he treated Tracy. You may not see it now because of course he was a 'good guy' to you, do you think he's stupid enough to abuse you when he knew he was on the chopping block? I seen the news report where you made the comment 'He told me this could happen.' Why would he have had to tell you that if he was innocent? Did Tracy ever tell anyone 'I could be arrested at anytime so be prepared.' No, I don't believe she felt the need to do that. Also, you said 'Ryan told me what happened, it was an accident.' Maybe you should go take a look at the publicly accessible files and see what his REAL statement was to the investigators. I don't know, maybe it will finally hit you when the trial comes and you get to see both sides of the story, and you get to see the evidence that he really was VERY abusive to Tracy. Maybe that might get it through to you that he was only using you to make himself look better. Yes, I can say all of this happen because I know him VERY VERY well. Rather if you want to believe it or not, the truth is going to be told, and he is going to get a small portion of what he deserves. Oh, and next time you all decide to have a sale to raise money, make sure you spell 'SALE' right on your signs. That just further proves how intelligent every one his 'supporters' are. It's not that I'm not sympatheitic towards his family, but HE put you all this situation."

Dawn of Danville wrote: "Im confused by the fact that Tracey and Ryan lived together and had a baby togeather yet Ryan is engaged to another woman. If i was Rachel i wouldnt allow that!! God be with them all. We all have our problems.." I can see why Dawn was confused; she had several facts in the wrong chronology.

On July 24, Sort of confused shared: "RE: Allhands. It would appear that the Investigating Officers and Attorneys who did some in depth questioning are the only people with the actual facts. All the ret is 'hearsay' and would not be admissible in any court, and should not be spread around here. People - thing about what you are doing, or being. Just a bunch of gossipers!"

Outside Looking In scolded: "There is absolutely no excuse for this to have happened. No matter who actually committed this heinous crime the fact remains that BOTH of these people who were in this child's presence are responsible. There is no man or woman worth losing a child over. As a survivor of both mental and physical abuse I can say this: Had my ex EVER even THOUGHT about abusing our children he'd have been very sorry indeed. I left when our children were 3 and 6 months. I had a choice and I chose to give myself and them a better life. The time for 'woulda, coulda, shoulda' is over and Reagan deserves justice."

On July 25, a poster named I support Ryan Allhands ALL THE WAY~!!!! explained: "The ONLY reason Ryan got arrested was because of all the articles that the Williams family kept putting in the paper. It made Frank Young look like he wasn't doing his job and that someone needed to be arrested for the loss of this little girl, It is a tragedy that she is gone, but when did people start getting arrested for being innocent?? Why is Ryan sitting in jail right now? If he can be arrested for this, why is Tracy Green sitting at home free as can be. Everyone keeps saying how Ryan is so abusive, its kinda funny the night before all this TRACY is the one that tried to hit Ryan. Why does everyone think Tracy is so innocent? She needs to be arrested and be charged the same charges as Ryan until the truth comes out! And for our States Attorney, shame on him for only making ONE arrest!! I think we all know that there needs to be another

Arrest made!!!!!!!! Its funny the only people that think Ryan did it are the Williams and the Greens family and friends!!!" Were any of these accusations true? Did Frank Young make a move a year into the investigation because of public scrutiny? Was an arrest made only because of newspaper articles? Did Tracy hit Ryan the night before? Were family and friends the only people who thought Ryan was culpable?

On July 26, another contentious day, just me posted: "rumor has it that tracy green's own mother has made comments that she doesn't think ryan did it......now come on!! And doesn't ryan have an older daughter? No allegations agains him abusing her!! He would get her for long periods of time because the mom lives in another state. she is alive and well. i just hope when they do prove him innocent, they haven't screwed up so bad and can't charge tracy."

A few minutes later, Ryan Allhands's supporter added: "I am a witness and a good friend of ryan's and knew tracy personally. the night before Reagan died tracy and ryan got into a horrible fight. Tracy pulled her hand back twice to punch ryan. ryan left with Bethany and stayed at his brother and sister in laws house. (stayed the whole night might i add). Tracy was livid about the whole thing. whose to say that out of frustration tracy grabbed reagan and shook her or hurt her? because whe was crying so much and tracy was upset. bethany (ryan's daughter), was there; in that house. don't you think she would give her dad away in some small way? she was there when the paramedics got there. When she sees a picture of reagan she says 'reagan has a boo boo'. She knows that something isn't right. And how was it that ryan had not had dcfs called on him when he had his daughter living with him for 5 months? and the time before that? why all of the sudden is he a baby killer now? i have suffered and still suffer from post partum depression and the thoughts you have are horrible. whose to say it wasn't an accident that this happened and tracy did in fact hurt her? her own parents have called dcfs on her. before she even got with ryan dcfs was called on her on 3 different occasions. ryan has never had a problem with that. anyone who knows ryan knows that he is a pleasant man and would give the shirt off his back for anyone. what about baby deegan? he's been in foster care since he was 2 months old. what's going to happen to him? what about bethany? her daddy was taken from her too. people need to understand that you're innocent until proven guilty. anyone who can comment on my thoughts, please do so but it won't make a difference because i know both ryan and tracy and their families and most of you folks don't. thanks and god bless!"

MC from Tilton responded to Ryan Allhands ALL THE WAY~!!!!: "You know, I don't disagree with you that there needs to be another arrest. There were TWO adult figures in the care of Reagan that weekend. But, I also believe it is very naïve and rude of you to think the only reason that they have arrested Ryan is because of all the news articles and positive things the Williams AND Greens are trying to do with a tragedy. They had nothing to do with the murder of their granddaughter. So, please stop coming down on them as though they had. Please try to put yourself in their shoes. What is that was your family member? Would you stop at nothing to demand justice? And, not ALL of the family and friends believe in Tracy's innocence. I agree with you that the truth will come out in the end. And I hope they will hold the correct person responsible. But the bottom line is, Reagan is still gone. We were robbed of a beautiful little girl. Please stop treating this as a popularity contest between Tracy and Ryan. Rest in peace our sweet baby Reagan."

Jello wrote: "To all of you who know the 'facts'. This world would be such a better place if you would take all of your negative energy, and apply it to something good…make a positive difference in someone's life. And if you're truly all psychic, and have all the answers…why didn't you wrap this case up over a year ago? If you could spare a free moment, I would love the winning lottery numbers for the Mega Millions…come on, help a girl out!...Suggestion to the Moderator: What are the chances of getting a message board on here to have areas of discussion about different topics? Maybe then some of us won't have to weed through this unbelievable mess?!"

Mark L. from Pensacola, Florida, asked: "Wasn't Ryan arrested on unrelated charges just recently? If I recall correctly, he was drinking and joy riding only to total the car he was driving and he fled the scene. I think it speaks of his character."

CN Reader soon responded: "Thank God rumors are just rumors…Why in the world would anyone with half a brain post a rumor? Well I guess I just answered my question."

Loose lips sink ships shared: "It's been mentioned before but don't you 'insiders' who are blabbing so openly here about details of the Reagan tragedy have a clue that you could be jeopardizing the entire case? Or are you actually hoping for a change of venue or a mistrial? In the name of justice, and decency, PLEASE WISE UP and

SHUT UP! I'm also disappointed the moderators are allowing all the BIASED TALK (for either side). Opinions are one thing: purporting to know 'the facts' and carelessly sling them around in another."

Crystal from Ridge Farm compassionately wrote: "I don't know anyone involved in this case. What i do know first hand is that people we have spent our entire lives with can do things you never thought they could/would ever do. Iam praying for everyone involved in this case. God bless."

A family friend, Kim Crouch, chastised Ryans Allhands Supporter, wondering who was behind that mysterious pen name: "How DARE you say the only reason he was arrested was due to the Green and Williams' familys involvement with the community to get awareness out there for this awful, awful truth that affects so many people throughout the country. You should seriously be ashamed of yourself. Why on earth would you publicly post things that many other people may not know, or that could be, in theory, complete lies and hearsay? I'm sure it's comforting to Ryan that you're sticking by him. But, unfortunately, for you and Ryan, the police arrested the MAIN suspect, the one that they had evidence for. They didn't draw names out of a hat. This isn't a chance for you to gain attention as the 'compassionate' friend.' Watch what you say, and stop being so inconsiderate toward the families of this tragedy."

Another poster, make it stop, pleaded for the "rather depressing" debate to stop: "…it's really all about the memory of this little girl…is this the way we want her to be remembered? With all this arguing? I hope we can all agree that this is not the place to have a trial for anyone…we should for the baby girls sake…let the court system do it's job…god bless."

Harold Van Duyn from Augusta, Georgia, mused: "I have just recently figured out the reason that the Reagan Williams case took so long for charges to be filed. It became crystal clear to me that everyone with ANY knowledge of this case has not spoken to the States Attorney's office. It appears that with all the experts who have first hand knowledge and insider information are spending their time on this guest book. If they had only gone to the authorities before now, we would have multiple convictions. Maybe since they know such much and haven't share it THEY should be charged with Obstruction of Justice. Yes this is all said in a rather cynical way, and for that I apologize, but it seems as if everyone knows more than the professionals. I said in an earlier post to please trust in the court system, while flawed is still the greatest on earth. Please people leave this subject alone in the future, as all that is being accomplished is the spreading of hatred. I am sure that is not the best way to honor the memory of this precious baby. Pray for her. Pray for justice. Pray for the police and Attorneys. Pray for the families. And last but not least pray for all of us, as none of us is perfect."

Seemingly in agreement, Tired of the bull…. wrote: "Kudos to you Kim Crouch and everyone else on here who has commented on the Reagan Williams case…not on behalf of the suspect in custody. I think it's way past time to give up all the he said/she said and just let the court system do their jobs. If you are so sure either one of them are innocent…it will be proven in court! The thing everyone is forgetting here is that beautiful little Reagan is no longer with us. Let her get the justice she deserves and rest in peace already!"

The activity on the forum waned. Perhaps the pleas to stop the hatred finally got through; more than likely the arrest in July became old news.

In September, however, the posts started up again when Ryan was released on bail due to oversights in the State's Attorney's office. Not every i had been dotted and t crossed in the preparing of the charges. Early posts were reactions to my being attacked on the forum. I appreciated those who came to my defense even though the attack seemed to have been a case of mistaken identity, the issue resolved and the confused poster withdrawing his accusations and apologizing. Soon, the topic turned to the mishandling of court procedures.

CN Reader, reacting to an article in the newspaper, wrote of how disgraceful and misleading the State's Attorney's office had been: "...I can truly say I'm not surprised at the lack of commitment, knowledge and foresight...Did they not go to law school at least? This is typical per Frank Young and his co-dependant Larry Mills. What a slap in the face to that poor child. And not seeking the death penalty as part of punishment? I'm not saying by any means that Allhands deserves it, but it just shows that the wheelin and dealin of that office has begun before a jury has ever been chosen or a trial has even begun. Aren't the plea's supposed to come DURING 'bargaining' and not before? And I have to ask why 'Judge' Anderson sent the letter requesting an outside court official? Formal complaints against the State's Atty office should be filed with the Attorney General's office and I certainly hope someone files a complaint in that baby's name. Instead of Young not running again it's too bad voting someone out isn't an option. It's definitely time for a State's Atty. To be FOR the people instead of against..I guess you get what you pay for..Nothing."

Another poster considered the Danville courts "slower than a snail." Still another was "just stunned that they let their skimmer leak and this person" would be released, also asking why the bail had not been set any higher and whether the time had come for "self-help justice. Certainly the thought of being prosecuted by this bunch" wasn't "a deterent to any criminal."

A former writer, lacey, though sorry for me and my family, was still open to the possibility that Tracy was the culprit, sure that the closure we longed for would be meaningless if the wrong person was punished.

In June of 2008, Jason Hubbard of Danville asked: "What the heck move the Allhands trial to another county for what exactly? He murdered a baby why is he not sitting on death row right now instead of wasting time and money. What do we really need a trial for just to prove how much of a cold blooded heartless killer he is. This is why justice is such a joke anymore and as much as I hate texas they got something right more then 3 creditable eye witnesses no trial by jury, no questions asked, just plain justice."

Dave of Danville posed: "Why have a trial for ALLHANDS anyway? He has already been found guilty by his pears. Why not just take him out and hang him? Didn't the fact be known that there were TWO people in that house when little Reagon died and her little brother was removed from the home and her mother 'lawyered up'. I don't know anyone from that family but I can bet you one thing. There is "reasonable doubt.""

Not that my opinion matters from Danville responded to Jason: "How do you know he killed Regan? Where you there and saw this take place? What about the mother? She has a questionable background. If I read the paper correctly at the time didn't the state have something against her for the littlest child. A son I believe. I do not know either party or any of the grandparents but I do know that I live in America where you are innocent until proven guilty by a court of law. This should never have happened that little angel suffered from whatever or whoever did this to her. What if the real killer is still out there free and this man goes to jail the rest of his life for something she did. I just think for someone who had a questionable background with DCFS already can't be that innocent." Ryan, babysitting when Reagan "fell" and hit her head on a coffee table multiple times, creating a circle of injuries which did

[528]

not match the coffee table scenario, also had that questionable background with DCFS as both mother and paramour were investigated. "It makes me sick to see the mother doing these public services about shaken baby syndrome when she had her son taken from her at one point. Does she have the little child back?"

Victim Impact Statement

Your Honor, you have already read my lengthy Victim Impact Statement in which I described how devastating the loss of Reagan was…is…to me, my wife, and our family. You have read about the physical, mental, emotional, and spiritual fallout of this tragedy. You have read about the sleepless nights, daily tears, dashed hopes, debilitating grief, and overwhelming guilt. You have also read about Reagan—a daughter, granddaughter, great-granddaughter, sister, niece, cousin. She was our Sunshine. Now she exists in our memories, in our hearts, in videos, in photo albums, in pictures hanging on our walls, on wristbands—nothing one can hug or kiss or comfort or rock to sleep or sing to or read to or play with. In our living room, there is an empty rocking chair which waits for an occupant; in our basement, there is a collection of toys waiting for an owner; in our bathroom, there is a mirror waiting for a reflection of a little girl and her Papa making faces and laughing. Our whole house waits for a light and a life that will never come again.

I have kept a journal for my granddaughter. I wanted to write about all the big events and the little moments that could not be captured on film. I planned on giving what surely would have been numerous volumes of this journal to Reagan when she was eighteen. In that journal I wrote about all that was the miracle of our little girl. Then there came a day when I was faced with writing something very painful.

[At this point I read several passages from the journal]

For those who say, "I know Ryan Allhands. He would never do this," well, I know Ryan Allhands, too. We spent hundreds of hours together. He was a student of mine, and as a student, he often had a disinterest in responsibility and a contempt for authority. We once talked about acting with honor and nobility of purpose and goodness. In him, I failed.

Your Honor, I ask that you consider the record of Ryan Allhands and his frequent disregard for the law. Leaving the scene of a car accident, for instance. And, when given his freedom in September of 2007 with the stipulation that he not consume alcohol, he flagrantly ignored that admonition, drank, and drove a car, becoming a potential danger to other motorists. I ask that you consider not only these prior actions but his miserable failure of a polygraph test he took just days after Reagan's death. I ask that you remember the efforts on the part of our family to get help, to intervene, to keep Reagan safe from harm, efforts that proved futile. I ask that you give to this bully and coward the maximum sentence so that others might think twice before reacting so carelessly, so heinously, and so violently. Perhaps other families may be spared this deep, deep darkness.

Yet, despite the rage I have toward Ryan Allhands, I know that good people eventually forgive. I will never forget what you took from us—all that you took from us— but I know that if I am to find peace in this lifetime, I will one day have to forgive you. I am not there yet, but it is a challenge that I must eventually confront. Ryan, here is a challenge for you. We—Reagan's family—have tried to bring some good out of something so horrible. We have tried to advocate for families- and children-at-risk. We have tried to educate the people of Vermilion County and beyond about domestic violence in all its forms, especially about Shaken Baby Syndrome. And we've done this without mentioning your name. So what good will you bring from this tragedy? How will you one day contribute positively to the world when you are released? You wrote on August 15, 2006, that you were a reformed man because of what happened in your household the previous month. Prove it.

My favorite photograph of Reagan is a close-up of her resting on her daddy's chest. She stares serenely, confidently into the camera. When I look in those eyes I see such wisdom. In my grief, those eyes have brought me comfort. In times of doubt, those eyes have led me to understanding. Were it not for that photograph, I might have perished. We all can look into those dark brown eyes and see what we've lost. But I think if we look again, we can also see her encouraging us to keep going, to keep living, to keep striving for a safer world for children, a world of peace and love. Like Dora the Explorer whom Reagan enjoyed watching so much, we have to face life's many challenges and obstacles, fend off those who would take what we hold dear and precious, and, finally, celebrate what we are able to accomplish together. We all have to do it for her.

Operation Shrink Charlie's Big Butt

TUESDAY, DECEMBER 22

How Reagan Rescued Me

Yesterday was one of the most emotional days of my life. My husband and I sat in a courthouse, surrounding a family and community who lost their two year old daughter, granddaughter, niece and sweet little angel- Reagan Williams- to shaken baby syndrome at the hands of a man who sat on trial. Yesterday was the sentencing hearing for the man's crimes of killing this precious baby.

I am going to bring you this message in the best way I know how, because at the moment I am so emotionally broken for so many reasons.

Reagan's life was short- too short, and in the 2 1/2 years she had on this earth, she endured the best of both worlds. She got to know the unconditional love of her father's family, and yet lived in the fear of the custodial home she knew. She never had the chance to go to her first day of school, her first dance, her own graduation. She will never see the love of her life waiting at the end of an aisle for her in candlelight. Her life was tragically taken at the hands of someone else. Someone who lived in the home with her and was supposed to protect her. But she never got that protection.

Her natural father and his family tried to pull her out. They tried to give her safety, protect her. But the nature of our overloaded courts and family protection services were too busy to take responsibility for this little girl in need of help. And they were wrong not to help. In their busyness, they turned little Reagan away, even though there were pictures and evidence of prior abuse. Their hearts should feel just as responsible as the man who created the fear and ultimately the end of Reagan's brief life.

So many of us have felt the effects of abuse in our own lives. Maybe we grew up with a father, grandfather, uncle, or even a stepmother who beat us, molested us, broke us. Maybe we have had boyfriends, husbands, ex-husbands, who chewed up what little hope we had and threw it on the floor, along with our hopes, dreams, and self-esteem, making our home a place that was void of safety and comfort.

I am here to tell you today that we are the lucky ones.

We made it out alive.

Reagan didn't.

She wasn't able to be a screwed-up adult because of abuse, like the rest of us. She wasn't able to gain a ton of weight, thinking that if she was fat or ugly her abuser would leave her alone. She never told herself while looking in a mirror "you are worthless" because someone told her that's what she was.

Instead, there is no longer a reflection in the mirror for her to see.

See, kids, yesterday, sitting in that courtroom, hearing that the man who killed Reagan was only getting 7 years in prison and screaming at the injustice- I realized something. I can no longer use my fears from my past to dictate my future. My fat has been my safety for far too long. I used it as a shield, protecting me from the bad things in life. No one could really get close to the person I am if I remain attached to my fat. No one would hurt the innocent child who didn't understand what was happening to her because fat made you ugly, and if you were ugly, no one would want you. Those are the thoughts that kept me alive, that gave me a chance at normalcy in life. The thoughts that keep holding me back from heading into a land that I have never known as an adult. The land of Skinnydom.

I know that if I keep hanging on to the fat- the emotional ties that binge- I will never have the opportunities in life that I deserve. That Reagan deserved. She deserved so much more than she was given, and yet I look at my own life and see the things I have squandered. I have selfishly thrown away chance after chance to change, because of my own fears of being hurt.

So as this year begins to draw to a close, I feel there is nothing left for me to do but be forced to shed all my feelings of inadequacies, fear, hopelessness. I made huge strides with my weight in 2009. But in 2010, it is time for me to do things as an adult I never thought I would. Take risks, live life to the fullest. Really really really work towards my goal of 100 pounds and become a survivor. A living breathing survivor who made it out, and helps others break free too.

When it is all said and done, Reagan's killer will be in prison about the same amount of time that Reagan was alive. A mere 2 1/2 years, thanks to our injustice system. I can't take on legal battles to correct that wrong. What can I do to help? Me? A mother, a wife, a writer and professional dieter?

What I can do is step up to the plate, embrace my kids, love my husband, and not let the after effects of my past abuse hold me back any longer. Those emotions can't tie me down. Not for one more day. I've got the answers to my unanswered questions, at last. And I saw them in the eyes of this little girl.

Reagan only got 2 1/2 years. But my own fears and past hurts have held me back for over 20 years. Yesterday I was filled with sorrow about that fact. Today- I am determined that I won't let it happen ever again. And it's time that life is embraced for all that it is. The wonderful joy of living every day to the fullest, to its full potential, and not letting my yesterdays loom over and dominate my todays. I'm breaking free from my fear and my fat.

So today, I say with absolute confidence that I will live life like it should be. With the faith and hope of a child. Reagan and me. One in heaven, one nothing more than a broken child at heart. Both of us safely in the arms of our Jesus, where we can't be hurt like this ever again. Bound forever in the throes of an ineffective courtroom where Reagan couldn't be saved, and I got my first taste of freedom. Reagan, sweet darling, you have rescued me. Your short life has forever changed mine. And when I get to heaven and see your precious face, I am going to throw my arms around you, lift you up in the air, and thank you for what you have done.

You may be gone, but your memory is far from over. You have given birth to new life, little one. Thank you.

So today- is for Reagan.

If you would like to know more about Reagan and the foundation her family has started on her behalf, please visit Reagan's Rescue for more information.

POSTED BY THE INCREDIBLE SHRINKING WOMAN AT 6:05 AM
4 COMMENTS:
Mary @ Giving Up On Perfect said...
Oh, friend. My heart breaks for that little girl and her family. As the mother of a 2 and 2 month-old little girl, I can only imagine too well what Reagan's family has gone through.
And my heart breaks for you, too. BUT - it also rejoices for the way you are breaking out of those chains and making a different life for yourself!

DECEMBER 22, 2009 AT 9:05 AM
faithWalker said...
Charlie, what a powerful post! My heart aches for Reagan's family. And at the same time I'm rejoicing for you...for God's healing, demolishing strongholds, for giving life.
You go girl!
Deb

DECEMBER 22, 2009 AT 2:28 PM

 Anonymous said...

Charlie, for a grandfather filled with so many emotions and for a writer who usually has plenty to say, I am without words here. Perhaps silence (listening with my heart) is the best way to respond to your beautiful thoughts. Thank you.

DECEMBER 22, 2009 AT 10:09 PM

 Anonymous said...

Sorry for not attaching my name to the previous comment.

Greg

The Sentencing

As soon as the sentence became public, the Danville Forum began to fill with debate. Some of the talk was informed, most of it hearsay, much of it incorrect. Passing off gossip as fact ruled the day. Everyone seemed to know the "truth." I read these opinions with both sincere gratitude and stomach-turning shock. I stayed out of it for as long as I could, but, eventually, eight and a half months later, I entered the verbal battle. I was Warrior 15. Our therapist had called me a Warrior for Reagan (at least now after she was gone). 15 was for January 5. I had to defend her honor and her memory.

Allhands Sentence: Baby Killing Is Decriminalized In Vermilion County
Posted in the Danville Forum

#1 Dec. 22 2009   **jarama1127**

Judge Michael Clary - a genius, a scholar, a gentleman. He is a true Renaissance Man. A robed Michelangelo. And in his finite wisdom, the judge effectively decriminalized murder in Vermilion County.

Despite the claims he made on paper this week, Ryan Allhands basically got a 2-year prison sentence for killing baby Reagan Williams.

Much like Judge Craig DeArmond's decision to aid the thief who stole all that money from Danville Mass Transit not long ago, our newest Savior hasn't got the guts to stand up to the criminals.

It's like giving bank robbers a loitering citation.

It's the equivalent of enforcing a noise ordinance against a man who beats his wife.

The police arrest these scumbags like they're supposed to, so we don't see the horrific hooliganism up close and personal. The sneaky slapstick comedy stylings of The Three Stooges comes at a later proceeding.

What starts out as a drama, very slowly turns into either a horror or a comedy (depending on your POV).

The judges whine, saying the police or the prosecutors didn't do their jobs. Or they say the General Assembly makes them act like weak-kneed dunces. Does it all boil down to fear?

If our judges can't stand up to baby killers, is there really Rule By Law in Vermilion County?

[544]

#2 Dec 22, 2009   **hate2loveme**

Well maybe if they had the right person arrested, there
would have been a heftier sentence. BUT since, of course,
there was hardly ANY evidence stating that Ryan, was in
fact, guilty, he got a lesser sentence. They just had to put
somebody, anybody, away for her death since kids I guess
don't hurt themselves anymore. There's always got to be
something more sinister behind everything. Well, people
need to realize that just because he was 15x heavier than
her, doesn't mean he did any harm to that little girl. I
happen to know Ryan Alhands personally and have seen
him with his children and, in my mind, there is no way he
could have hurt Reagan. Why didn't they look into Ms
Tracey's past with children services? #3 Dec 22, 2009

#3 Dec. 22, 2009   **jarama1127**

Oh yes, I forgot, babies often bash their own heads in. How
silly of me to have thought someone else could have done
it!
And of course they had no evidence Ryan did that. Other
than the fact that he was abusive of Reagan in front of lots
of friends and family, and there were several complaints
going back over many months, calls to DCFS and such.

And, naturally, we all know Tracy's past never came out. Uh, er, except for the fact that it was gone over with a fine tooth comb and repeatedly talked about in minutiae by me and all my neighbors in Tilton.

Tracy wasn't innocent. She knew what type of guy Ryan was all along, and obviously dismissed it, even when family tried intervening. But, it doesn't change the fact that your "friend" is a murdering dog.

You're a true blue, loyal friend to Ryan Allhands. You're extremely biased, and you should be. If I was his friend, I have little doubt I might "jump the shark" on reality as well.(We all do when we get overly emotional!) I'm not friends with any of the people involved, so I can't defend Reagan Williams's family or their inattention to her. They misjudged the situation, and maybe a few didn't really care either. I don't know for sure, but I am sure they have to live with the consequences from now on.

Sadly, Ryan Allhands doesn't.

You can turn a baby killing into a He Said--She Said contest if you want. It doesn't change the fact that he got away with murder.What about the skelton's in her closet? Of course none of that came out.

#4 Dec 22, 2009   **Kati**

I think Ryan was guilty, however, I think that Tracey was culpable also. She knew what was going on and did nothing to stop it. She's as guilty as Ryan is. I think they should both do time. It's really sad that they said the crime wasn't serious enough for a longer sentence.

#5 Dec 22, 2009   **Justice**

Hopefully he will be given a big welcome as a baby killer in prison.

#6 Dec 22, 2009   **Doug Brown**

I Agree.

#7 Dec 30, 2009   **hate2loveme**

No one will know what really happened. There's only three people who really know. Thats the only thing we can assure.... right?

#8 Jan 6, 2010   **Standing up**

Excuse me? There was dire evidence against Ryan Allhands and unless you know the family personally like i do. You have no right to even talk about.You do not know them to be judging them. You do not know that they are going through. Don't point your fingers at another person unless yours are clean.

#9 Jan 6, 2010   **Standing up**

Your right you don't know the family to be saying anything about it. But i can say one thing, the family may have over looked him, or misjudged him, But that is not excuse to let a baby killer, get away with killing an innocent child. That child had a family. And grand-parents who would die and take her place. So forgive me if you find me rude, but he belongs in prison for more then 2 years. In my opinion, he deserves the needle. That child had a future. And Ryan took it away from her. If it was you wouldn't you want some one to stand up and defend you.

#10 Jan 6, 2010   **unjust**

Personally I believe this is the most corrupt judge ever. He is very impartial. He apparently does not like women or care for children (I can attest) and always seems to help defend the men- JUST AS HE DID IN THIS CASE!
I am absolutely outraged that even with a life loss- a dear innocent child- that Clary would continue to be leanient!

Leanient toward a monster who could inflict such an unforgiving act.

I guess that's why he'd not allow to change venue- he questionably has MOTIVES! It doesn't surprise me. I do not see how his unsound decisions can continue to be accepted by the circuit court; nor how his questionable practices have not already raised more suspicion.

I seriously question this judge's mentality.

#11 Jun 13, 2010   **Holly**

All I know is that a coroner is elected in Vermilion County Hee-Hah town. I could get elected coroner and so could you if we were popular enough. Sorry, unless it's a medical examiner I just doubt whatever they say. Peggy whatshername or whatever has zero credibility with me.

#12 Jun 14, 2010   **Cheryl**

Cheryl, you are right. A coroner is a political office and you only have to convince enough people of your qualifications to get elected. A lot of them get elected and then get training for their new job before they take office. A medical examiner is a medical doctor (usually a pathologist) with special training in forensic medicine. They do a better job in criminal investigations, but they also command a much larger salary. Small cities can't justify the cost vs. the very small need for such expertise. Large cities require an M.E. It is the middle-sized cities that have to make a decision cost vs. quality.

UNJUST, I think you meant to say the judge is "partial" instead of "impartial". Otherwise your point is good.

#13 Jun 14, 2010   Cheryl
Sorry, in that last post, I meant to direct my first comment to Holly, not me. Damned fingers have a mind of their own!

#14 Jun 28, 2010   Mr Savage
It's so curious to me that all of you were present when this poor child was hurt, and yet none of you testified at the trial. Why?

#15 Jul 31, 2010   Standing up
For one, we all knew what was going on. Why do you think we interviened. For two, DSFS was called sever times. That family has gone through hell with everything that has happened. Tracey has to live with the fact every single day of her life, that the man she chose killed her baby girl. And

you are right, the judge does need looking at. That baby had another brother, she will never grow up with him, go to prom, or even enjoy the little things that people get most out of life. Reagan ha two families that loved her to her death. And still get together to talk about her every single year.She may have made a bad mistake. But that mistake doesn't give any man,woman or child to be murdered. Any parent, relative, family friend of a victum of SBS will tell you , that they live with that every single day. But we could of never expected , nor seen the future of what was going to happen.Because trust me, if we could, that baby would be alive enjoying life. And there was evidence. A baby cant brutely shake itself. Tracey was sleeping at the time. Ryan was awake with the child. It takes all of 8 seconds to kill a baby of SBS. SBS is 100% preventable.

To learn more go to reagansrescue.com

#16 Jul 31, 2010   Standing up

It's times like this that people want to stand up and knock common sense into people. Four years has gone by since the beginning of court. That family was forced to sit in a room, where everyone was judging them, instead of the criminal. Everytime they went back to court, they had to see him. And watch him deny the fact that he murdered that baby girl. Outrage isn't the word to describe what they went through. In fact no one can really relate to it unless they have lost a child. There will forever be a whole in her heart. The hardest part is Deagan getting older , and her having to explain to him about everything that happened. How do you think he will take it. The judge that held the case is sexist. Several cases have been put in front of him and he has always sided with the male. But would he do the same if his baby was brutely murdered. Grandparents who will never get to see her have children. How many children have to die and not get justice, due to the sexist eye of the court?

#17 Aug 12, 2010   **hate2loveme**

DCFS was called on Tracey (and her family), not Ryan and she was not asleep, she was in the shower. And it can take up to 24 hrs for the results of SBS to come into full effect.

#18 Aug 12, 2010   **Warrior15**

hate2loveme, where do you get your information from? The DCFS investigation was conducted on Tracy and Ryan. The amount of new bleeding in Reagan's brain indicated that this was an injury done to her minutes before her death. Ryan stated in court that his action did, indeed, lead to her death. Let's deal with facts then debate whether killing a child is okay.

#19 Aug 13, 2010   hate2loveme
WHAT ACTION?! If he's going to pretty much "confess" in court, why the hell didn't he PLEA?! And she had DCFS inv. before her and Ryan were TOGETHER.

#20 Aug 13, 2010   hate2loveme
And BTW don't worry about where I get my information.

#21 Aug 19, 2010   Warrior 15
I see that you are devoted to your ignorance, so these last facts will be it for me. Ryan did plea to manslaughter. He admitted in court that he caused Reagan's death. Were you there? Did you hear him? As for the DCFS investigation, have you read the DCFS report? Have you met with investigators? Have you met with the state director? Tracy was not visited before "her and Ryan" were together. Again, it is your right to be ignorant. I'm guessing you also think President Obama is a Muslim.

#22 Sep 22, 2010   **Warrior 15**

First of all, Ryan Allhands did plea. He confessed in open court to manslaughter. He said aloud to all those in attendance that he did, indeed, take action that caused Reagan's death. Also, DCFS did not investigate Tracy before "her and Ryan" were together. You are obviously relying on hearsay. Were you in the courtroom? If so, did you listen to the testimony? Have you seen the DCFS files or the accident reports from when Reagan was injured in October 2005 (while in Ryan's "care")? Have you spoken directly to the Director of DCFS in his office in Springfield or seen the Office of Inspector General report on the mishandling of the case? Out of respect to this little girl, forever 2 1/2, you should stop spreading rumors.

#23 Sep 22, 2010   **Kentucky Whiskey Shark**

hate2loveme wrote:

And BTW don't worry about where I get my information. In other words, disregard your posts. Thanks for the tip.

#24 Nov 30, 2010   **Truth**

I know Ryan personally, he's a very good family friend. I also know Tracy very well. You wanna know why Ryan got a lesser sentence? It's because everybody that knew anything about the entire situation, knew that Ryan wasn't guilty but they had to put somebody in jail. They knew that Tracy's story didn't add up at all, and had changed at least four times. And now because of her, he is sitting in jail for something she did. She'll tell you she never laid a hand on her kid, but if that was true, then why was DCFS called on her for the baby having bruises on her? Think about that one for a minute while you have nothing better to do with your lives except for judge and criticize a man you know nothing about.

#25 Dec 3, 2010   **hate2loveme**

thank you TRUUUUUTH!!! THANK YOU SOMEONE FREAKIN KNOWS WHAT THEYRE TALKING ABOUT!!!!

#26 Jul 29, 2011   **Keri**

He IS guilty. He ADMITTED to it at his sentencing, jackass. But not to worry. Your little friend is now a free "man". Lock your doors and hide your kids. You know where I got MY info? FIRST HAND. Look that up in your Funk and Wagnalls. Why are you ashamed to show your NAME?

#27 Aug 10, 2011   **hate2loveme**

There are no freaking kids in danger. He is not a dangerous man.. I ALSO know FIRST HAND. Why don't you go fear monger around all the freaking sex offenders in Danville?! They're way more dangerous than Ryan is.

#28 Aug 13, 2011   **danville**

Warrior15 wrote:

hate2loveme, where do you get your information from? The DCFS investigation was conducted on Tracy and Ryan. The amount of new bleeding in Reagan's brain indicated that this was an injury done to her minutes before her death. Ryan stated in court that his action did, indeed, lead to her death. Let's deal with facts then debate whether killing a child is okay. mabe you should jet your info right !!!!!

#29 Aug 13, 2011   **danville**

Maybe you should get your info right corrners report only showed 1 place on bleed when you are shanken you have two and dcfs was only on tracy not ryan

#30 Apr 18, 2012   **cutie84**

DCFS was called once, because of a time that Ryan was watching her and she ended up with bruises....I love how all you know so much about the case but when the family presents facts we over look them? If you were accused of killING someones child...would you plead guilty if you didnt do it? ever? of coarse not. But all these link card-loving mom's he knows still lets him babysit their child? That's a bad mother. Danville trash. BOOM.

#31 Apr 18, 2012   **cutie84**

hate2loveme wrote:

DCFS was called on Tracey (and her family), not Ryan and she was not asleep, she was in the shower. And it can take up to 24 hrs for the results of SBS to come into full effect. And her family??? WTF are you talking about??? C'mon girl; im SURE you've had DCFS on you at least once....did they go for your hole family? You sound dumb.

#33 Apr 18, 2012   **cutie84**

hate2loveme wrote:

There are no freaking kids in danger. He is not a dangerous man.. I ALSO know FIRST HAND. Why don't you go fear

monger around all the freaking sex offenders in Danville?!
They're way more dangerous than Ryan is.
^^^^......wow. I hope you dont have children.

#34 Apr 19, 2012   **cutie84**

hate2loveme wrote:

WHAT ACTION?! If he's going to pretty much "confess"
in court, why the hell didn't he PLEA?! And she had DCFS
inv. before her and Ryan were TOGETHER.
Hate2LoveMe.....Ryan DID plead guilty, thus confessiong
to his crime....wtf are you talking about??? Lol

35 Apr 19, 2012   **cutie84**

Truth wrote:

I know Ryan personally, he's a very good family friend. I
also know Tracy very well. You wanna know why Ryan
got a lesser sentence? It's because everybody that knew
anything about the entire situation, knew that Ryan wasn't
guilty but they had to put somebody in jail. They knew that
Tracy's story didn't add up at all, and had changed at least
four times. And now because of her, he is sitting in jail for
something she did. She'll tell you she never laid a hand on
her kid, but if that was true, then why was DCFS called on
her for the baby having bruises on her? Think about that

one for a minute while you have nothing better to do with your lives except for judge and criticize a man you know nothing about.

Sorry to break it to you "Truth" Ryan was the one questioned changing his story, Tracy told the same story she was in the shower...thats why she wasnt a suspect for very long at all, and Ryan was the hole time, fucking duh. DCFS was called on Tracy one time, for a time that Ryan was baby-sitting her and she "fell off the couch and hit her head on the coffee table." Think about that one while you have nothing better to do with your life you link-card loving hoe. Want to know how I know that without even knowing you? Because your friends with that low-life alcohic. Ever wonder why EVERYBODY that knows Tracys will tell you she didnt do it...but everyone that knows Ryan will tell you he's always been an angry heavy-drinker piece of shit. The only people who stick up for him EVER are people that are his skanky friends.To bad the dude that BEAT THAT ASS at Juliees didnt give that bitch some karma and done him in....btw if any one knows who that was I would love to know...I need to shake this man's hand!! ;) Now go ahead and try to come back at me with your obviously biased "facts" so I can shut your ass back down again. I promise I know more about this than you...you only hear word of mouth. Now go wait in line for you food stamps ;)

#36 Apr 19, 2012   cutie84

And do you people honestly think shakin baby syndrome takes atleast 24 hours? Dude shook her so hard he broke her fucking neck instantly and her brian started to bleed. That is not going to take you 24 hours to die from.....seriously people your on a computer on this site time to figure out google!! Its not hard!!!

#37 Apr 19, 2012   Sara

Yet Ryan is a good person? If someone thinks a good person kills a little baby and lies about it, that person is either severely mentally retarded, on meth, or in need of in-patient, psychiatric care (preferably for the long term).

#38 Apr 19, 2012   cutie84

danville wrote:

Maybe you should get your info right corrners report only showed 1 place on bleed when you are shanken you have two and dcfs was only on tracy not ryan

"Danville" ...your name is Danville and by reading your comments you obviuosly never even made it to high school. The coroners report said that her neck was broken causing bleeding of the brain from being shaken. You have obviously never seen this report, and are talking out of your ass. Now please for the sake of the community go get a fucking GED.

#39 Apr 22, 2012   **cutie84**

That's fine, cutie84. That's the beauty of living in a free country; everyone is entitled to their opinions. I refuse to sit here and argue and belittle people in an online forum. I continue to keep my stance on this subject of: Only three people know what happened that day(s), and one isn't here to tell her side.

So continue to call people names and be verbally abusive. It is, after all, a free country.. and I will continue to be a friend. A real friend. Go ahead, tell me I'm friends with a baby killer. Maybe I am. But I'm still a friend..

#40 Apr 22, 2012   **hate2loveme**

BUT another thing to consider (again, without me being abusive): You bet your ass I'd trust Ryan with my child, wouldn't you?? Think about it this way: Ryan is not a serial killer. He didn't "get off" on it or anything. If anything, it was an accident.. it wasn't on purpose. You think he's gonna serve more jail time for "killing another kid"?! He's gonna watch that kid like A HAWK and make sure nothing happens. If he were a sociopath or something, sure.. but he's not. He doesn't go trolling school yards for little kids he can kill and dispose of.. I;m just trying to say, there are sicker, more deplorable people in this community and world than Ryan Allhands..

#41 Apr 22, 2012   CSUGrad

Cutie84 is always verbally abusive, knows nothing but acts like she knows it all, and sounds like she survived a shaken baby episode herself.

#42 Apr 22, 2012   TrollKiller

CSUGrad posts under multiple fake names to defame other people and makes herself sound like an idiot. She also works at the crummiest restaurant in the world, MEGDIS in Tilton,IL when shes not working at Joejin Spa(dont worry you can get a happy ending at both). So pay no attention to her!

hate2loveme wrote:

BUT another thing to consider (again, without me being abusive): You bet your ass I'd trust Ryan with my child, wouldn't you?? Think about it this way: Ryan is not a serial killer. He didn't "get off" on it or anything. If anything, it was an accident.. it wasn't on purpose. You think he's gonna serve more jail time for "killing another kid"?! He's gonna watch that kid like A HAWK and makc sure nothing happens. If he were a sociopath or something, sure.. but he's not. He doesn't go trolling school yards for little kids he can kill and dispose of.. I;m just trying to say, there are sicker, more deplorable people in this community and world than Ryan Allhands..

Hate2LoveMe..I honestly agree with you that yes, I bet it was an accident. I'm willing to bet he didnt mean to kill her that day at all...but he was SO ANGRY with a 2 year old child that he shook her hard enough to break her neck. Someone with anger issues like that I would NOT trust around my child!! And as to belittling and name-calling, what have you been doing to Tracy this hole time? You just sound so ignorant. You said that Tracy got DCFS called on her and her family...uhhhh that doesnt make sense. You have NO facts right at all. I promise. You would trust him around your child? God forbid I hope you dont have children.

#44 Apr 22, 2012   **Cutie84**

CSUGrad wrote:

Cutie84 is always verbally abusive, knows nothing but acts like she knows it all, and sounds like she survived a shaken baby episode herself.

CSUGrad from GeorgeTown is obviously illiterate because my hole argument here is that shaken baby syndrome kills you quickly......

#45 Apr 23, 2012   **CSU Grad**

You said "hole argument." You are in that! Hehe. I was ridiculing not your whole argument but your hatred. Now I'm illiterate. Anyone that disagrees with you gets called names like a two year old. Real mature, which is why I added the barb about you suffering from shaken baby syndrome. It was in poor taste, but I wanted to give you a taste of your own medicine.

#46 Jan 9, 2013   **Standing Up**

The point isnt whether or not where they were or what they were doing , its who killed reagan and why werent they put up for justice.

#47 Jan 18, 2013   **hate2loveme**

Look up SBS on webmd..

"Symptoms can start quickly, especially in a badly injured child. Other times, it may take a few days for brain swelling to show symptoms. Often the caregiver who shook the child puts the child to bed in the hope that symptoms will get better with rest. By the time the child gets to a doctor, the child needs urgent care. In some cases, the child may be in a coma before a caregiver seeks help."

Anywhere from immediately to a few days.

Afterword

At the end of this long process, the question remains: Why a book?

I believe that a brief life is not an incomplete life and that Reagan can continue to matter.

I believe that clear, detailed memories begin to fade. They dull and diminish. That is a second type of loss. In writing about them, however, you don't lose them. They are always there in black and white.

I believe that one of the advantages of loss is that I can comfort others who are where we have been. My experiences, my collected memories, can be of some use, perhaps even a blessing to another person who is grieving.

In this test of faith and in the ongoing search for answers, I believe there are resources beyond ourselves, whether words uttered by a friend or acquaintance or ideas found in print or visually displayed. We must continue to look for help and recognize it when it appears.

Lastly, I owe it to Reagan. She saved my life.

And so...

The journal writing goes on.

On Christmas Eve 2014, I made my annual trip to Reagan's grave. Feeling lonely at that hour of the night, I sent a text to Ian: "Just wanted to connect with you across the miles for a second. I love you, son." He immediately responded, "Love you too, dad." I didn't feel so lonely then. An hour later, while watching *A Christmas Carol* with Alastair Sim, I received another text from Ian: "It's still really hard, but I'm so happy now. i'm standing in front of our house and i know this is exactly where i'm supposed to be. best feeling ever." His message was the best Christmas gift I could receive.

In April of 2015, I spoke at my dad's church at a service commemorating Child Abuse Prevention month. As I looked around the sanctuary filled with blue and silver pinwheels, I could not help but marvel at how a little girl gone for so long could still be so very present in all that we do.

In May of 2015, Ian married Dani, his soulmate, in an historic chapel at Kennekuk County Park outside Danville. A small picture of Reagan in the yellow dress from that last Easter stood next to a white candle on a glass holder (lit by Aubrey) atop an old pump organ. As there was no electricity in the building, the flame provided the only light, its tiny, flickering presence all the more powerful. Though it rained buckets for most of the afternoon and evening, our Sunshine was very much a part of the many rituals of the day. After so much heartache and loneliness, Reagan's daddy had finally found happiness, marrying into a wonderful, loving family.

As I sat at a table watching Ian dance with Marsha to the recording of "Somewhere Over the Rainbow/What a Wonderful World," I reaffirmed my belief that it *is* a wonderful world which happens to contain great pain sometimes as well. Then I looked at the family gathered at the reception—four generations, the oldest beginning to slow down but still hanging in there. I saw in our parents where Marsha and I were headed, and I wished for our children happiness, love, and fulfillment and for our grandchildren safety and security. I also remembered those separated by death but bound to us eternally. I knew that they were standing around Reagan, smiling down, watching over us.

In April of 2016, Ian graduated from Weber State University in Ogden, Utah, with a Bachelor's Degree in Social Work. During the ceremony, my eyes filled with tears as my heart filled with pride in the accomplishments of my son who chose to go back into the belly of the social services beast in spite of (and because of) being so ultimately let down by its inefficient and ineffective bureaucracy. I am in awe of the courage, conviction, and compassion he has demonstrated!

On July 2, 2015, the ninth anniversary of Reagan's passing, I visited Reagan's grave, marking, precisely, 12:25 p.m. like I had done each time before. My solitary vigil was interrupted by a former custodian at Danville High School and his grandson who were visiting the grave of the man's granddaughter who died at 2 ½ from pneumonia. We talked about the love of grandchildren, the difficulty of loss. He then explained to his grandson what happened to Reagan. As the grandfather walked away, he added, "So remember that when you have children of your own. Never shake a baby. Smack anyone who does."

An unforeseen blessing on a challenging and emotional day.

I am not alone in so many ways.

No one is.

Little stars still climb.

Acknowledgements

There are so many people to thank, many of them mentioned in detail within these pages. I am especially grateful for the following:

My family and friends—If I don't say it enough, I hope you know that I treasure you all.

Barbara Greenberg and Julia Megan Sullivan—When I needed moxie, you were there with support and encouragement.

The Central Christian Church congregation—Your love enveloped us.

The Shaken Baby Syndrome (Abusive Head Trauma) network of child advocates—The guidance you provided and the interest you showed gave us the answers we needed and a reason for living.

State's Attorney Randy Brinegar—You approached our case with compassion, sensitivity, and professionalism, putting a human face on the justice system.

Noelle McGee—Your continued interest in our story and your beautifully written, evocative articles in *The News-Gazette* kept Reagan from being too soon forgotten.

Sarah Durst—Through your wisdom and faith, you pulled me up time and time again.

The cast of Danville Light Opera's *The Secret Garden*—
You brought a withered soul back to life.

Brian Morris—As I approached publishing, you were
there with your customary positive outlook to allay my
doubts and fears.

Patsy Jones, Stefanie Grubbs Igo, Erin and George
Halls—You saw so much of this firsthand you became
family.

My grandchildren—When Pandora opened her box and
let evil escape into all the world, a tiny creature called
Hope flew out, too. Although you cannot take the place of
Reagan, you each have a special place in my heart for you
give me hope for the future.

My children—Reagan's legacy is that she brought us
closer together and taught us how not to take each other for
granted.

Marsha—You became my best friend.

About the Author

Greg Williams is an educator, writer, actor, director, and child advocate from Danville, Illinois. He holds degrees from the University of Illinois in Urbana-Champaign and Francis Marion University in Florence, South Carolina. He and his wife, Marsha, are co-founders of Reagan's Rescue, a 501(c)(3) public charity, its mission to spread awareness of Shaken Baby Syndrome (Abusive Head Trauma) and to meet the needs of families- and children-at-risk. Greg and Marsha have five children and five grandchildren.

Please visit www.reagansrescuefund.com for more

information about Shaken Baby Syndrome (Abusive Head

Trauma). Remember, never, *ever*, shake a baby or a child!

51456270R00320

Made in the USA
San Bernardino, CA
22 July 2017